ALAN VILLIERS: VOYAGER OF THE WINDS

ALAN VILLIERS

VOYAGER OF THE WINDS

Kate Lance

with a foreword by
Sir Robin Knox-Johnston

NATIONAL
MARITIME
MUSEUM

First published in 2009 by the National Maritime Museum,
Greenwich, London SE10 9NF

www.nmm.ac.uk/publishing

Photography credits appear on pages 289–91.

A CIP catalogue record for this book is available from the
British Library.

ISBN 978-0-948065-95-8

Printed and bound in England, by Cromwell Press,
Trowbridge, Wiltshire

9 8 7 6 5 4 3 2 1

To my sons,
Alex and Joe

CONTENTS

FOREWORD

I think that anyone of my age group who had any interest in the sea knew of Alan Villiers. By the time I began my Merchant Navy apprenticeship in 1957, there were no square-rigged vessels left on the British registry, so real training in sail was no longer available to us. The Germans still ran the *Pamir* at the time, but there were no openings for British trainees, so we trained in modern motor ships for the main part. That same autumn the *Pamir* sank 500 miles from us in a storm in the north Atlantic, and apart from the Russians and the Japanese, sail training for Merchant Navy men ceased.

Perhaps it was the absence of opportunity that made sailing ships more romantic. Although we rarely saw one, we were still expected to know the various types of sailing vessels and be able to calculate their course from their lights and wind direction when we went up for our second mate's certificate examination at the end of our apprenticeships. There are not many books about the sailing of the square-riggers, so Alan Villiers' account of his voyage with the *Joseph Conrad* was part of a small library available to those of us who were curious.

It was when I went out east to sail between Bombay and all the ports to Basra and met up with the Arab dhows still in use at the time all over the Persian Gulf that I became aware of Villiers' book titled *Sons of Sinbad*. We frequently met these dhows, often showing no lights at night or a pathetically small oil lantern that was barely discernable, and with unreliable radar it kept us very alert on watch. They still traded from the Persian Gulf to Pakistan and India, providing an alternative service to our four British cargo/passenger vessels, which were the main means of communication prior to the introduction of cheap air travel. Some could still be seen in Mombasa and Zanzibar, carrying on the trade that Villiers himself had seen before the Second World War. Often they were under power, but occasionally we would overtake one under sail – which was not always easy, as they had a good turn of speed.

It was to understand more about these beautiful-looking craft that I read Villiers' book and immediately got round to wondering how

I could make a similar voyage from the Gulf to Zanzibar whilst the dhows still operated. That led to thoughts of building one and sailing it home at the end of my contract. Having no knowledge of sailing in the UK – all my sailing had been in and around the Indian Ocean – I wrote to the only person I felt I could trust for sensible advice. Within three weeks, a long, handwritten letter arrived from Alan Villiers. A nice idea, he said, but there would be no market for such a craft in the UK, so far better to build a yacht and sail her home. I took heed and thus *Suhaili* was born. Although I did not sell her when I got her home, I have always been grateful for the advice given very freely to a young, unknown Merchant Navy officer by someone who had plenty of other things to occupy his time.

I wish that we had met. Our times as trustees of the National Maritime Museum in Greenwich did not coincide, but Villiers does not pull punches when commenting on people there during his tenure. In his personal writings, he appears as irascible and impatient as I can sometimes be, and he was prepared to take risks, the way seamen will, and particularly when told by non-seafarers that they cannot do something. He had the best of it, sailing a square-rigger during the twilight of commercial sail, and before health and safety officials had begun to snuff out the character development that comes through using initiative and taking risks.

Kate Lance's extensive research, using Villiers' own journals and papers, will help those who did not know him to a better understanding of this remarkable man. Young people reading this book will realise that there was a time, not so long ago, when true adventure still existed – but you needed to be a man like Alan Villiers to take advantage of it.

Robin Knox-Johnston

INTRODUCTION

Alan Villiers was only in his mid-forties when he wrote his autobiography *The Set of the Sails*, but by then he had already lived a life that made it well worth reading. In 1920 he went to sea on square-riggers, but an accident forced him into life ashore as a journalist. At twenty-five he sailed again on a four-masted barque around Cape Horn: a thrilling race and a female stowaway made his book of the passage a bestseller.

A shocking death blighted his next voyage in 1929 but gave Villiers another memorable book. By the mid-1930s his writings, films and lectures had made him famous, but after the agonising failure of a love affair he set off for two years to sail around the globe in the exquisite full-rigged ship *Joseph Conrad*.

His public rationale was always the urgency of recording the fast-disappearing ways of sail; Villiers never mentioned the private depressions, loneliness and self-doubt that also drove him. He rarely questioned the racial and sexual stereotypes of his era, yet he lived amicably among people from all over the world in sometimes extreme privation.

Villiers at last found happiness in marriage at thirty-seven, then spent six arduous wartime years in the Royal Naval Volunteer Reserve. Afterwards he became a media star of the '50s and '60s, captained the *Mayflower II*, sailed movie ships for Hollywood and lectured internationally. He inspired ship-lovers worldwide to preserve their remaining historic vessels, and today his unique images enhance a renowned museum collection.

Oddly, despite further significant work and extensive travel, he never published an updated autobiography. This book is the first study of his life as a whole – the myth-making, the achievements and the consequences.

Alan Villiers was not simply a voyager. At a pivotal moment in maritime history he worked aloft as a seaman and abaft as a master, observing and recording an age-old body of wisdom. The result was an extraordinary memorial: to the greatest sailing ships ever launched and to the talented man who loved them.

AUTHOR'S NOTE

Villiers' diaries contain outdated nomenclature, random British or American spelling and occasional errors. For authenticity and readability I have left quotations as they appear in the diaries, without indicating his variations by '[sic]' except in potentially confusing cases. However, an ellipsis '...', which means omitted text or a significant pause, is shown as '... [sic]' where Villiers himself has used it for significance. The other instances occurring in this book indicate text I have omitted for brevity, and appear simply as '...'.

I

HELL AND
MELBOURNE

One moment I was working away, full of pleasurable thoughts. Next moment
the rigging was flying past me, and a tar-covered wire hit me a grazing clout. I
felt myself striking other rigging. Then the deck. It seemed to me, in a last instant of consciousness, that the deck was surprisingly soft.

It was not the deck that was soft. It was I.[1]

In a life of accidents and injuries and sudden shocks, none was to bring
such a change of fortune to Alan Villiers, able seaman on the four-
masted barque *Lawhill*, as the moment the vessel ran aground near
Port Lincoln in 1921 and threw him from aloft. He was eighteen and
feared he might never walk again.

He had always yearned to sail on the square-riggers, never accepting
their days of glory were lost forever beyond the void of the First World
War. In an era intoxicated with the new there were few enough sailing
ships left working in the world – there were none for a half-crippled
seaman.

Alan Villiers was a stoic, stubborn boy. He went home to Melbourne,
forced himself back to his feet, and took a job on a grim little Bass
Strait ketch. Then he tried the easier labour of steamships: he made
one tedious voyage to Europe and loathed every moment.

He knew finally he would never become a master in deep-sea sail,
and he could not bear to work in steam. His dream was over and he
must leave the sea behind. He started again in Hobart, Tasmania, and
talked his way into a newspaper job at the age of nineteen. It was 1923
and the world of the wind ships was finished, he believed.

———

Villiers was correct. By 1923 one of the greatest periods of human ingenuity was coming to a close. From the days the world was flat and
order spread at the point of a sword, sailing vessels had been the engines of civilisation. Only ships could fly (by grace of God), with
parchments and news, perfumes and silk, weapons and gold, from
port to far-flung port. Entire economies were driven by the species of
trees a country could harvest for its fleets, and entire cultures knew
themselves in terms of those fleets.

Shaped by the physics of air and water, sculpted through centuries
of cruel experience, wooden vessels reached their perfection in the
clipper ships of the mid-nineteenth century. With their long slim
hulls, dashingly raked masts and cloudstorms of canvas, they were (to
most minds) the finest creations of the age of sail. They set speed
records as they raced the year's first crop of fragrant China tea to
England, or immigrants to Australia and wool bales home again. On
one trip the terrified crew begged the master to reduce sail in a great
storm; he famously replied, 'To Hell or Melbourne!'

Wood was part earth, part liquid, part breathing green life; perfectly
at home within the flux of great waters. But the Chinese tell us whenever an element has reached its peak another is growing stronger quietly beneath; and even as wood mastered the seas, metal was being
forged to take its place.

It was a good joke at first – floating metal! – but by the mid-nineteenth century iron ships with ingenious propellers and puny engines
had appeared, and every year those engines became more powerful. Yet
the sailing world adapted. Iron hulls were large and strong, and iron
masts could carry canvas. God's wind needed no bunkers, and even the
best steamships were no faster than the square-riggers.

But in 1869 the balance shifted forever when the Suez Canal was sliced
between Africa and Arabia, and made voyages around the Cape of Good
Hope a thing of the past: a thing of the past for steamers at any rate. The
big wind ships could not negotiate the canal without costly towage and
were forced to keep to their old highways of the Roaring Forties. The
postal lifelines between distant colonies shifted to steamships, and passengers began to prefer their reliable passages. Understandably, a trip
through the tropics – no matter how fever-stricken – was a more attractive prospect than the gales and icebergs of southern seas.

Only one market remained open to the square-riggers – carriage of bulk goods from remote ports, where slow loading and lack of facilities made the tight schedules of steamers too expensive. They began to specialise in coal, saltpetre, ore, timber, grain and guano: filthy, labour-intensive cargoes.

In the late 1880s ship-building steel became available in quantity. It led to major advances in steam but also made possible the creation of a kind of wind-driven vessel that had never before been imagined: one of vast rigging and even vaster capacity, a massive four-masted warehouse that could be driven through even the roughest of waters.

To many these vessels were simply industrialised horrors, lacking the grace and glamour of 'real' sailing ships; to others they were romantic anachronisms – surely any fool could see that the future belonged to steam? But the new square-riggers were surprisingly useful – crews were cheap and the market for bulk commodities booming – and shipowners were anything but fools. They commissioned over four hundred of those extraordinary vessels and worked them hard, until the First World War brought their epoch to an end.

By the Second World War just twenty or so of the giant four-masters were still afloat, taking grain to Europe from isolated ports in South Australia, the far Antipodes. The great wind ships had been an expression of the highest in human art and skill and intelligence, but like the dinosaurs, their day was done.

———

Alan John Villiers was born in Melbourne on 23 September 1903. He was the second of Annie (Anastasia) and Leon Villiers' six children. His elder brother Noel was born in 1902, young Frank in 1906, Edith in 1907, Lionel in 1909 and Enid in 1912. Six babies in ten years – poor Annie! – but his mother is only an anxious shadow in Villiers' memoirs; he never mentions her by name.

Leon was a gripman on the cable trams, once the marvel of old Melbourne. They were propelled by metal cables running constantly in narrow tunnels beneath the road surface, between the tracks. The 'grip' was the device that reached through the slot in the side of the tunnel to grasp the moving cable, released by the gripman when the tram had to stop or coast, thrillingly, around corners.

Cable trams were quiet, cheap and very frequent, did not smell of oil or petrol, and glided, it was said, 'with a swan-like motion', along seventeen routes and more than sixty miles of track. Every small boy in Melbourne wanted to grow up to be a gripman: every small boy but Alan Villiers. He saw what happened to his father.

Beyond his long working hours, Leon was a tramways union leader and unsuccessful Labour parliamentary candidate for the seat of Waranga. He was also a passionate poet and writer. 'His poetry was about the bush and the strivings of man: the articles were to point the way to a better world,' said Villiers, who felt that his father was over-loaded with 'a great deal of the donkey-work for a movement which, great as were its early aspirations, sometimes came regrettably short of carrying out its ideals.'[2]

Leon was 'a tall square man with a high forehead and a black mous-tache'. Alan always remembered his 'doctrine of good citizenship – be resolute: give your ideas: go after peace of mind, gear down to simple things. Be not possessive or avaricious. Discard all shams. Love simple things.'[3] Leon believed that education for the workers would lead in-evitably to progress, and that his children must aspire to a better life: he trusted in The Future. He was appalled to discover that his son longed instead for The Past, and the labours of a common sailor.

He should hardly have been surprised. Alan wrote that his earliest memories were not of his own home but of a house on Spencer Street belonging to his Ballarat Irish aunts and uncles (from his mother's family) which had an amazing balcony – one from which the little boy could watch the square-rigged sailing ships along the Yarra River at the end of the street, and in Hobsons Bay off Port Melbourne and distant Williamstown.

The uncles at Spencer Street were gold prospectors, 'tall, brown, bearded men', who would take Alan with them to visit the docks, 'a very small boy trudging along beside some very large uncles in the shadow of a full-rigged ship'. Alan's father was of more reserved English stock: he liked ships well enough, but visits to the docks were opportunities for lectures on geography and politics. He preferred camping in the bush to the sea, and tried to turn his son away from his growing passion.

When Alan was small, the family moved from Buncle Street, North Melbourne, to a tiny house near Flemington racecourse, in Collett

Street, Kensington. Ships were still his greatest love, and he would walk to the docks and back – 'only four or five miles' – by himself or with his little brother Frank. He kept a secret book of his drawings of square-riggers.

Once Leon brought home a gripman, an elderly sailor whose job was to talk Alan out of his passion for ships: instead, to Leon's dismay, they enthused together for hours. Villiers later imagined the old man dreaming of Cape Horn gales, where 'silent ships under a press of trade wind sail followed each other through sunlit days', while he was 'jammed in the driver's pew of a cable tram'. Such a prospect filled him with horror.

Alan Villiers' family always called him by his second name, John, or more usually 'Jack'. His sister Edith Hazel was 'Hazel', brother Lionel was 'Leal', and Enid Marjorie, for some reason, became known as 'Bill'.

To help support his family, Alan had a paper-round from the age of nine, starting at 5.30 in the morning. A boy in one of the children's novels he later wrote 'was very quiet and paler than he should have been: a hard life had left its marks ... for eight years – six days a week, for two hours in the early morning, he had trudged four miles throwing people's newspapers on their verandas and poking them beneath their doors.'[4]

He needed the money for schoolbooks, and the few pennies left over went towards second-hand books on ships, which he read obsessively. He loved to go to Royal Park near the Melbourne Zoo to climb a favourite tree from which he could see the square-riggers. When he was nine, he and his little brother Frank were chased away by a park ranger on horseback, who flogged them with a stockwhip he kept for impounding stray cows.

'I can hear the creak of the saddle-leather now', he wrote in an unpublished draft of his autobiography, 'thirty years afterwards and 12,000 miles away, and see the suffused blood grow on the ranger's saturnine face ... This incident befouled Royal Park for me. Never again did I climb the tree to look at ships.' Villiers ran to his father to show him the welts and blood. Leon dashed to the park and confronted the ranger, who simply sat on his horse and, humiliatingly, ignored him. Leon was powerless. Alan wrote, 'That stinging stock-whip lashed deep & even today I find the sight of Melbourne depressing and dispiriting.'[5]

At the age of eleven Alan tried to join the barque *Hippen* as an apprentice, but was dissuaded by the mate, who had signed on at ten. He was 'bewitched' by the five-year-old daughter of the captain of the Norwegian ship *Asmund*, a white-blonde angel 'as remote from humdrum everyday life as the lovely ship she sailed in, and the great man her father who sailed the ship'. But now, in the years of the First World War, *Hippen* and *Asmund* sailed without him, and both went missing. Villiers does not clarify whether storms or German submarines were the reason, but U-boats certainly had as little mercy for graceful square-riggers as for warships.

When Alan was twelve he started work with his older brother Noel in the long summer holidays at the glass-bottle factory in Spotswood, on the Yarra River leading to the docks. It was hot and hellish, with much night work; but square-riggers towed past and that was compensation enough. (Sailing ships were rarely spoken of as 'being towed' – too passive a term, perhaps.)

He was a clever, adaptable boy, awarded a scholarship to continue at high school, and hopefully to go on to university. He flirted with the idea of joining the Royal Australian Navy but lost interest when he found out that they no longer sailed their last full-rigged ship; and in any case, they did not want him.

Then, when Alan was only fourteen-and-a-half his childhood ended, and even the loss of the blonde angel from the *Asmund* could not have prepared him. His father went suddenly to hospital, was operated on for cancer, sewn up and sent home to die. He did so within a week, on 10 April 1918, aged only forty-five.

Leon Villiers was laid out in an open coffin in the front room, and Alan recalled 'his manuscripts, his *Songs of Labour and Love*, his poems of the Australian bush, now never to be revised. All his great hopes for his country and for us, his sons, were in that coffin too ...' But at the burial all he could think was, 'Oh God, now let me out of Melbourne! Let me go!'[6]

Leon Villiers' own father had also died at an early age, and his mother had left Australia with her four younger children. The three eldest stayed with relatives at Warrnambool but, wrote Alan, they 'committed my father and two of his sisters to an institution miscalled a home ... his greatest dread was that he might die young and leave the six of us to suffer one.'[7] Leon's worst fears had come true, but the Labour movement was able to help establish widowed Annie in a small suburban grocery shop. Alan, respecting his father's wishes, stayed reluctantly at school for almost another year.

As in many Australian families of the time there may have been some inter-denominational tensions – Leon was Protestant and Annie Irish Catholic. Alan and Noel identified themselves as Protestant, but after Leon's death the four younger children were raised as Catholics. (Edith Hazel changed her name to Hazel Mary, Enid had numerous children, and Lionel bitterly resented what he saw as an imposition.)[8]

In late 1918 the deadly global pandemic of pneumonic influenza escaped quarantine in Australia and broke out in Sydney, Perth and Melbourne. Alan fell ill early in 1919, then the rest of his family also succumbed; Annie lost the shop. 'My mother went to work for a Jew in Flinders Lane, for she was handy with the needle. Brave soul! She worked hard there for years.'[9]

Villiers wrote a number of varying accounts of what happened next, which present some interesting anomalies. The first version of his final year in Melbourne appeared in the 1937 book *Cruise of the Conrad*. When he wrote it he was deeply depressed: he had lost a woman he loved and a ship he loved even more, and the book is suffused with anguish, self-doubt and financial desperation.

In a chapter bitterly entitled 'Local Boy Makes Good', memories of the life he had fled sixteen years before came back to haunt him. He recalled losing his school cap and being humiliated 'time and again'. His widowed mother was too poor to replace the cap, so he worked at the glass factory to get the money. He would watch ships on the river, yearning desperately to escape, and finally – as simple as that – he did so.

A second version appeared in a 1938 piece Villiers wrote for a twenty-fifth anniversary magazine for his high school, Essendon, which by then regarded him as its most eminent old boy. From February to August 1919 the school was used as an influenza hospital, but classes continued at another school in Wilson Street, Moonee Ponds.[10] He recalled, 'the school was taken over as a hospital, when the influenza epidemic was so bad, and we were all bundled off to a new school at Wilson Street, or somewhere … it was about that time that the chance of a cadetship came in the barque *Rothesay Bay*, and I was off.'

The third telling is in his 1949 autobiography, *The Set of the Sails*. Here there was no mention of lost caps or Wilson Street, but instead a strange tale of sexual humiliation. He wrote that his school had been closed and he was working in the glass factory until the official notification came that it was open again. After months had passed Villiers suddenly realised his school had re-opened but he had not been informed, when he saw a pretty blonde classmate, with a look of the *Asmund* angel, in uniform one morning on the train. He was filthy, just off the night shift and embarrassed to be recognised, and he simply never returned to the school.

This published version of events puzzled a classmate, who wrote to him saying, 'I could have sworn you actually began your leaving certificate year and stuck it for one term at the school in which we were temporarily housed when ours was appropriated as an emergency hospital. I thought you started on Chemistry and Latin, as you thought you might take up Medicine, but also did History, as you were keen on it.'[11]

The complete story seems to be that he attended Wilson Street school for at least the first third of 1919, then dropped out and worked at the glass factory until the end of 1919. During the year he had an embarrassing meeting with a classmate he was attracted to. He started learning sailing skills halfway through 1919 with the Melbourne Ancient Mariners Club at Albert Park Lake, and actually joined his first ship on 11 January 1920, according to his discharge certificate.

Minor discrepancies, certainly. Still, what is the significance of his tale that other students were informed that school had resumed, while he was not? There is an air of grievance about it – his close friend Fritz

Egerton would chide him gently about his 'inferiority complex' – but it might have been just a story he told his mother to account for dropping out of school, one that expressed his sense of exclusion and became entangled in his memories.

What is undeniable is that in this frustrating period he yearned to 'sail away' from his bereavement, poverty and emotional pain. His various tales express compulsion – just get away from the hell of Melbourne! – and anything and everything around him seemed to offer a justification.

———

Villiers needed a Board of Trade certificate to learn sailing with the Ancient Mariners. Dated June 1919, it states that he is fifteen, 5 feet, 10½ inches in height (he would grow a little taller), with fair complexion, fair hair and grey eyes. He had passed his vision tests and had an 'eagle and flower' on his left forearm: tellingly, at the tender age of fifteen, he had already committed himself to the stigma of a sailor's tattoo.

The Ancient Mariners found a sailing ship willing to take him on as a cadet – *Rothesay Bay*, sailing between New Zealand and Australia. (Villiers pronounced the ship's name crisply as 'Roth'sy Bay', as he did his own, 'Vill'yers' – two syllables, not three.)[12]

In early 1920 sixteen-year-old Alan took the train to Adelaide, South Australia, and a steamer to the small port of Edithburgh. He felt guilt at leaving his struggling mother – it was true that one less child around would make it easier on her, but she wanted him to study as his father had wished, and he knew that his leaving for a sailor's life would hurt her.

All mariners' memoirs at this stage seem to retell the same scenes: the sad farewells, the looming ship, the awkward baggage, the unfriendly mate, the grim berth in the apprentices' half-deck, the awful food, the inevitable seasickness: and Villiers' story retells them too, except that from the moment he first saw the 'very ordinary' three-masted barque *Rothesay Bay* – all bluff bows and ugly grey paint – he discovered a great happiness. As if in a dream he recalled the vessel setting sail, all of the hands cheerfully drunk, a few of them having fled from a much harder ship:

They ran along the yards, scorning the footropes, and they danced and sang, laughing to think themselves free of their great Cape Horner and in this handy, small Australian barque ... They went at everything with such a will that they never finished a chanty, and the chanties they sang were such as I had never read in any books ... What a going to sea![13]

Later, when a week or two of wretched seasickness had passed, standing at a masthead he thought, 'Spiritually I felt nearer the Creator of things on the high yards and astride the bowsprit-end than I had ever felt ashore. This was the life! Drive on good barque, I am where I want to be! This is contentment.'

Happiness from the first few ships he knew was to colour his view of the sea for life. He would bring all of his father Leon's passionate trust in the innate goodness of the working man to a vision of the ship as a near-perfect world, content in its firm, wise hierarchy, safe from the deceits and illusions of the shore.

Rothesay Bay, 'this handy, small Australian barque', was one of a greatly diminished fleet sailing southern coastal waters with timber, coal, fuel and provisions. She was a classic three-masted iron barque, built in 1877 in Glasgow; 187 feet long and 772 gross registered tons.[14] We may know a little of *Rothesay Bay* from another of her kind, *Polly Woodside*, the 'prettiest barque ever built in Belfast', which is marooned today on the Yarra River in Melbourne beside the unlovely bluster of an exhibition centre.

Polly Woodside is an iron barque from 1885 of 678 gross tons. She was in the same Tasman Sea trade as *Rothesay Bay*, but the year after Villiers first went to sea she was turned into a coal hulk. In 1968 she was rescued by the National Trust of Australia and restored by a group of passionate volunteers. The World Ship Trust awarded *Polly Woodside* the International Maritime Heritage medal in 1988, placing her in the company of vessels such as *Cutty Sark* and HMS *Victory*. Sadly, her museum site was closed in 2006 so that another convention centre could be built on it.

Melbourne seems to have forgotten it was once – and still is – one of the great port cities of the world, but few residents ever think of the docks now except in terms of real estate. What used to be the heart of the city – alive with odd vessels and mysterious people – is now a high-rise wasteland. The freighters (so ugly), the trawlers (so smelly), the tugs (so noisy) have been banished to less desirable environs, and today barely a soul in trendy Docklands would know a brig from a barquentine, although once any child in Melbourne could have told them.

In the days of merchant sail every kind of ship had its own terminology. Even the word 'ship' itself meant precisely a vessel with three masts and a bowsprit, carrying rectangular ('square') sails on *all* of the masts – a 'full-rigged ship'. A major innovation of the nineteenth century was a move from square sails on the rearmost mast to 'fore-and-aft' sails, set along the length of the vessel, which were more easily worked. Hence a two-masted full-rigged vessel was a 'brig', but with fore-and-aft on the rear it was a 'brigantine'. A three-masted full-rigger was a 'ship'; with a single fore-and-aft mast it was a 'barque', with two it was a 'barquentine'.

Those carrying four masts were simply termed four-masted barques or ships. They were usually constructed of iron or steel to cope with the structural stresses. Four-masters could load far more cargo than three-masters but they were comparatively rare – out of a 1901 list of sailing vessels only 3 per cent had four masts.[15] In total, amongst the thousands of square-riggers of that era, only 414 metal four-masters were ever built: they were the elite of the wind ships.[16]

Today, *Polly Woodside* floats unvisited beside a construction site in Melbourne, her hard grey bulk and outstretched yards looming tall above the mud. She is vast in a puzzling way that simply has no scale of comparison to modern eyes. Yet when likened to a four-masted barque, pretty *Polly Woodside* is as a dolphin might be to a whale.

———

Alan Villiers grew lean and sinewy, utterly content in his new life on the barque *Rothesay Bay*. He learned of the true seaman's passion for neatness and cleanliness and well-organised gear, and the importance to ship stability – and survival – of precise cargo stowage. He liked both his young fellow cadets and the weathered ancients who ran the ship.

They sailed 1,000 tons of gypsum to Whangarei in New Zealand, unloaded it and filled up with timber for Sydney. The passage was expected to take two weeks but poor weather turned it into two months. When they arrived their desperately ill captain went to hospital and the first mate, who had sailed the ship safely through atrocious conditions, was fired. So was Villiers, after only half a year at sea, but the first mate found him a berth in the barque *James Craig* – 'a lovely little vessel, as much a clipper as the *Rothesay Bay* was a warehouse'.

James Craig had been launched as *Clan McLeod* from the Glasgow slips in 1874 and was still crewed by a number of Scots. An iron barque like *Polly Woodside*, 180 feet long and 671 gross tons, she was 'a lively, lovely, and highly responsive thoroughbred of a ship … She tacked like a yacht and ran like a greyhound.' *James Craig* had already done time as a coal hulk in New Guinea but had returned to service for a firm of Tasmanian jam merchants. Her first port of call was Hobart in Tasmania, and Villiers 'took a great liking to the clean southern city at the foot of Mt Wellington … an attractive and cheerful spot, full of small ketches and schooners'.

In Hobart Alan also met a girl, Daphne Kaye Harris. In the little notebook he kept at this time, in a different, childlike handwriting, are the words 'D. Harris, 193 Davey St Hobart'.[17] He liked Daphne enough to send her the following Christmas a copy of a posthumously published booklet of his father's poetry, *The Changing Year and Other Verses*.

James Craig loaded timber for South Australia and battled the Southern Ocean for a month to get it there. In Port Adelaide Villiers saw a four-masted steel barque, the first he had ever seen, registered to an unknown port named Mariehamn – 'a massive ship, manned by young fellows with white hair and pale yellow eyebrows'. The barque flew a flag with a blue cross on a white background, that of newly independent Finland.

'The little Craig tramped pleasantly around the Tasman Sea for several voyages', wrote Villiers in *Set of the Sails*. 'It seemed to me that the fo'c'sle of a happy sailing-ship at sea was one of the more pleasant abodes of labouring man, where the sailors of all nations had learned through the centuries to work and live amicably together. Here there was true democracy, true international co-operation.'

Then in December 1920, less than a year after Villiers had first gone to sea on *Rothesay Bay*, they sailed into Port Phillip with a cargo of

New Zealand timber, and towed up the Yarra to find out that *James Craig* would sail no more. She was laid up in Hobart for four years, became a coal hulk in Recherche Bay in southern Tasmania, and in 1932 was beached in a storm and abandoned.

In 1949 Villiers wrote about *James Craig* in his autobiography, and passed on his memories of the 'happy sailing-ship' to a new generation of maritime enthusiasts. In 1972 volunteers from the Australian Heritage Fleet refloated *James Craig* and towed her to Hobart for repairs. In 1981 they took her to Sydney for an extraordinary job of rebuilding, and today she is a working excursion vessel.

James Craig and *Polly Woodside* were the lucky ones. They could easily have gone the way of so many others: the way of *Rothesay Bay* perhaps. She was hulked in 1921 and dismantled in 1936, her remains dumped on an island near Auckland, unidentifiable among those of thirteen other vessels.

———

It was still just possible for a naive lad to dream of a career in sail when Alan Villiers first went to sea in 1920, although the path to ship's master was not easy. The first step was four years of apprenticeship at sea, followed by nautical academy to prepare for examinations for second mate. Next came more sea time, then another set of exams for first mate, followed by at least a further year as a watch-keeping officer, and finally the test for Master's Certificate. Command was still not assured, either – many ships' mates were qualified masters hoping for a position.

By the early 1920s the cruel truth was emerging. Since the war, the world had an abundance of new steamer tonnage; the merchant fleets no longer needed sailing vessels. Not only the handy little iron barques had been superseded by steamships, but even the great steel four-masters were living on borrowed time.

Still, Villiers and his friends searched for another sailing ship. They had no wish to go in a 'Yankee' schooner – American ships were notorious for their casual brutality – or a 'Squarehead' (Scandinavian) cadet ship, which would have no need of apprentices. They went to Williamstown, the old port town at the mouth of the Yarra, to look over two four-masted steel barques loading bags of grain at the railway pier, *Bellands* and *Hougomont*.

Villiers thought that *Bellands* was the better option. She was 3,145 gross tons, five times the volume of *James Craig,* and had a 'Liverpool' deckhouse – a dry, central living quarters that would break the dangerous rush of seas on deck. Best of all, *Bellands* carried Jarvis brace-winches to ease much of the heavy labour of taking-in and paying-out the braces, the wires that swung the yards to the best angle for the sails to catch the wind.

In January 1921 Villiers and several of his friends joined *Bellands*; Villiers as ordinary seaman at the good wage of £8 10s. per month. Their only quibble was that she was a 'lime-juicer', a Limey: British ships were well-known for their scanty food and rigid class distinctions, so unlike the informality of the small barques.

Once they set sail, however, they found that work on the gigantic *Bellands* was little harder than that on *James Craig*: as well as the wonderful brace-winches she had twenty-four crewmen and a donkey-engine to raise the anchor and the heavier sails. But soon disappointment arose: the ship's passage was not to be around Cape Horn as Villiers had assumed, but the slower route westwards to England via the Great Australian Bight, the Indian Ocean and the Cape of Good Hope. They might enjoy thrilling sailing that way too, but to miss out on the classic Cape Horn voyage was bitter – for young Alan at least (the more experienced seamen sighed with relief).

Astonishingly, there was a young woman on board too, the first of those bizarre creatures Villiers would encounter throughout his life that simply refused to comprehend that a woman had no place at sea. She was the niece – or perhaps the 'niece' – of the captain and lived aft with him.

> The crew … did not care for the niece, who trod the poop haughtily and frowned upon the lot of us as if we were the scum of the earth … She never spoke a word to any of the dwellers of the foc's'l throughout the voyage; the crew had a grudge against her that she wanted fool things done, at inappropriate moments, in order that she could photograph them. It rankled to have to come out in a broiling sun from a decent job of splicing or something and fool around aloft with a tops'l for a blessed girl to take a photograph; she was by no means popular, though I don't suppose that troubled her.[18]

The captain's ship-handling was excessively cautious and he misjudged the trade winds, making the voyage longer than necessary. That was bad enough, but worst of all he had carelessly neglected to replenish the stores of tobacco before leaving port. The sailors were in despair: hunger was one thing, but no tobacco for months was simple torture!

The captain's neglect had a more sinister side, however. In the mid-Atlantic they saw a large sailing ship on fire in the distance. Instead of going to help as custom and law demanded, to the horror of the crew, the mate and the captain insisted that the smoke was from a steamer, and sailed on.

Villiers later found out that the burning vessel, *Lysglimt*, was abandoned once *Bellands* had passed her by, but her lifeboats were rescued by another ship; the crew were unusually lucky. He had two shipmates sign his diary to witness the accuracy of the outraged account he wrote. When they got to England the three boys went to Lloyds to report the incident, but their story was discounted as an attempt to smear the captain.[19]

By the time they reached St Nazaire, France, on 7 June 1921, Villiers was 'heartily sick' of *Bellands*. A few days before he had listed gloomily in his notebook:[20]

149 days at sea
No sugar
no butter
no milk
no jam
no rice
no burgoo
no dried fruit
no lime juice!
no spuds
nothing at all!

Still, it was not the barque's fault, he later argued, for 'her tobaccoless voyage, her ham-fisted sailing, her food shortage, her long swelter in the doldrums', but that of poor officers: the demands of the First World War 'gave commands to some who were unfitted for them'.

'What annoyed me,' wrote Villiers, 'was that the stupid privations practiced aboard, the whole unsatisfactory spirit of the ship, were so unnecessary. The voyage was, at any rate, a good object lesson in what not to do, if I ever became a sailing-ship captain myself, as I surely proposed to do.'

———

On joining *Bellands* Villiers had noticed that the ship's bell had been cast with the Scots name 'Forteviot' but her lifeboats bore the painted-over words 'Werner Vinnen'; she clearly had some history behind her. He learned that she had been launched as *Forteviot* at Liverpool in 1891, then renamed *Werner Vinnen* when sold to German interests in 1910. In the early days of the First World War she was taken as a British war prize, became *Yawry* for a year, then was sold in 1916 and renamed *Bellands*.

The life of *Bellands* under different flags was far from unusual; sailing vessels from Britain made their way into many national fleets. But what was unusual was the sheer preponderance of British ships among the iron and steel four-masters: only 414 such vessels were ever built, and of those, an astonishing 349 – 84 per cent! – were launched from British slipways. Even more surprising, two-thirds of those vessels came from a single region – Scotland's River Clyde, with its shipyards from Glasgow to Greenock (see Appendix A, Figures 1 and 2). Despite their famous sailing fleets, France only ever built twenty-nine four-masters and Germany eighteen; and in the whole of the prosperous United States only eight were ever launched (Appendix A, Figure 3).

The epoch of the metal four-masted vessels was brief too: it lasted for only half a century, from the 1875 Glasgow iron ship *County of Peebles* to the 1926 German steel barque *Padua*. Throughout the 1880s, ten to twenty four-masters per year were built – a mixture of iron and steel ships and barques. Then in 1889 the numbers of steel vessels exploded and barque rig was the only game in town. The peak arrived in 1892 when sixty-seven four-masters were built, but the bubble collapsed just as suddenly as it began.

A brief recovery took place in 1902 with seventeen four-masters, but the party was over by 1907 (Appendix A, Figure 4). After that, only the Germans would seek to build four-masters – seven superb steel barques – but no more Clydeside sailing giants would ever again be launched.

At St Nazaire, the crew were paid off and sent to England, a 'home port' for Commonwealth sailors; foreigners were forbidden to seek work in France. In Paris, Villiers wrote in his autobiography, 'our score-odd of lusty seamen descended from the train from Nantes with a whoop and a wild exuberant surge ... Three of us from *James Craig* stayed together, and though we had our fling in Paris too, in due course we went on.'

This is the only hint Villiers ever gave that he might have enjoyed the life of a young sailor let loose in a big city. Just one year later James Joyce would publish *Ulysses* and revolutionise the frankness of the written word, but Villiers' books were always as coy as a maiden aunt: in his 1949 autobiography he fails to mention the name of his first wife, the presence of a woman he loved on a major voyage, or even the very existence of his second wife and three children.

The young sailors reached London on 12 June, and again started searching for a ship. They stayed for a while at a friend's house in Golders Green and would walk nine miles to the docks and back every day: 'The summer of 1921 was hot and glorious in England, and each morning as we strode across the Hampstead Heath the great metropolis looked wonderful and romantic, spread out before us.'

The boys found lodging and potential work on a four-masted iron barque named *Omega*, but could not sign on because a coal strike prevented her loading. 'The summer months of 1921 continued warm and pleasant until there was a serious drought in London,' recalled Villiers. Finally a shipmate suggested that Villiers go back to France to seek work on a vessel named *Lancing*, and 'a couple of weeks later I slipped ashore quietly by night from a little weekly steamer at the port of Nantes ... in the early autumn of 1921.'

There then followed wonderful adventures with a sailor who travelled with him, a Finn nicknamed Lusitania – 'twenty-six, dark, lean, lithe ... a very strange young man ... His features were sharp and determined, and there was a fierce glow in his dark eyes'. But they could locate neither the elusive *Lancing* nor even any working square-rigger. All they found were 'lovely big barques, ships and four-masted barques ... moored in dejection together in tiers along a canal'. They sheltered for 'weeks and weeks' on one of the ships with other illegal foreign sailors, then decided to walk south to Bordeaux, a distance of around 180 miles:

> The weather continued fine; the days were long, and each worth while for its own sake. The sun rose and we washed in streams, and the birds sang and the countryside was lovely ... To roll in a blanket with the sweet smell of hedges in my nostrils and the clear stars above, after a long day's tramp, was very satisfying so long as we were not hungry ... it took us about ten days, as far as I remember, to reach Bordeaux.[21]

There Villiers found *Lawhill*, the ship that would change everything. At first he and Lusitania were refused work, but they talked their way into jobs, accepted at last because *Lawhill* was undermanned. To his surprise, Villiers said, he was even signed on as able seaman, despite not having the sea time for that rating.

This all sounds perfectly reasonable, except that if they arrived after a long English summer at Nantes in autumn, starting the third week of September, by Villiers' own reckoning it must have been at least October before they reached Bordeaux. Yet his discharge certificate states that he signed on to *Lawhill*'s articles a scant five weeks after he landed at St Nazaire, on 7 June in *Bellands*. He joined *Lawhill* on 12 July 1921, in early summer, not autumn. He had his diaries and seaman's papers to check the dates, so how could he so poorly remember the timing? And more interestingly – why?

The obvious explanation is that he simply made a mistake. His book came twenty-six years after the event; on later occasions he would scold himself for slap-dash writing, and perhaps that was all there was to it. Yet in these memoirs he is lovingly precise about the seasons, the weather, the days spent travelling here or there.

Or perhaps the reason was that this bittersweet time loomed so large in his memory. He was only seventeen or eighteen, after all. He had escaped from stifling Melbourne to a thrilling new life: one that would soon be struck down by the accident on *Lawhill*. It is not surprising he might recall every sunlit day as if it had been weeks. But no, the truth appears to be simply a case of authorial embroidery. Basil Greenhill, a friend of Villiers, wrote:

... while in London, looking for a berth in another sailing vessel, he called at Clarkson's, then famous as ship-brokers in the city, who looked after the affairs and interests of Scandinavian and Finnish ship-owners in Britain ... Clarkson's sent him to Bordeaux to join the Finnish four-masted barque *Lawhill* as an able seaman (the account of this development which Villiers wrote in his autobiography, *The Set of the Sails*, is somewhat more romantic).[22]

Villiers' own diary notes the job and how he got to the ship:

Lawhill in Bordeaux, bound to Port Lincoln for orders (ballast) ... British & Foreign Wharf below Tower Bridge, SS Petrel for Bordeaux direct fare £7-0-0 ... Left wharf 2 pm Sat [actually a Sunday] July 10, fine hot day ... clear of Thames by 8.15. Next day warm, no wind. Arrived Bordeaux 10.10 am on Tuesday morning – Lawhill away to the devil down the river.[23]

It may have taken him a long hard trek to get to *Lawhill* but he must have found her, as he signed on to the ship's articles the day he arrived. So his yarns of walking for ten days from Nantes, fast-talking his way into *Lawhill*'s crew and his 'surprise' at being rated able seaman, were simply not true; although the enigmatic Lusitania apparently did exist.[24]

Sadly, the long idyllic tramp through the French countryside was complete fantasy. While his father Leon loved camping in the bush above all, that was a pleasure young Alan never shared with him. What he wrote later may not have been his true experience, but perhaps it was what he might have wished it to be.

2

THIS WAS SAILING!

Lawhill was often called 'lucky *Lawhill*' and so she was, to most people but Alan Villiers. Yet he was fast enough himself to hang nicknames on vessels: he called *Grace Harwar*, unfairly, a 'killer ship' for years. It was true that people died on her, but people died on square-riggers all the time. Even in everyday conditions they could all be killers: a giant metal shell tossing around in the most mutable of elements was never going to be a bastion of health and safety in the workplace.

Lawhill was a four-masted steel barque of 2,942 gross tons, launched at Dundee in the boom year for barques, 1892. For twelve years until 1911 her master was the ingenious Captain C.B. Jarvis, inventor of the labour-saving brace-winch. She did not carry royal yards above her topgallant sails ('bald-headed' rig), so had a squarish and inelegant appearance. Just before the start of the First World War, *Lawhill* was bought by August Troberg, one of the major shipowners of Mariehamn, the capital of the Åland ('Or-lund') Islands, 6,400-odd granite specks in the Baltic Sea, midway between Sweden and Finland.

Since the thirteenth century Sweden had ruled Finland, including the Åland Islands, but after devastating Russian invasions in 1714, 1741 and 1808, Sweden finally ceded Finland to Russia. When the 1917 Russian Revolution began Finland grabbed the opportunity to declare its independence, but then suffered a civil war between communists and monarchists in the first half of 1918.

During this time, Finnish ships in foreign ports were regarded as stateless – unflagged and potentially unfinancial – and many were confiscated until their legal positions were clear. In June 1918 *Lawhill* was seized by the French government, rigged down and laid up for a year in Brest. But even that was lucky: it probably saved her from destruction in the last months of the First World War.

At the start of hostilities in August 1914 there were only 229 four-masted iron or steel vessels still existing worldwide (a few of the total of 414 had not yet been built, the rest had already been lost). By the end of the war, sixty-six of those 229 ships – 29 per cent – had been destroyed in action: torpedoed, shelled, bombed or scuttled. Such a loss rate is appalling, even for merchant shipping in the 'war to end all wars', while the thought of sleek killer submarines stalking unarmed square-riggers is grotesque, like a time machine gone mad. Still, in a period when medieval cathedrals were casually obliterated, there could be little concern for mere sailing ships – they were but a tiny fraction of the greater tragedy.[1]

During the war another twenty-four metal four-masters were lost in the usual wrecks, collisions, strandings and disappearances, while a handful were converted to motorised tankers, albeit with far handsomer lines than most. In total, only 141 four-masters survived the conflict, including lucky *Lawhill* and two that were built in Germany during the war. Two more square-riggers would be launched in the 1920s, but they were the last of their kind. Everyone knew they were finished: everyone but shrewd Gustaf Erikson.

———

Captain Gustaf Erikson had bought *Lawhill* in October 1917. He was one of the clever, tenacious Ålanders, whose farmlands were sprinkled over so many tiny islands that every household needed a boat, wrote Elis Karlsson, an Ålands sailor and author who met Villiers in the 1930s.[2] The Ålanders were fine seafarers who prospered enough as farmers, fishermen and timber traders to start building up their own fleets of sailing ships from those supplanted by steam.

At the start of the First World War, little Mariehamn was the port of registry of over seventy vessels, of which twenty-six were iron or steel square-riggers. In 1913, at the age of forty-nine, Gustaf Erikson – known as Gusta' – had retired as a master mariner and begun carefully building up his own fleet. When he bought *Lawhill* in 1917, he already owned a schooner, six barques and a full-rigged ship, the much-maligned *Grace Harwar*.

Erikson employed Ruben de Cloux as captain of *Lawhill* in 1919, and de Cloux sailed *Lawhill* on four successful voyages which were said to have been Erikson's financial salvation. De Cloux had been born in 1884 and was married to Elis Karlsson's sister – most Ålanders were related to each other – and was to become a good friend of Alan Villiers. They first met briefly in 1921 when Villiers joined *Lawhill* and de Cloux was handing command over to a different captain.

Erikson vessels were noted for their hiring of 'boys' as crew: teenagers were energetic, good-natured and well used to heavy work. When Villiers visited Mariehamn in 1933 he wrote, 'It's a hard life here: a Cape Horn voyage must be a holiday to a boy brought up on an Åland farm.'[3] Most European countries still required their merchant officers on steamers to have apprenticed in sail, so clever Gusta' was even able to charge a lad's family for the privilege of labouring on his square-riggers.

He saw that the only expenses for these ships were stores and equipment – the vessels themselves were going cheap and could be sailed uninsured. If they survived at sea they could be worked until they no longer passed classification and their cargoes became uninsurable, then sold without sentiment to the breakers. And while the rest of the world was rushing to embrace steam, Erikson just kept on buying three- and four-masted barques, until he had assembled the last windjammer merchant fleet that would ever exist.

———

Oddly, there is no convincing explanation for that word 'windjammer'. It was said to be a non-nautical, landlubber's name for square-riggers,[4] but it was also supposed to be a steamer crew's sneer at sailing-ship men, so it did have nautical usage after all.[5] People who talked too much in the trucking or oilfields trades were called windjammers, as were circus musicians, who blew loud and fast into cornets, clarinets and trombones.

Some claimed it was because sailing ships had to 'jam' their yards tight against the backstays to drive into the wind.[6] Villiers himself was infuriated by a coffee-table book which said 'they jammed themselves into the wind however hard it blew'. He wrote sharply, 'Any vessel which jammed herself into the wind would stop.'[7]

In fact, the earliest usage is from about 1870, meaning 'horn player'. It comes from the German (or Dutch or Norwegian) words for wind and 'moan, cry or lament'. Applying the term to square-rigged vessels in general was rare before the First World War, when precise distinctions between rigging styles were important. But by the 1920s, with so few sailing vessels left afloat, 'windjammer' came to be used by landlubbers and sailors alike. Yet that was usage, not rationale; and nothing so far explains why 'windjammer' came to mean 'deepwater sailing ship'. But perhaps the sailors themselves can tell us.

Villiers recalled, 'A score-odd notes are here, if you listen closely, if you listen carefully into the sullen great roaring ... there is the plaintive moaning at the rigging screws, each with a different note; the sighing through the slackened running gear; and the mad roar at the wet and powerful backstays.'[8] And Elis Karlsson wrote, 'the icy wind played the music of the square-rigged ships in their rigging, a music no square-rigged sailor ever forgets.'[9]

That music was the wind's lament in saxophone, cello and shimmering percussion; and the ship itself – the windjammer – was the soulful musician.

———

Villiers was astonished at the youth of the *Lawhill*'s crew – fifteen-, sixteen- and seventeen-year-olds. Apart from the captain, mates, bosun and carpenter, there were only nineteen seamen 'to work 2750 ton square rigger 14,000 miles in ballast! Can't do it,' he wrote gloomily in his diary. Still, he stayed. They loaded the ballast quickly then sailed:

> Friday July 29 1.30 pm. Leave Bassens Pier Bordeaux, tow of tug Callus ... Dip ensign to ex Captain de Cloux who came to see us off. Drop the pick [anchor] 11.30 pm off Verdun at mouth of Garonne.[10]
>
> To get that big ship to Australia with her small crew was not going to be a picnic for them, or anyone ... What was I letting myself in for? I very quickly found out. I was embarking upon the smartest piece of deep-sea sailing it has been my good fortune to enjoy.[11]

He was charmed at the ease with which the young Ålanders took *Lawhill* to sea:

[T]he morning sunshine found us slipping gently along under every stitch we had – twenty-three sails – with as little fuss as if we had been an onion ketch bound for La Rochelle instead of a deep-water four-poster, outward bound to-wards Australia. Whew! So this is a Finnish ship, I thought.

When conditions worsened and *Lawhill* did not have enough sea room to manoeuvre near the Spanish coast, Villiers expected her to seek a safe anchorage. Instead, to his surprise, she was handled with great skill:

What, I thought, they aren't going to tack her, surely? ... Sprays were breaking over the huge wall of her weather side ... Tack her? That's just precisely what they were doing. Into the wind she came, as if she loved it, like a gigantic yacht – no trace of the clumsy windbag now ... *This* was sailing – sailing as it was meant to be ...

The work was hard but shared out fairly, Villiers wrote. The food was plentiful and the watches well organised. The barque was 'a master-piece of labour-saving devices on deck and aloft', which Villiers cred-ited to her captain of ten years before, Brace-Winch Jarvis. Even though he was the only non-Scandinavian on board, Villiers mixed easily with the other crew, helping them with the English they needed to learn for their officer's certificates. He soon picked up some basic Swedish, which had remained the Ålands' language despite Finland's sovereignty. Although he did not know it then, he was gaining entry into a society normally closed to outsiders.

It took four weeks for *Lawhill* to get to the Equator, then the winds picked up and they passed the Cape of Good Hope forty-eight days after leaving Bordeaux. A few weeks later they were off Spencer Gulf in South Australia.

We had seen ice and the road had been rough and hard on the boys. The *Lawhill* was driven hard despite the smallness of the crew; but her master knew what he was doing. We blew out no sails. We had no accidents ... I was feeling very pleased ... I liked the big *Lawhill* and was well accepted aboard.

As the barque approached the scattered lights of Port Lincoln in the dark, Villiers was aloft with several other sailors, stowing the fore lower topsail. Standing by at the anchor, the mate suddenly cried out in Swedish, 'I believe we sail ashore!', and let the anchor cable go with a roar.

And immediately, too, the forefoot of the big ship came up on the beach as she hit Australia with a gentle thump which quivered the masts and all the rigging. Caught off balance, working with two hands, I was pitched from the yard and hurtled to the deck.

———

Like a confident child, Villiers had never dreamed of the possibility of falling. The sailors carried him in a piece of old canvas to a bunk, then refloated the barque.

I have fitful memories of that long night, of waking in some dulled pain and hearing the wind in the rigging and the cries of the sailors, my shipmates, as they went about their work. I was past caring what happened to the ship, or for the moment, to me.

Still, he had been fortunate, his fall broken by the rigging, the damage relatively minor, he thought: 'a wrenched pelvis, some internal injuries, and a nasty jab in the left thigh where I had fallen on a ringbolt.' (An X-ray fifty years later showed he had actually broken his pelvis at this time.)

It was a few weeks before he could even walk again. In the meantime the ship was sailed to Port Adelaide to load wheat for the return journey to Falmouth; there was no possibility Villiers would be going with it. He was paid off on 15 November 1921 and took an agonising train ride back to his family in Melbourne. Despite his injuries, three weeks later he signed on to a run-down little ketch named *Hawk*, which carried cargo to and from Tasmania across the Bass Strait.

Hawk was more than fifty years old and undermanned. Villiers helped load her with tons of superphosphate and a deck cargo of inflammable benzine. To his horror the other hands calmly lit a firebox on the top of the volatile benzine to boil the billy, and the poor state of *Hawk*'s lifeboat suddenly seemed irrelevant. The weather worsened. The cargo shifted, the ketch leaked, the sails were rotten and everyone was seasick. After two days they reached Launceston and unloaded, then stacked timber for the return passage.

Villiers made one further unhappy voyage on *Hawk*, then left just before Christmas 1921. In January 1922 he worked for two weeks at Henderson's Motor Spring Works, then decided to try a berth on a steamer. He joined the Seamen's Union and on 8 February 1922 signed on to a 3,121-ton cargo ship named *War Spray*. They went to Newcastle, loaded coal and took it to Geelong, went back to Newcastle, loaded more coal and took it to Melbourne. He hated it, left after a month and never mentioned the ship in his writings.

––––

Next came *Erriba*, a steamer of 3,345 gross tons run by the government's Commonwealth Line. She was a grey 'ugly lump' taking grain to Europe, and on 5 May 1922 Villiers signed on as able seaman. *Erriba*'s cargo capacity was not much more than *Lawhill*'s but she needed twice as many men to run her.

They loaded wheat in South Australia then had a 'rotten' passage across the Indian Ocean. They stopped for two days in South Africa: 'Found Cape Town very interesting but remarkably foreign for a British possession,' wrote young Alan. *Erriba* spent a few days in the Canary Islands then made for Falmouth, arriving on 23 July 1922. They unloaded the grain and took on coal for French Somaliland.

In Djibouti Villiers noticed the large graceful local vessels, the dhows. Here he caught malaria, which would trouble him occasionally throughout his life. His nineteenth birthday came as they steamed back across the Indian Ocean, finally reaching Melbourne again on 24 October 1922.

That was all he recorded in his diaries, but he recalled in his autobiography the dreadful monotony of the voyage – 'a week of this was longer than a month of the *Lawhill*'s watches ... for sheer boredom the second and third mates' jobs aboard that tramp must have been hard to equal.' The master rarely appeared and the unionised seamen were truculent: 'I had been brought up to put the ship first ... that sailors should have reasonable conditions and just rewards, all fair-minded men will agree. But to lose all sight of their duties in a great profession is to lose their place as honourable seafaring men.'

He wanted no part of a life on steamers. His *Lawhill* injuries made a return to the fo'c'sle on a sailing ship unlikely, and even remoter were the chances of becoming a master in sail – he had been shocked to see ports in England without a single square-rigger tied up at their wharves. He decided it was time to give up his dream of sailing ships, to leave the sea and swallow the anchor. At the end of 1922 he caught the Bass Strait ferry to Launceston in Tasmania, then the train to the pleasant little city of Hobart, where the Cape Horners did not go.

———

Villiers had over £100 in pay from his *Erriba* voyage, so had funding enough for the move. He boarded at 37 Campbell Street, near the waterfront, and started work at a new factory rigging scaffolding. When that ended he took on a casual job in a jam factory. In his autobiography he wrote that one day he noticed a prosperous-looking young man going into the newspaper office. A friend explained he was a reporter for the *Hobart Mercury*, and 'it came to me almost with the suddenness of a bomb-burst that newspaper reporting was just the thing that I could do.'

He approached the paper and discovered that before he could be a reporter he had to serve a three-year cadetship, and before that he had to first work twelve months in the proofreaders' room. There were no positions currently for readers and half a dozen hopefuls were lined up ahead of him. He waited and waited for a vacancy. On 15 January 1923 he started at Zercho's Business College, to learn the typing and shorthand he would need as a reporter, 'with a group of merry Tasmanian girls whose studies were not always confined to the curriculum of the business school.'

Perhaps Hobart's attraction was not so much the lack of Cape Horners but the presence of Daphne Harris. They had become friends three years before but now things were apparently more complicated: the day he joined Zercho's he wrote in the back of his shorthand notebook, 'Met Daphne but unfortunately wasn't speaking to her.'

At last, Villiers' persistence won him a lowly job at the newspaper as a night copy-holder, reading aloud from manuscripts for the proofreader to compare and correct the proofs. He seemed destined to remain a copy-holder for years – 'the three youths ahead of me were smart young fellows, and the whole editorial staff was radiant with health.' He graduated to revised proofs, corrected proofs and daytime work. He got to be a racing editor, providing tips for winning horses – he would select those with names like ships and his tips 'were as good as most'.

After six months or so he was becoming restless. Then in November 1923 five strange little vessels came into the wharves, named *Star I* to

Star V. They were 'small, lithe steamers, with high flared bows and lovely lines ... in the bows of each was a small stubby gun.' They were followed later by a larger steamer, her decks 'a clutter of boilers and curious gear ... unlike any other steamer I had seen.'

The 'tough-looking' crew spoke Norwegian, which Villiers could follow with his *Lawhill* Swedish. He found out they were on an expedition to a new secret whaling ground in the Antarctic, and were short of men. Villiers thought the expedition had the makings of a great story, and signed on as a whaler's labourer, for £4 a month and a fraction of a farthing per barrel share in the oil: 'This was Opportunity, knocking loudly, and I was in.'

That was Villiers' version, anyway. The photographer Jack Cato wrote in more detail:[12]

> One of my friends was a young reporter on the *Hobart Mercury*, a quiet unassuming man who hated cities and loved the sea. Later the world knew him as Captain Alan Villiers.
>
> His rounds as a reporter always included a call at the General Hospital for news of accidents. Here one day he heard that the captain of a ship at sea had wirelessed for an ambulance to meet them and take off two sailors injured during the voyage. Villiers ... assumed that this was a secret expedition to the Antarctic for whales, by a fleet that had not touched port since leaving Europe. It turned out that he was entirely right; also that it was obvious they would require two men to take the place of the injured sailors ...
>
> But Alan Villiers had to have pictures and he had never taken one in his life. He didn't know a lens from a hypo dish and I had just one hour to teach him. Obviously then it had to be the simplest camera ever made. I got him a Kodak 'Brownie' box camera for 10/6, told him to point it at any subject full of snow and ice and water and press the lever to release the shutter, and wished him luck.
>
> Many months later when he returned, I developed a great mass of films and they were marvellous ... ideal under the conditions of that intense reflected light ...

———

The mysterious Antarctic fascinated the public, but it was far from obvious that the technology of slaughtering its whales would ever be of interest, and it was clever of Villiers to sense the possibilities. He went to work on the mother ship, the 'infernally comfortless' *Sir James*

Clark Ross, an old cargo steamer that would 'fold up like a large tin can', should it be caught in the ice. His job was to clean coal holds to prepare them for whale oil – if they got any.

For some weeks pack-ice stopped them reaching the Ross Sea. When it broke up, they could not find a safe harbour, and without sheltered waters the flensers could not work beside the mother ship. One of the little 'chasers', *Star II*, disappeared one night and did not return. They searched for her for days without luck and finally gave up hope; at that point the small ship turned up again. Finally the expedition anchored at an inlet, a split in the wall of the Great Ice Barrier:

> [A] thousand miles of ice, like a fantastic elongation of the Dover cliffs all frozen and pitted with caves ... Sometimes whole miles of the Barrier crumbled away without warning, and tumbled into the sea, a lovely cascade of shining blue-green ice which shimmered and scintillated as it fell.

Villiers yearned to go with the doctor and scientist on their brief expeditions ashore, but 'I have no chance of even asking to go. I am no one here, and I have no help and no privileges, no instruments and "no nothing". So be it ... I shall do quite well despite that and it does not damp my enthusiasm in the slightest degree,' he wrote earnestly in his diary.

The sights of Antarctica fascinated him, especially the changing light. Of one sunrise he wrote, 'I shall never lose the impression of it, although it is quite beyond the power of any useless pen to describe it.' In a list of the beauties of the wild Antarctic, one was 'the great ship's decks a picture of man's courageous industry among Nature's wastes', followed by this grim description:

> [R]ound the deck a hundred men toiling cutting blubber, feeding it to slicing machines whence endless chains like those of a bucket-dredge scooped the rashers and fed them to the square steel boilers ... the embryo of a well-formed whale ... lying pathetically on its back in a welter of its mother's and its cousins' blood ... Steam gushed from countless pipes; the chain-drive of the blubber-hauling machinery clanked; and the men, oil-skinned and heavy-booted, hacked with their flensers' knives at tons of creamy blubber.

'Courageous industry among Nature's wastes' was the conventional view, and Villiers would probably have been unusual for his time to see it as anything different, although even in those days some people did. He wrote, 'I was happy in the Ross Sea. Indeed, I was extremely happy … the whole thing was a grand adventure for me, and I revelled in it.' Nonetheless, it turned out to be a hard and meagre season, and soon it was over.

> Sometimes the mirages in the inlet were almost frighteningly fantastic. The place began to get on the people's nerves. The smaller penguins had all gone. The whales had gone. The seals were gone, and even the few birds. The whole lifeless, threatening waste was like a continual nightmare, and the whale-ships' men daily became more savage and morose.[13]

They had killed little more than two hundred whales, when they had hoped for a thousand. After they sailed to New Zealand, Villiers cabled an account of the expedition back to Australia.

———

Villiers' wages and share of the take came to £28, barely enough to get him home again by steamer in April 1924, and far from any hoped-for profits. However, back in Tasmania fortune of another kind was waiting for him: for the first time in his life he had achieved minor fame. His cabled account of the voyage had been sold around the world and he quickly wrote fifteen articles that were syndicated throughout Australia and New Zealand, receiving £200 for them. Even better, he was appointed as a newspaper reporter without the customary three years' cadetship.

He was certainly happy at this time. He loved the work of a junior reporter – police courts, hospitals, interviews, meetings – and he liked the old *Mercury* office: his friend Daphne Harris was on the staff too. There are jocular asides in the social column of the *Mercury* in early December 1924, 'now that everything is out about our literary hero of "The Frozen South" and the lady of the commercial department', which mentions a presentation from the staff to Villiers 'on the eve of his marriage'.

Daphne and Alan married on 6 December 1924, when Villiers was twenty-one. He wrote breezily in his autobiography:

Within less than six months, with that two hundred pounds behind me, I was married and trying to settle down. I married a girl on the *Mercury* staff. She was a blonde. I liked blondes and never looked at a brunette or a redhead in those days. I suppose I still had some remnant of my childish admiration for the little Norwegian girl in the ship *Asmund* ... In the absence of Norwegians, a Tasmanian blonde would do very well.

He wrote this two decades later, when he had been happily married for eight years to a beautiful Australian brunette, Nancie Wills. Perhaps the casual tone was for Nancie's benefit.

—————

Villiers' friend Jack Cato took a remarkable portrait of him at around this time, posed against a studio backdrop of snowy mountains, wearing a fur cap and heavy coat. He is barely twenty-two: his eyes are calm and determined, his mouth vulnerable, with just a hint of humour.[14]

The *Mercury* re-issued his whaling articles in a booklet, *To the Frozen South*. It was to lead to his first 'real book', Villiers wrote. In his autobiography, he tells of a sly Hobart lawyer who knew a British literary agent who would publish an expanded version of the booklet. The lawyer persuaded Villiers to give him the rights over anything he might write about the whaling voyage, offering him half the book's earnings less expenses. He hastily agreed, and expanded the booklet – too quickly and carelessly, he later maintained.

The resulting book, *Whaling in the Frozen South*, was published in 1925 by Hurst & Blackett in Britain, and Bobbs-Merrill in America, and it sold well. Villiers' judgement was far too harsh: it is a striking and important record of extraordinary experiences – naive, curious and observant – and unlike anything ever before written about the Antarctic.

Then Villiers was told by the lawyer he called 'Mr Scrooge' that he was obliged to submit the next two books he might write through them. Villiers wrote, 'In sunny, pleasant Tasmania it was difficult to believe in Mr Shyster Scrooge, setting up office in the heart of Hobart, and pushing sealed messes of crafty verbiage across dusty tables to me', but he signed, expending four pages of his autobiography on his indignant recounting of the tale. In 1970, however, Villiers said in an interview:

[T]o my great astonishment some optimistic person, a woman of all things, in some place called Indianapolis in Indiana wrote to me having seen these [whaling] articles ... and she said 'Look, fella, how's about doing a book for [inaudible] here in Indianapolis, Indiana?' and so forth and so on. A book? Well, it was her idea, so I sat down and wrote a book.[15]

It is difficult to reconcile an American woman (of all things) with the dodgy Hobart lawyers, but as the book's American publisher, Bobbs-Merrill, was based in Indianapolis, perhaps this is how the US edition came about. Among Villiers' papers are the contracts with the Hobart lawyers and they are certainly unfair: indentures which gave the lawyers all rights over his book and also took half of any small author's profits it might generate.

However, what probably annoyed Villiers most of all was that he had carelessly signed away the rights to his next two books, and his brother Frank had given him a very good idea for a story.

———

Villiers' little brother Frank, last seen toddling loyally after him on his wanderings to the docks, and being whipped with him out of Royal Park, had by now followed him off to sea. He sailed in Scandinavian vessels and on an Antarctic whaling ship, then on *Hougomont*, the four-masted steel barque that Villiers had seen moored at Williamstown in 1921 beside *Bellands*.

Hougomont had been launched from the Clyde in 1897. She had had a fairly ordinary career – two strandings and two dismastings – until she was bought by Gustaf Erikson in 1925. Frank kept Alan in touch with the doings of Gusta's growing fleet, but Villiers was still battling to keep thoughts of the wind ships at bay; although he would sometimes stop at the Hobart wharves and gaze at an old coal hulk lying there – *Otago*, the 'lovely barque' whose master was once the writer Joseph Conrad.

Then one day a full-rigged ship sailed into Hobart harbour. She was named *Hamburg* (ex-*Marechal de Castries*), French-built and now German-owned and, Villiers wrote, he and Lusitania had briefly sheltered in her:

The year was 1925; I had been married less than twelve months; I thought I was done with the sea ... The sun shone on her high, white sails, and she was a picture of beauty as she came creaming along. Her hull was silver-grey ... her pillared white sails stirred me far more deeply than I thought they could, and I found myself turning over in my mind wild schemes for a return to the sea.

As a reporter he had access to files and government archives and had begun researching Tasmanian maritime history. He noticed that most writers 'treated the romantic Cape Horn sailing-ship as already a thing of the remote past. The handful of such ships still sailing was ignored ... perhaps because they were nearly all Finns and Germans, with a few Swedes.'

Then in 1927 Frank told him of *Hougomont* taking part in a 'race' around Cape Horn with other Erikson vessels as they carried grain to Europe. Villiers wanted to write about them – 'I liked the idea of the handful of surviving ships making a race of it, undermanned as they were, deep-loaded around the Horn. It was a brave gesture.'

Yet time was slipping away like the ships themselves – beautiful full-rigged *Hamburg* went to the breakers after this voyage – and Villiers was still struggling in the clutches of the wily Hobart lawyers. Also, he wrote,

> My married life was not a conspicuous success, for the practice of marrying the first attractive blonde one thinks one knows, at the age of twenty [actually twenty-one], is not really to be commended ... I had no compunction about leaving the company of the young woman who had mistakenly married me, on the poor glamour of some Antarctic whales. We had long given up the attempt to make a home, and I was a boarder in her mother's establishment on Liverpool Street. This suited me. My hours were long and I made them longer.

Villiers' diary from 1935 in Sydney tells more of the pain behind these casual words. Daphne's mother had apparently run a poker school in her 'establishment on Liverpool Street', and one of her old friends visited him:

> ... a poker-mate of the dreadful Mrs Harris in the nightmare Hobart days ...
> Fat Osborne's fancy woman – yet upright and fair enough in her own way and possessed of more than the ordinary share of good qualities. I do not care to dwell upon the useless scenes that she recalls – the haggling poker school, with its false jocularity and bitter hatred among bitter hags: the Hobart days, when I steadily worked on dreadful novels to get myself out of the Butler-Listner

contract ... and tried at first so desperately to be happily married and to settle down ...[16]

After five years ashore Villiers yearned to sail away again. He had been appointed the Tasmanian representative for the Australian Journalists Association, and in December 1927, at the age of twenty-four, he went to Melbourne for a conference. As the ferry docked, he noticed two square-riggers moored in the swinging-basin on the Yarra.

One was the 'lovely silver-grey *Beatrice*' of Sweden, and near her, 'a beauty of a four-masted barque' flying the blue-crossed white flag of Finland. It was the most famous square-rigger in the world, *Herzogin Cecilie* – the Duchess herself.

———

Herzogin Cecilie had been built in 1902 at Bremerhaven and named after the sixteen-year-old Duchess Cecilie of Mecklenburg-Schwerin, betrothed to the eldest son of the Kaiser. She was designed as a training ship for cadets, with a distinctive long poop deck that, compared to most vessels, housed the crew in great comfort. Her captain's saloon was luxurious, with 'brass railed sideboards, dark red velvet upholstery, brass lamps hanging in gimbals, leather armchairs ... carefully placed mirrors, richly panelled teak bulkheads ... and in her early days, aspidistras [house-plants] in stands'.[17]

Herzogin Cecilie was large – 3,242 gross tons – painted white, and always beautifully maintained; a handsome showpiece for her owner, Norddeutscher Lloyd. At the start of the First World War she was interned at Valparaiso in Chile, then handed over in 1921 as part of the war reparations to the French, who promptly sold her to Gustaf Erikson for £4,250. (Ålanders would pronounce her name as Cecilia rather than Cecily – 'Hair-tso-geen Se-seel-ia'.) As on all of Erikson's ships, framed portraits of Gustaf and his wife Hilda were mounted on the panelling of *Herzogin Cecilie*'s beautiful saloon, but Villiers probably didn't notice that when he abandoned his conference and rushed to the barque.

In the saloon all he saw were 'the huge shoulders and square head' of Captain Ruben de Cloux. Elis Karlsson wrote of his brother-in-law Ruben's 'ruddy-blond complexion, twinkling sea-blue eyes and calm,

imperturbable disposition. Simple and retiring by nature, he totally
lacked the so common desire to impress; yet … one sensed that this
half-amused remoteness hid an uncommonly powerful personality, as
powerful in its way as his herculean physical build.'[18]

Herzogin Cecilie had become the favourite of Erikson's fleet. De
Cloux, now forty-three, skippered her on fast profitable voyages and
was so well-regarded by Gusta' that he was paid more than any of his
other captains. In the early days with Erikson the Duchess carried
Scandinavian timber and South American saltpetre, but in late 1924 she
embarked on her first voyage to Port Lincoln for a wheat harvest. For
the next twelve years she took grain to Europe and brought timber to
Australia: much of Melbourne's mellow Baltic pine flooring, so beloved
of renovators and real estate agents, arrived on Erikson barques.

Fewer and fewer wind ships were now sailing: Britain no longer had
a single steel square-rigger in her merchant fleet. By the time Villiers
boarded *Herzogin Cecilie* in December 1927 only fifty-four four-
masters remained in the world, plus a single five-master. In the nine
years since the end of the war more than 60 per cent of the surviving
four-masters had disappeared – most of them lost to the breaker's yard.

Yet the fact that the great sailing ships were increasingly rare began
to work in their favour. They had laboured unheeded for decades but
now they had almost gone they were suddenly news – fodder for the
mass media of the 1920s: silent movies, the wireless and the newspapers. Their sailing times had always mattered to their owners but
now the world was eyeing them with speculative interest too. A
Swedish paint company, Holzapfels, offered a trophy to the ship making the fastest time to England with Australian grain, and elegant
Beatrice and handsome *Herzogin Cecilie* both hoped to win.

Once again, Alan Villiers heard the gentle tapping of Opportunity.

———

'First I had to work out some way in which I was free to join. There
were three serious disabilities – my contracts with Mr Scrooge, my
job, and my wife.' They weren't obstacles for long: a sympathetic mag-
istrate explained to Villiers that he need not be bound by contracts like
those of Mr Scrooge. His editor jumped at the offer of some articles on
the European apple markets (of great concern to Tasmanians) in

exchange for six months' leave, £100 and his job back at the end of it.

Daphne, however, 'thought he was mad' to give up 'an assured future on the *Mercury* for a wild-goose chase around Cape Horn in some frightful ship which did not even have an engine'. This was a not unreasonable attitude in a young wife, but Villiers wrote, 'I had faith in my ideas … I packed my sea-bag and departed.' 'Daphne' in this case probably represented all of those who might have held Alan back from his destiny. In reality his personal diary of the voyage has a number of entries about letters or cables he sent to her, while her birthday (6 April) was noted and a letter especially sent, so they were probably not as cool towards each other as his retelling implies.

After all, it's not easy to set out on a Noble Quest if everyone thinks it's a fabulous idea. Some opposition is demanded, at least for dramatic effect, and Villiers rather enjoyed dramatic effect: he wrote that after he was free of Mr Scrooge he tore up all of his unpublished novels 'and never wrote fiction again'. This wasn't true literally – on the coming voyage he would rework a story, 'The Lady of Lansdowne Crescent', a half-finished novel he abandoned called 'The Teacher' and 'Kensington Hill's Last Voyage', eventually published as *The Wind Ship*. A year later he was still writing 'The Sailor', which he ditched overboard in disgust from *Grace Harwar*.[19]

It wasn't true even metaphorically: he was to write a certain amount of fiction in the future but he labelled it memoirs instead. It was not that he deceived deliberately, but he would leave meaningful events out of his stories and polish what was left to a gloss that neatly obscured his deepest feelings. And sometimes, when he mourned for the passing of the wind ships, it was not the wind ships for which he was mourning.

3

WHAT COULD A
GIRL LIKE ME DO?

Villiers wrote his first bestseller, *Falmouth for Orders*, on the *Herzogin Cecilie* itself. Chapter One was finished three days after they left port, Chapter Two two days after that. He kept up this rate of production for the whole voyage, almost completing the entire book before they reached England. The first chapter was poetic licence. It vividly describes *Beatrice* and *Herzogin Cecilie* in mid-December 1927 racing to Port Lincoln from Melbourne, but Villiers did not witness it. He joined the Duchess a few weeks later in Port Lincoln on 10 January 1928 as an able seaman. 'The first day's work – Hell! ... going aloft for the first time in 6 years today; shackling on sheets, one of the rottenest breaking-in jobs possible.'[1]

While the ships were being loaded with grain, a committee of Port Lincoln ladies organised a dance ashore for the sailors, and both *Herzogin Cecilie* and *Beatrice* held dances in return on their decks, great social occasions for the small town. Still, Port Lincoln must have been pleasant enough – the year before Captain de Cloux had met a small group of Adelaide teachers visiting the town for their annual holiday.

There had been dances the previous year too, and one of the teachers had asked to go on the Duchess to England then. It was a 'school-ship' after all, she'd said earnestly. The cheerful first mate, Harald Lindfors, joked that the only way she'd get to sail with them was by stowing away – and how they'd all laughed at the idea of a fashionable young lady on a Finnish square-rigger!

The teacher had turned up again this year too, and had even made a bumbling attempt to board the ship dressed as a boy. Harald Lindfors recognised her and sent her away, humiliated. He recalled (ungallantly) in 1975:

> I spotted a funny figure with long trousers, in those days girls did not wear trousers, and I recognised Miss Day because she was so broad behind. So I said to her she could not come on this trip either. So she started to cry, and I told her that wouldn't help and she had better go ashore or I would call the police.[2]

They finished loading and moved *Herzogin Cecilie* from the quay to the roads (the off-port anchorage) to prepare for sailing. They left in the afternoon of 19 January 1928. *Beatrice* had gone before them that morning and at first could be seen ahead. The weather became stormy but de Cloux took a daring shortcut past Kangaroo Island, and next day, clear and fine, *Beatrice* passed out of view; they would not see her again until England.

The ships were not really racing each other to Falmouth – the competition lay in the total passage times taken along what might be wildly varying routes. The usual way was via South America using the westerly winds to round Cape Horn, but sometimes a master would choose the opposite path via South Africa if the weather demanded it. It was not only *Beatrice* and *Herzogin Cecilie* taking part in the 'race' either: the other grain ships that year were *Ponape*, *Melbourne*, *Archibald Russell*, *Garthpool*, *C.B. Pedersen*, *Penang* and *Favell*. It could be a great story, and Villiers wrote in his diary when he joined the ship, 'I must make £200 out of this voyage not to show a loss, and I owe it to my wife to do that. Perhaps it is a chance to make a name?'

They were more than usually short-handed as two apprentices had deserted. Villiers had to work far harder than on *Lawhill*, because *Herzogin Cecilie* was a ship built to train cadets. She had had no need for labour-saving devices like brace-winches because her sailors in past days had numbered well over one hundred. However, on this voyage she carried a mere twenty-six men. And one woman.

––––––

> Stowaway discovered aft – that <u>infernal</u> woman dressed as a man, consternation, desperation, damnation!

This was Villiers' first response when the bedraggled woman emerged from the hold on the morning of 20 January, the day after *Herzogin*

Cecilie had sailed. Would they have to take her back and lose precious time? De Cloux decided to carry on. Stowaways were quite common on the grain ships and often became useful members of the crew. Still, what use could a woman be? It actually took Villiers four weeks to re-alise that, far from being a handicap, the woman was a gift from the gods of publicity. She loaned him her journal,

> turned down some pages that I was not to read – and I did not – and said I could read the rest and do what I liked with it … and such a story! My journal-istic instincts as I read told me that it was the best 'copy' I have yet stumbled on. So I shorthanded the whole damn lot of it – good old shorthand! – and, em-bellished, romanticised and dramaticised to the utmost degree, it is going to make an extremely interesting chapter of *Falmouth for Orders*.

There are five versions (at least) of the stowaway's story: Villiers' di-aries of the voyage in 1928;[3] his 1929 retelling in *Falmouth for Orders*; his autobiography *The Set of the Sails* of 1949; his recorded interview in 1970;[4] and the reminiscences of the first mate, Harald Lindfors.[5] The stowaway herself never gets a word in edgeways.

Her name was Jeanne Day (not Jean or Jennie as sometimes stated). She was a high school music teacher from Adelaide, born on 22 September 1904 and exactly a year younger than Villiers himself, although he says unkindly in his diary, 'she is older than I too, a darn good bit older, I reckon, though she says not'. She was probably unlike any woman he'd previously met – certainly she was no blonde.

Her hair was dark, glossy and cut short with a long wave at the front, a fashionably shingled boyish style. She was slim with shapely legs, thought-ful eyes, a strong nose and a shy smile. One English newspaper called her 'pretty and vivacious', another, 'cultured'. While they might wish to glam-ourise her for the sake of the story, it is hard to see the twenty-three-year-old as the sexless harridan that Villiers goes on and on – and on – about:

> [I]t might be all right if she were pretty. But she isn't, and she has the sex ap-peal of a bar of soap. (Diary)
> It would be idle to dilate upon the girl's complete lack of attractiveness. (*The Set of the Sails*)
> Her face was green, her nose red and long unpowdered, and the wisps of her mouse-coloured hair flicked in the wind like recalcitrant straws on a worn-out broom. (*The Set of the Sails*)

The journal, though, reveals this woman in a new light – she is obviously pretty intelligent and must be rather clever. She looks neither; there is utterly nothing attractive in her. (Diary)

Villiers has forgotten his Shakespeare: there appears to be rather too much protesting going on.

———

In these days of ambiguous fashion, we forget how dislocating the sight of women in men's clothing once was. Villiers quotes a transcript of Jeanne Day being interviewed by the first mate, who said, 'Didn't you think it was wrong – very wrong – for a young girl to come alone in such a ship, with only the clothes she stood up in, and those not fit for a girl to wear?'

Villiers wrote loftily, 'She made herself some dresses out of an old cloth from the cabin table, and good dresses they were; and before we had been very long at sea the sight of her sitting on the after hatch making a hair-net or a hat – she was always doing something – excited no comment at all.' Once Jeanne started wearing a dress 'like a woman' everyone relaxed. The crew found old jumpers and spare fabric for her to sew, and the captain made her a pair of shoes out of sailmaker's leather.

The transcript Villiers took in shorthand of the stowaway's interview with the first mate is the only statement in her own words of her reasons for stowing away – although it may be less than reliable, as she lied at that stage about how she got aboard. She claimed that, dressed as a boy, she had asked a fisherman to take her out to the ship at three-thirty in the morning, and that she knew where to hide in the hold from previous social visits.

In the transcript Lindfors questioned her relentlessly, but all she replied, over and over, was 'No' or 'I don't know', and often she was simply silent. Lindfors persisted: 'Whatever on earth made you come here?' Jeanne finally burst out, 'I wanted to go to sea, and what could a girl like me do? … I said I wanted to go to sea. I did not want to go in a steamer; I wanted to go in a ship like this.'

———

The woman was blamed when the wind dropped but was given no credit when it rose again. They struck hurricane weather sixteen days out from Port Lincoln, as they were passing from New Zealand waters into the southern Pacific. The lads struggled up the rigging to shorten the sails:

> Green seas fell upon the lower rigging as we climbed; the sprays drove over us high aloft. Every now and then the ship lay so far over and the wind blew so terrifically that we could not climb at all; we had to hang on for our lives, and wait our chance. Then up we went again; up, up, always up …

They moved out onto the yards to try to secure the wildly billowing sail and struggled for more than an hour. Next day they replaced blown-out sails with fresh ones and flew before the wind at great speed, covering 240 to almost 300 miles each day. They went further and further southwards, to 55°, then struck fog and wallowed, blind and fearful of icebergs, for two days. The wind rose again and on they went through the cold and rain and hail towards Cape Horn.

On 21 February Villiers noted, 'I took photographs of the captain, the officers, of the stowaway aloft – how scared she was! – and of both watches in all their Cape Horn gear.' He still showed little kindness towards Jeanne, although just the day before she had given him her journal and the scoop of a lifetime.

They passed fearsome Cape Horn in bitterly cold but unusually clear weather. 'It was all very grand and very beautiful, and rather pleasant and infinitely attractive in the morning. Who would not be here, one thought, in a great sailing ship racing around Cape Horn?' That was the day too that Villiers completely rewrote the first version of Chapter Five of *Falmouth for Orders*, now calling it 'Her Story', an interview with the stowaway. It was complete guff.

———

Villiers says himself in the diary: 'What a remarkable woman! people will say if ever "FFO" is published and they read that chapter. What a dam' liar of a writer they really ought to say.' Chapter Five tells us more about Alan Villiers than Jeanne Day. At times it reads like a cross between music hall sentimentality – 'She Was But a Girl Who Went Where She Should Not' – and *Carry On*-style innuendo.

The purported interviewee struggles against fatal premonitions and aches with Freudian yearnings. She trembles, cringes, weeps, and on the ship cuddles 'a little golden kitten' she finds in the hold (living off the wheat, perhaps?). She 'liked to see the clear skins of the sailors and the distance of blue waters in the sweep of their eyes … to hear the lithesome boys … talking in their musical foreign tongue'. Deep passions are stirred, she fights her strange urges, she is almost mentally deranged; but she chooses Life!

She dresses as a boy, whistles at a female friend like a 'bold bad beach sheik', smokes 'manfully', tries to board and is turned away by the first mate. She collapses dejected in the sandhills, then, resolve renewed by the beauty of the ship, she hides in a fishing boat. When the fisherman sails out in the early hours she pretends to be a drunken apprentice who needs to get back to the ship.

The vision-impaired fisherman obliges, she hides in the hold – hungry, terrified, comforted yet by the magical kitten – until she emerges at last upon deck to the wrath of the 'six-foot-something mate'. She tries to stop her lip from trembling – deliciously – as he scolds her.

But at last she is satisfied. 'I wake … to feel the roll of the ship as she flies on. I snuggle down in ecstasy of bliss. I know there is a longfelt desire in me that now is being fulfilled.'

———

It took thirty-three days to get to Cape Horn – an excellent time – but then another thirty-five days passed in the South Atlantic before they reached the Equator. 'Calms, light winds, rain, head winds – these were our lot for weeks, with us toiling like Trojans in the midst of it all to get our ship on, and getting nowhere.'

The weather became warmer, 'Soon we came to wear as little as possible – it would have been nothing at all if the woman had not been aboard.' That spoilsport! And the deceitful minx had even brought out a suitcase of clothing from the hold when it got hot. Villiers wrote in *The Set of the Sails*, 'all hands were disgusted with her. Why had she allowed us to tear up our few things for her when she had so much?'

There are several possible reasons. To bring out the suitcase at the beginning would have undermined her 'drunken apprentice' story; or it probably held only light clothes as it had been mid-summer when they sailed; or the first sign of softening in the crew's attitude towards her had been their gifts of warm clothes and shoes, so she would not have wanted to reject them.

Or perhaps the suitcase didn't really hold much at all: a few weeks later for a 'special occasion' Jeanne wore a dress she had sewn on board, 'made out of white flour-bags ... trimmed with little wooden buttons, painted green, that she had made too'. If that was her dress for special occasions she clearly didn't have a lot of other options. Whatever the explanation, Villiers regarded her only with coldness. On 15 February:

> I had almost forgotten to chronicle the fact that on Sunday Zimmerman strode naked across the deck coming from his bath ... and did not know that the girl stowaway was looking at the foredeck. She blushed when she saw him and turned away. Nobody asked her to come here anyway.

After reading Jeanne's journal, Villiers broadly accepted her fisherman story though he could see its inconsistencies: '"He agreed to take me," she says; either she agreed to pay him infernally well, or there was someone else who did, I say ... I shall try to see that there are no obvious holes like that in it when I am done.'

He became more suspicious when the suitcase appeared, and became convinced that she was a discarded girlfriend of First Mate Lindfors, who had danced with her at Port Lincoln although he was engaged to the secretary of Gustaf Erikson himself. Villiers wrote, 'It appears that the mate had been with her a bit on the ship's last visit to Port Lincoln, and she, being even sillier than most of her sex, was struck on him more than she ought to have been.' Jeanne herself seems to have been unaware of Villiers' attitude. She trusted him enough to ask his opinion of her, worried that she was not perceived as a lady. He pontificated later:

> A woman in a ship must sooner or later cause trouble, even if she is as sexless as the specimen that sails with us ... I am not accustomed to laying down the law to young women, particularly laws of morality! Here, two months at sea with a hysterical woman in whose eyes there always appears a bit of insanity; what am I to tell her when she asks me do I think her 'decent'?

There is no indication of Jeanne's 'insanity' from anything else Villiers reported on the voyage. He gave her Chapter Five to read, and she 're-turned later very pleased and obviously also a bit surprised, I suppose mainly because she discovered she had met a better liar than herself'. But he was still wrong. A month later she told him the full story and he headed his diary entry: 'I Hear the Truth About the Woman – And Am Not Surprised. Lies, Lies, Lies!' Neither a fisherman nor the hap-less Lindfors was responsible for her presence; instead, it was the Finnish sailmaker, twenty-nine-year-old Vilho Savolainen.

In a Finnish ship, with crew from Australia, England, Germany, Sweden and the Swedish-culture Ålands, it was odd that the only true Finn, Savolainen, was thought of as the most 'foreign'. Unlike the blond Scandinavians, the ancestors of many Finns, like mysterious Lusitania, were dark-haired, pagan, nomadic Laplanders.

Jeanne had begged Savolainen for help. If he would not, she threat-ened to kill herself in front of him, and haunt him for the rest of his life. It was threat enough. Villiers wrote that Savolainen told him that Jeanne had said 'she and the first mate were in love and she could not live without him ... she raved, and screamed, and howled, and acted, and carried on'. Even if the Finnish sailmaker had used such unlikely colloquialisms as 'carried on', he would probably have exaggerated the situation in any case to minimise his own complicity.

But Villiers was not much interested in his story anyway: 'It would be madness to write the truth [about the sailmaker], it would spoil the book ... why should I write the truth, and expose myself to libel and all kinds of trouble, when untruth can be much more interesting, harmless and avoid trouble for everyone.'

Certainly such a desperate and manipulative side to the stowaway's personality would be highly inconsistent with the simpering ninny of Chapter Five, who sits around on the most handsome square-rigger in the world whipping up hats and hair-nets; so in *Falmouth for Orders* he sticks to the line that Jeanne stowed away with the help of the mythical fisherman.

Yet it is extraordinary that in *The Set of the Sails*, published twenty years later, he still does not mention the sailmaker, and implies that it was all the fault of Lindfors. Perhaps this was because Savolainen had also claimed that Jeanne had spent a night in the first mate's cabin in

Port Lincoln, convincing Villiers that Lindfors was indeed the original culprit:

> The blustery first mate … was an ass of the sort who found it impossible to scorn any reasonably youthful female; at that dance of ours, a night or two before sailing, the stowaway was there. She had passed well enough in that crowd, painted and dolled up a little.

———

Passed well enough? Jeanne, dolled up a little, was apparently nowhere near as repulsive as Villiers so often complained. She had certainly appealed to Lindfors (before he realised his fiancée might hear about it) and she appealed to others on the ship too. One was the twenty-four-year-old third mate, Bertel Jefrelius, who Villiers thought 'looked like a cowhand' – although his smile is handsome and friendly, photographed sitting close to Jeanne on the main yard. Another was the English seaman Stewart Winter, also twenty-four years old, described by Villiers as 'loud-mouthed, garrulous, vile-tongued and bombastic'.

Winter was undoubtedly tactless enough. He and Jeanne were the only two in the ship who had never crossed the Line in a sailing ship before, so Villiers was planning to use the Father Neptune ceremony as a chapter of his book. That day, Villiers wrote, Winter asked Jeanne to sleep with him. She retorted that he was no gentleman. He said he could judge the type of woman that stowed away in ships. She 'howled'. He was 'kicked aft to apologise … So there wouldn't be any Neptune business after all. Damn the Englishman!'

When they met up with *C.B. Pedersen* on 24 March, Villiers wrote unkindly in *The Set of the Sails*, 'we showed our stowaway to their incredulous and envious gaze, but when de Cloux offered her to them they would not take her away. They rowed across for a look; that was enough.' But in the diary another tale emerges. The *C.B. Pedersen* sailors were fascinated by the woman, and their captain brought her a jar of sweets and a formal invitation to visit his ship. Jeanne was treated with courtesy.

Winter was still attracted to her – on 5 April 'that damned Englishman began another row today over the woman. He came out worst'. Some time later when Winter hurt his head slightly in a fall,

Villiers wrote, 'I do not think much of it really, but shall, of course, make the most of it in the book.' And he did.

As Villiers had done on *Lawhill*, Jeanne taught the sailors English. One moonlit evening Villiers noticed her in the mizzen rigging with Jefrelius, the third mate. He wrote, 'It was rather a romantic setting for just an English lesson. I wonder if that was all it was?'

When Villiers found out about the sailmaker he wrote, 'What a cad the woman is! I have never trusted her; I never would trust, respect, like, or do any other darn thing about her, to her, or with her.' But why does he deny so furiously that he could have the slightest interest in an enterprising young woman who loved sailing ships? Perhaps it was no more than a clash of very different personalities, but if he were truly indifferent to her the question would not arise.

Or was it he himself he was trying to persuade? Could it be that it stung, just a little, that like the pretty schoolmate on the train or the scornful girl on *Bellands* Jeanne did not seem to want to do any darn thing about, to, or with him?

———

They passed the Equator without ceremony on 27 March, and immediately were rained upon or becalmed in the doldrums. Light winds came and went. Two weeks later they found themselves becalmed again among the seaweed of the Sargasso Sea. The winds finally came and they began to make good time again. North of the Azores they were hit by a vicious thunderstorm:

> With appalling suddenness the sky seemed to burst into a sheet of flame that lit up the whole ocean … queer blue lights danced about the steel rigging and on all the steel yardarms … Looking up from the deck at the boys climbing aloft and laying out the yards was especially interesting, with the lightning-sheets playing on them at intervals and the eeriness of the blue lights silhouetting their oilskinned forms against the pitch blackness of the hour before the dawn.

The storm cleared. Villiers reported 'a yarn' with the stowaway. Some of it was undoubtedly true – 'I was never happier in my life' – but most of it was pseudo-girlish gush that was probably not even very convincing at the time. 'Jeanne' is terribly understanding about why sailors don't want women on board, although some clearly hadn't minded in the slightest.

She found it 'pretty natural' that the sheer presence of a woman is undesirable and sure to cause trouble; 'that the "nervousness" and "intuition" of women is bad for the *moral* [sic] of the ship'; and that woman's more delicate nature, lacking strength of character as well as physical strength, simply renders her – well – unfit. The counterfeit Jeanne is barely restrained from smiting her forehead and exclaiming 'How could I have been such a fool not to realise this before!'

'She' goes on to express contrition at the 'rotten trick' she had played on the crew – 'they hadn't the faintest idea that anyone would ever do anything so out of the ordinary as to stow away in their ship,' wrote Villiers without a blush, at a time when stowaways on grain vessels were common. 'We see things in their proper perspective at sea, and the little things stay little, and the big things grow big,' she confides, all wide-eyed innocence, and ends with a lengthy paean to the ship, 'a creation of beauty indescribable' – which can hardly be said of Villiers' prose at that point.

Still, they were getting close to land. Jeanne said she hoped to see something now of Europe and de Cloux joked that he expected 'a big fat policeman would be waiting with an irate message from her parents and a return passage to Australia'. Jeanne said she wouldn't go. (That sounds more like it.) The Duchess sailed on, 'the sea turned an ugly green, and the trawlers came, and we knew we were not far from port'.

Ninety-six days out of Port Lincoln, they sailed into Falmouth on 24 April 1928 to the glorious news: *Beatrice* had not yet arrived and *Herzogin Cecilie* had won. *Beatrice* took 114 days – it turned out she had gone the Cape of Good Hope route.

———

Jeanne Day had been having the time of her life. Perhaps she was not pretty in the fluffy manner; but she was young, friendly, educated, courageous and fierce enough to blackmail her way on to a great ship. She had signed on to the articles as a 'cabin boy' and cleaned *Herzogin Cecilie*'s living quarters every day for over three months.

Villiers insisted that de Cloux bitterly resented her being on the barque. He certainly would have feared any disruption, but he also had a teenage daughter of his own, Ruby, and even Villiers cannot ignore his many kindnesses towards Jeanne. De Cloux was concerned about her reputation – Villiers reported him telling her that 'as soon as they heard of her mad escapade people would snigger and wonder whose mistress she was'. Villiers could not restrain himself from jotting the interjection at that point, 'As if anybody'd have her!'

> Jeanne replied that she only came because she knew that everyone on board was a gentleman. The skipper told her it was a good thing they were … How could any young woman imagine that she could stow away in a ship of men for a four-month voyage and keep her good name? The fact of her doing such a thing is a pretty sure indication that she never had a good name to keep.

It must all have been so different from her previous constrained life. Villiers reports her 'saying' – and the sheer ordinariness of this scene among the excesses of 'Her Story' suggest it was probably true – 'I had never gained any distinction greater than to see my photograph published in an obscure newspaper, as one of a crowd looking on at an extremely uninteresting football match.' Everything was about to change.

When they docked on 26 April at Cardiff to unload the grain, officials and reporters swarmed aboard. The barque's winning of the race would have been news enough, but now there were 'worried-looking chaps with motion-picture cameras who did not care a hang for the ship when once they heard there was a woman stowaway on board'. This gloom at the superficiality of the reporters in the published account was not reflected in his diary, where he wrote cheerfully, 'I hope they come in the morning, the more publicity for the ship the better for the book.'

In *The Set of the Sails* he writes: 'The newspapers got hold of her and made a great fuss, photographing her in the rigging where she had never been at sea.' But she had, with Jefrelius, and for Villiers' photographs if nothing else; and perhaps she might have spent more time aloft had she not been told so often that being a woman made her unfit to even be on a ship.

> In a day or two she found a relative somewhere in England who, intrigued by the cheap publicity, forgave her the queer manner of her coming and undertook to look after her, to the satisfaction of the immigration authorities … I saw her later driving an elevator at Australia House in London. She was a very fortunate young woman.

In a diary more than a year later he is even more dismissive: 'The woman got a job in Australia House, took a flat somewhere near the Brompton Road and proceeded to go to the dogs.' He does not indicate what particular rack and ruin he had in mind, but her sexual life clearly intrigued him. But if sex were to be her downfall then she had a lot of catching up to do; for when she arrived at England, aged twenty-three-and-a-half, she had never had a lover. Jovial Harald Lindfors said:

> When we came to Cardiff, we were met by the police and people from the Health Department. They thought we had shanghaied the Day woman ... two female doctors wanted to have a look at Miss Day in private and I let them into my cabin. When they returned they laughed and said that you people from Scandinavia are a funny lot. You have had a woman on board for three months and she is still a virgin. So I said, Praise the Lord! As you know, we had Germans, Englishmen, Finns and Swedes on board so anything might have happened.[6]

It was not hard-boiled experience that had brought Jeanne Day to a ship full of men; it was innocence. 'I only came because I knew that everyone on board was a gentleman,' she had said, and in the end her faith had been justified. Whatever crude speculation took place in the fo'c'sle, she had been protected by her own naivety and the strict hierarchy of the ship. If Savolainen's story that Jeanne had spent a night in Lindfors' cabin was true, clearly nothing much had happened: it seems more likely that the sailmaker was lying or mistaken.

But Villiers could never forgive Jeanne Day. He had yearned to write an epic about magnificent ships and a noble competition, and instead her presence had turned it all to farce, at least in his eyes.

———

Within two days of docking in Cardiff Villiers was in London trying to sell his manuscript of *Falmouth for Orders* to publishers. He had his films developed and most were 'magnificent'. All of the newspapers wanted interviews and photographs of Jean, Jane, Jeinne and (occasionally) Jeanne. The *Evening Express* said she was 'a pretty picture with her red jumper and navy blue skirt, and it was seen that her hair was, as it should be for a cultured girl, shingled'. The *Western Mail* said she was 'twenty-two, a brunette, keen, cultured and intensely musical. She has long experienced the call of the sea.'

As soon as he got to London, Villiers visited Jeanne to interview her for the *Daily Mail*, and a week later received eight guineas for 'Log of a Happy Girl'. She was asked to write several stories and wanted Villiers to help her. The *Daily Mail* of 2 May 1928 printed 'Why I Stowed Away by Jeanne Day', and on the clipping that Villiers kept in a scrapbook he inserted 'AJ Villiers for —' before her name. He heard that *Wide World* was paying Jeanne £20 for her story – 'must do more!' he wrote in his diary. He was annoyed that Nash's wanted an article from Jeanne but had rejected one from him; she submitted his article in her name and it was accepted. He sent 'stowaway article' to Hobart. *People* printed something he wrote in her name.

It must have been infuriating to find fame via the stowaway but it was also a thrilling time for Villiers. The story had wide publicity and his book was almost certain to get a publisher. He was to go to Europe in late June for a fortnight to do interviews on the apple market, then in August he would return by steamer to Australia. And best of all, he had stumbled upon Goldershurst.

———

In Villiers' books *The Sea in Ships* (1932) and *Last of the Wind Ships* (1934), there is a fold-out drawing, a 'Sail and Rigging Sketch of a Four-Masted Barque'. The barque has a name on her bow – *Goldershurst* – but you may search the maritime records in vain, for Goldershurst was never a ship. It was 'the happy little boarding house' at 35 Hoop Lane, Golders Green, where Villiers lived for three months, the first of several significant times in his life.

On 11 May, he wrote in his diary, 'The Golders Green establishment learns of *Herzogin Cecilie* & is very interested.'[7] There he met 'some splendid people, chief among whom were Betty and Alan Deverall of Johannesburg', who were brother and sister, not a married couple. By late May the three of them were going on outings to films, plays, museums, parks and palaces all over London with a Miss Bolton and a young seaman, Hawkins.

In one four-week period they managed to see *Ramona*, *The Gondoliers*, *The Desert Song*, *Two Arabian Knights* and *The Vagabond King*; they went to Trafalgar Square, Pall Mall, St James's Park, Buckingham Palace, Whitehall and the Changing of the Guard; they visited the Natural

History, War, Science and Victoria & Albert museums; they boarded *Beatrice* at Victoria Docks four times for yarns with Villiers' friend, the mate Mr Svensson; and walked in Hyde Park, Hampstead Heath, Hadley Woods, Golders Hill Park and nearby Hendon Aerodrome.

While this might not be an action-packed programme for someone on holiday, during this same period Villiers was also writing articles about sailing ships, the grain race and the stowaway; completing *Falmouth for Orders*, revising the novel that became *The Wind Ship*, visiting publishers and his literary agent Michael Joseph, getting photographs developed and printed, submitting stories to magazines in Britain and Australia and interviewing dealers in the fruit business in London and – over a five-day jaunt – those in Hull, Liverpool and Manchester.

Then on 29 June he set off to interview fruit dealers in Europe. In the next two weeks he visited Antwerp, Rotterdam, Amsterdam, Bremen, Hamburg, Stockholm and Oslo. By the time he steamed back to Hull he had already written eighteen articles based on his fruit interviews, and would write another six before returning to Australia.

He returned to Goldershurst to receive the marvellous news that publisher Geoffrey Bles would take *Falmouth for Orders*, and five days later he heard that Hurst & Blackett would take *The Wind Ship*.

———

Villiers had begun *The Wind Ship* some years before. In *The Set of the Sails* he says that in order to fulfil his contract with the dodgy Hobart lawyers he decided to write two novels of such 'indifference that no publisher would look at them'. This was with harsh hindsight – on *Herzogin Cecilie* he had still hoped something would come of them:

> Well, two books have been written and are in London – a first novel with Antarctica as the theme, called at present 'The Frozen Continent', and a sailing ship story called 'Kensington Hill's Last Voyage'. 'The Frozen Continent' was hawked around London with no success ... therefore when I reach London I shall see Mr Joseph and discover what he thinks of them.

Probably on the strength of the *Herzogin Cecilie* publicity, 'Kensington Hill's Last Voyage' was accepted. It was renamed *The Wind Ship* and published by Hurst & Blackett in late 1928. Villiers' judgement of it as 'indifferent' was not unreasonable: he also called it a 'very, very bad novel' in his diary. In the course of a single voyage on a great square-rigger, the hero – a medical doctor – gets promoted through accidents and murder, from seaman to mate to captain. The previous captain's beautiful daughter just happens to be aboard too.

The *Tasman Motor Sport and Dramatic Review* of 22 March 1929 remarked dryly that the book 'smacks of melodrama, to which the author too frequently descends. There are occasions when the long arm of coincidence is sorely jerked from its socket.' Another review, from the *Australasian* in February 1929, mentions perhaps the most bizarre aspect of the novel:

> [Villiers] reveals too, a certain bitterness towards women, which also may be based upon personal experience, and which suggests that he is still young in experience of many aspects of life. Roger Winspear, the hero of the story, is a graduate in medicine at Melbourne University, who finds it impossible to obtain a post or a practice, chiefly it seems because of 'the number of young ladies who had also qualified for the profession'.

His father Leon had hoped he would study medicine rather than go to sea, and in fiction he could do both and still get the girl. But all those worrying lady doctors? The mind boggles at the implausibility of the labour market being swamped, in the mid-1920s, by female medical practitioners: and also a little at the world-view of young Alan Villiers.

———

The final four weeks of Villiers' stay in London would become 'the happiest of days'. Not only because of the two book deals but, perhaps more importantly, because of his growing closeness to his friends at Goldershurst. He was liked and admired. They called him 'Alan John' to distinguish him from Alan Deverall, or 'Duke', probably because of his ship, the Duchess. They took long walks, played gramophone records over and over and stayed up yarning till after midnight.

Alan Deverall did a painting for the dustcover of *Falmouth for Orders* and his sister Betty drew the map for the endpapers. They designed a coat of arms for their little group, jokingly labelled the Purity League – 'a chicken rampant on a field of turnips'. Villiers revelled in the light-hearted social life he had missed through his youthful labours and early marriage. There are hints in his diary that he was particularly fond of Betty, and when he finally left Goldershurst and Britain on 7 August 1928, he wrote:

> The sad, sad business of parting today. I never thought that I would mind! But —. Left St Pancras 10.20 hung around Tilbury for tender for hours; boarded *Jervis Bay* about 1 p.m. and put to sea 5 p.m. ... Memories of the brave, brave figure that went around the corner.[8]

We cannot be certain who the 'brave, brave figure' was, or why their parting was so very sad, but on the endpapers of that diary Villiers listed every outing he took with his Goldershurst friends, and (for the first and only time) three emotional stanzas of poetry by Emily Brontë.[9]

He stayed in touch with the Deveralls – Betty did the endpaper map for Villiers' next book, *By Way of Cape Horn*, and may also have drawn the mythical barque 'Goldershurst'. Even forty years later, when Villiers and his wife briefly stopped over in South Africa, they took the time to meet up again.

———

He was clearly touched by the few thrilling months that had brought him loving friends, a happy summer in London and Europe, two new books and dozens of articles published worldwide. It was all so remote from provincial Hobart and his unhappy marriage; and on *Jervis Bay* he wrestled with his feelings.

'Passed an awful night last night – worst in life.' The following day: 'Still thinking things out and coming to certain conclusions.' They steamed through the Mediterranean and into the Red Sea: 'Still trying to solve some problems', and again, 'It is ... very difficult to do anything save to think, and that is not wholly pleasant or desirable.'

Nothing on board interested him. He disliked the steamer – 'The only thing that ever happens in this damned ship is that 700 people eat three meals a day.' After reaching Ceylon his spirits began to rise with a pleasant shore excursion, but then he became ill with a fever, 'Indian Ocean – Malaria: hell! Temp 105.4. Quinine 15gr.' They reached Fremantle on 7 September 1928. He was interviewed by reporters, one of his articles was highly commended by *Bulletin* magazine, and there were 'pictures in *Western Mail*, *Observer*, *Queenslander*. Hobart public has taken my fruit stuff seriously and the job is big. Alarmed at prospect of returning.'

He was desperate to get to Melbourne quickly, but when the ship arrived at Adelaide it was 'to find place deserted and in throes of strike. Damn Australia! Next time I leave – and I hope that is soon – I stay.' He took the train to Melbourne where he was met by Daphne and his brother Frank. He and Daphne caught the *Loongana* and passed a 'stormy night in Bass Strait'.

On Sunday 16 September they 'arrived Hobart abt [sic] 9 o'clock in heavy rain: Jack, Thelma, Ron Walker and his car there'. This is where Villiers' 1928 diary ends – on the name of Ronald Walker, soon to become so significant.

4

HE IS DEAD

Villiers had spent a lot of time 'thinking things out' on the ship home. His time in London had shown him happier possibilities in life and probably contributed to the greater emotional depth of his next book, *By Way of Cape Horn* – but at this stage he had probably decided to let it all be; to pick up the threads of his four-year-old marriage and enjoy his new consequence as an author.

Back in Tasmania, however, he was startled to discover he was now considered an authority on European fruit markets and expected to serve on advisory boards, which did not interest him at all. Within six months, at the age of twenty-five, he was ready to go to sea again.

A fellow reporter on the *Mercury* was tall, fair, pleasant-looking Ronald Walker, only twenty-two years old. He suggested to Villiers that a moving film of the square-riggers would have wide appeal, but they must act quickly as others were also considering the possibility. Walker had sailed on yachts but, like Villiers, had never touched a motion picture camera in his life – there was not one to be had in the whole of Tasmania. Still, they found some funding and bought 6,000 feet of film and two cameras costing £40 each from Sydney.

Villiers wrote in *The Set of the Sails*: 'This time my wife gave me an ultimatum. I could choose the sea or her. This was a choice already made. My sea-bag was packed. (It had never been unpacked.)' Brave words, but since the marriage continued amicably for another few years – and Daphne herself sailed around Cape Horn with him in 1932 – their estrangement was probably again being exaggerated for effect.

Villiers hoped to film a ship without modern enhancements such as brace-winches, halliard-winches or wheelhouses, to depict the square-rigger life of earlier days; he thought that the Finnish four-masters had less 'pictorial value' than older vessels. Thus the fateful decision was made: to sail in the three-masted full-rigged steel ship *Grace Harwar*, the last of her kind in the Australian trade.

Grace Harwar had been launched in 1889 at Port Glasgow, and Gustaf Erikson had bought her in 1916. She was only 1,816 gross tons (less than two-thirds the volume of *Herzogin Cecilie*), and carried elegant royals over her topgallant sails. 'I cannot recall a lovelier old ship ... Her three masts have a graceful loftiness and the sweep of her deck is entrancing to the sailor's eye,' Villiers wrote in *By Way of Cape Horn*, the account of the voyage on *Grace Harwar*. Less lyrically he recalled in his 1949 autobiography, 'My heart sank at the sight of the old full-rigger.'

Rusty and unkempt, she had been tramping around the world for two years, heavy with seaweed and barnacles. Her previous cargo had been caustic, cordage-rotting guano, and her rigging was 'full of the long splices which tell of worn-out rope ... She was a killer and had been for years washing sailors overboard, knocking their heads off with parted wire, dropping them out of the rigging. She was always in trouble.'

Not always: *Grace Harwar* was benign and well-behaved for the remaining years of her life, but Villiers would never forgive her – or himself – for what happened on this particular voyage.

———

The utter ruthlessness of the sea had never been more apparent than in those first few months of 1929, when the world was gradually realising that *København* – one of the finest sailing ships ever built – had mysteriously disappeared, along with her fifteen crew and forty-five teenage boys. Villiers wrote about the mystery of her loss in his 1956 book, *Posted Missing*.

In 1928 *København* was the last five-masted barque still in existence, out of only seven five-masters that had ever been built. The Danish East Asiatic Company ran her as a sail-training vessel, with watertight bulkheads, a fine auxiliary engine and a long-range radio, pumps, boats and life-saving gear. She had been surveyed to Lloyd's highest class, and over seven years *København* had already made nine successful cargo-carrying voyages. Her captain and officers had years of experience on the ship, and even most of the cadets had been under sail for one or two years.

In late 1928 she took cargo from Denmark to Buenos Aires, then was ordered to sail in ballast (without cargo) to Australia via the Cape of Good Hope and the Indian Ocean. She left Buenos Aires on 14 December. A week later, from the mid-South Atlantic near Tristan da Cunha, *København* radioed that 'all was well' to the steamer *William Blumer*, 100 miles to her north.

Then nothing. No radio reports, no lifeboats, no wreckage; no *København*. For a full year other ships were diverted or chartered especially to search the surrounding waters, the remotest islands, the furthest paths she might have floated, from one side of the Atlantic to the other.

It was as if the magnificent five-masted barque and her forty-five boy cadets had never existed. An unseen iceberg may have opened her steel hull like tin; an extraordinary squall may have overwhelmed her before anyone could reach the radio: whatever the cause, it was sudden and inescapable and catastrophic.

The occasional loss of an undermanned, poorly equipped grain barque was grimly tolerated, but *København* was different. If there had ever been any small hope for merchant sail's future viability – and most European navies still saw it as fundamental training for their officers – then that hope had vanished now as completely as *København* herself.

When Villiers joined *Grace Harwar* in March 1929 he was appalled at her decrepit state. The sailors, even the apprentices, were drunk on a Saturday afternoon on board. She had been reduced to begging for food from steamers on the inward passage; her young sailmaker had died suddenly in Peru, her captain had broken a leg. When the crew was finally counted, apart from officers there were only thirteen men – ominously numbered and ludicrously few – left to sail her.

Villiers kept a diary during the voyage, the most immediate account of its terrible events.[1] He wrote *By Way of Cape Horn* just afterwards in 1930: it aimed for the romantic heroism of *Falmouth for Orders* but he could not hide his bitterness. His 1949 *The Set of the Sails* is more honest about the deficiencies of ship and crew, but from years of yarning has gained a little too much glibness: for instance, Walker has a 'premonition' when he boards *Grace Harwar*; 'I don't remember that he smiled again, from the day that we joined.' Yet photographs in *By Way of Cape Horn* show Walker smiling quite cheerfully on board!

They left Wallaroo on 17 April 1929. Sailing a full-rigged ship like *Grace Harwar* was different from the four-masted barques Villiers had known before. On 22 April he noted: 'She is good to steer and handle after that big brute *Herzogin Cecilie*.' The weather degenerated as soon as they left port and stayed that way – they spent weeks battling the rain, cold and seasickness. The skin on their hands was always wet: 'Deep, bloodless cuts and splits in the flesh appeared in the palms and along some of our fingers, and remained there malignantly ... they never healed, and never made any change, except sometimes to be more painful.'

Their oilskins and sea boots were hopelessly inadequate, and even this early in the voyage the ship began running low on supplies. Crewmen were discovered drunk on at least two occasions. Villiers praised their good fellowship in *By Way of Cape Horn* but actually disliked some of them intensely: he suspected the mess boy of having tuberculosis, and was much irritated by a Swedish-speaking West Indian 'nigger', Adolphus Fox.

The poor condition of *Grace Harwar* worried Villiers intensely. In *The Set of the Sails* he praises Captain Karl G. Svensson, who 'acted like a good officer with a group of men in a front-line trench. ... the cut of his face was gentle and almost saintly, though he was no saint. His blue eyes were clear and open as a boy's. His voice was soft, and he never raised it.'

But perhaps Captain Svensson should have raised his voice more often instead of tolerating the behaviour of the crew and the dreadful state of the ship. No matter how tightly Erikson kept the purse-strings, there was always money for at least adequate food and fundamentals like sails and rigging, and a good master made certain of it.

The winds forced them to pass through Cook Strait, between the north and south islands of New Zealand. For a while the weather was fine, and they cleared the Strait three weeks after leaving Australia. When not on duty Villiers spent part of his time writing a maritime history of Tasmania that became the book *Forgotten Fleets*. Its commission from Hobart businessman E.H. Taylor had paid for the cameras and expenses of the voyage.

The rest of his spare time was spent with Ron Walker, filming *Grace Harwar*. It was Walker who knew most about photography, especially loading the camera, 'guiding the raw film over its spools and cogwheels' in their darkened cabin. The light was poor and the days were short during winter at high latitudes, but they filmed when they could.

They shared a tiny cabin in the foc's'l. Waves swept frequently aboard and water seeped and spurted through the poorly fitting steel door and puttied-up porthole. The voyage came as a shock to Walker. Villiers had at least known easier and happier passages in the past; this, the worst of times, was Walker's first, and he wrote in his diary (quoted in *By Way of Cape Horn*):

> It is a wonderful experience, though horribly and cruelly miserable ... I was aloft on the mainmast an hour to-day and my hands were so cold that ... when I touched anything I could not feel it, yet all the time my hands were burning as if scalded ... I had no idea what pain – real pain – was until I came here; no one could possibly imagine ... how these lovely and graceful ships drag one, immerse one, and perpetually stifle one in the very dregs of hell ... And yet I'm glad I'm here in spite of everything.

When they had been just over five weeks at sea they had an utterly depressing day – their cabin was soaked, the camera jammed, the evening's soup was burnt, and their few books were wet mush. Walker was low and Villiers made him a supper – cocoa with stolen milk, charred bread with jealously hoarded honey and a piece of plain cake from the cook. They shared the feast contentedly while the ship rolled onwards in the dark. That memory would be a small comfort to Villiers in the time ahead.

———

On a ship with three masts – the fore, main and mizzen – the large sails nearest the deck were named the foresail, mainsail and crossjack. Above them were the topsails, then the topgallants and finally the small royals. Each sail was named for its mast, for example, the fore topgallant.

As vessels had grown larger, some topsails and topgallants were divided into two – upper and lower – making them easier to handle. *Grace Harwar* carried double topgallants on her fore and main masts and a single on the mizzen. The yards, the cross spars that carried the sails, also doubled. The lower yard would remain fixed in place, while the upper yard was movable – when an upper topgallant was being set, its yard would be hauled up the mast. When the sail was not in use the upper yard could be let down the mast, to rest close to the lower.

Although *Grace Harwar* was small compared to a four-master, her topgallant yards were substantial, about 50 feet across. They were heavy steel tubes tapered at both ends, with the girth of a man near the middle. Their massive weight was lifted by the halliard ropes, wound on to a capstan as sailors slowly pushed the capstan bars around.

At about 4.20 a.m. on 25 May 1929, Villiers and Walker came on deck to help set the upper topgallant on the foremast. Villiers went to the capstan with three of the crew. Walker was sent up the rigging to help another man, Finila, loosen the sail before its yard was hauled upwards into place. It was still dark but the moon was nearly full, Villiers wrote in his diary. The wind was light, the air icy, and the ship was 'slipping along a quiet three or four knots in the most perfect Cape Horn running weather I have known'.

Aloft, Walker and Finila freed the sail, then waited while Villiers and the other men began tramping around, pushing the capstan bars. The upper topgallant yard slowly rose, but when it was a few feet from the top it slowed. The second mate noticed a gasket, a securing rope, caught on one of the lower corners of the sail and shouted for it to be cleared. The men at the capstan stopped.

Walker climbed down to the yard of the lower topgallant, and standing on its footrope, reached up and released the gasket. He called out that everything was clear. The sailors began pushing on the capstan again and the upper topgallant yard started moving easily into place.

> Suddenly, when everything was going well, something carried away with a wild rush, the fall of the halliards broke and wildly unrove, and the yard fell down from its hoisted position onto its lifts ... we around the capstan cleared for our lives, not knowing what had carried away and expecting the heavy blocks, or the chain tie, or the yard itself, to descend about our ears.

Finila called out something that Villiers did not catch, but with the others he jumped into the rigging to clear whatever damage had occurred. He went to secure a dangerously swinging halliard block. One of the men called out to him to bring some water; he hurried down, starting to wonder if 'something rotten had happened', filled a coffeepot with water and carried it up to the others clustered at the top-gallant yards.[2]

> There I found a ghastly scene – Frenchman and Finila holding Walker up by the head and shoulders while his feet still rested on the footrope, with the moon's pale light reflected on his paler, unconscious face. ... I tried to revive him with the water and by other means; I bathed his temples, and massaged them, for half an hour, while the ship rolled and the others clung to him desperately, to hold him there. Nothing happened.

Walker had been struck by the plummeting upper yard. It had fallen to within a foot or two of the lower yard; he was held loosely between them, but the sailors were able to free him easily. Their hands were so cold they could not feel his pulse but they believed he was simply unconscious. They put a rope around him and gently lowered him to a blanket on the deck. The captain felt his head and heart, and said, 'He is dead.'

> Saturday May 25: 38 days – Walker was killed today ... it seems impossible and unbelievable and I write this, sitting in our cabin, in a queer unnatural belief that he really still lives and will come in here again; but he is lying in his oilskins on a rough sailor's bier beneath the foc's'l head, and he will never come in here again, nor speak, nor anything. He died suddenly without warning and without sound; without pain, too, by the mercy of God ... It just happened, and he was killed.

Walker had remained leaning on the lower yard when he should have moved away – on his first voyage he did not know that he should never stay beneath a hoisting yard, and in the dark no one had noticed him there to warn him. Finila, above him, said that all he had heard was one soft moan. Villiers told himself, over and over, that Walker had been gazing at the moonlight on the sea, thinking about filming; or at peace, thinking of nothing at all.

Next day Captain Svensson and Villiers examined Walker's body. He had bled from the nose and mouth, his back was heavily bruised, his neck and shoulder blade were perhaps a little awry. Neither could see any obvious cause for his death. They washed him and wrapped him in a sheet, then the second mate sewed him into a canvas shroud. Over that was a Finnish flag, for there were no Australian flags aboard.

They buried him in the sea that afternoon. Except for the helmsman the whole crew was at the service. There were hymns and readings in Swedish and English. The captain addressed Walker, saying, 'Here we are just children, going through our school; and you have qualified.' Then they tilted the hatch he was lying on and he slid into the water.

> The Captain and I have cleared up all his gear to take back to Hobart; the sea stuff, of course, I shall not take back and I have done with it what he would do. It has gone to those without in the foc's'l – Finila, Berqvist, Beckmann, Jim, all of whom were horribly off for clothes down here. I hope I have done right in his people's eyes.

Where the topgallant halliards had broken, the ropes could be shredded by hand, even though they had recently been tested, turned and appeared quite normal. They had probably rotted through from the guano that had been *Grace Harwar*'s previous cargo, as guano dust mixed with salt water becomes acidic.

Villiers tried to pick up the thread of the filming but had great trouble loading the camera. He slowly mastered it, but the light was rarely good enough, and now with one man less there was even more work for everyone to do. He feared that the project would fail in his hands. He wrote, 'His blood is still on the fore lower t'gallant.'

———

They had a few days of good light winds a week after Walker died, but then found that the ship had begun leaking, and the slow tedious labour of hand-pumping began, for hours each day. The conditions were too gloomy for filming. Everyone was subdued; there was no more drunkenness.

The second mate, who had been the one to send Walker aloft that terrible night, told Villiers that once he had been helmsman on a ship when the mate and the rest of the watch were swept overboard by a huge wave in a gale. He could not leave the helm or the ship might have foundered, and the other watch asleep below could not hear his cries. When they emerged at dawn there had not been the slightest chance of saving anybody for hours.

Villiers listed in his diary the numbers of sailing ship deaths he knew of over the previous five years: *Archibald Russell* had killed four men, *Penang* and *Grace Harwar* three, *Olivebank*, *Greif*, *Ponape*, *Garthpool*, *Fennia*, *Pampa* and *Killoran* two, and *Hougomont*, *Winterhude*, *Lawhill* and *Herzogin Cecilie* one man each. Twenty-five had been lost from *Port Caledonia*, and 'all hands of the French Barque *Eugene Schneider* are to be added ... and God knows what has become of *København*'.

They were still hundreds of miles from Cape Horn, with the winds frustratingly against them. Villiers wrote sardonically, 'Everybody is so wet the best way to start the watch is to go and lie in the scuppers; you'll end up there so you might as well begin.' There was so little light that he began to think he might have to get his 'Cape Horn' footage in the Atlantic. A few days later he wrote, 'The film jammed on me today, dam' it, and I can't help being a bit depressed about it all. I don't even know if I put it in the magazine right way round ... But I think I <u>can</u> write that other book.' He began planning *By Way of Cape Horn*.

They reached the Horn on 13 June, fifty-seven days out from Wallaroo. That evening they held a feast in the foc's'l to celebrate. They had typed-out menus, sheets on the table, candles, clean shirts and brushed hair; and the unfortunate 'nigger', Adolphus Fox, got stuck with the job of waiter. 'We had gin (from the slopchest), Kraft cheese, honey from Mr Lindsay, cocoa, cake, biscuits, tinned pine-apple and tinned plum pudding, cigarettes and wine.'

———

The air seemed a fraction warmer, the wind a little kinder: 'One can venture out on deck without three coats on, though still with three guernseys.' The winds were excellent for a week and the ship made her best times of the voyage, 1,100 miles in six days.

Then 'a heavy shrieking gale came out of the north ... It was the fair hell of a day, for everybody; standing soaking in cold blood at the wheel, and lying sodden over streaming wet yards, clothes blown off your back, hail cutting you, fighting wet maddened canvas.' It rained again the following day – 'I never put in such a horrible wheel turn as 1–2 this morning; I couldn't keep from shivering violently, though it was not cold …'.

But they were on their way to the Equator, and the gale was the last spiteful gasp of Cape Horn weather. Soon it was Midsummer Eve (in Scandinavia) and 'the kids are making a great night of it tonight. The sea and wind have dropped and there is a glorious moon; midnight finds them singing hilariously on the foc's'l head.'

Next morning 'we can see some good in life today! For the weather is beautiful; there is a drying sun; we have Midsummer Holiday (though it is midwinter here); and the cook has made pancakes for breakfast, and roast salt pork for dinner.' Days followed of beautiful weather, light breezes, flying fish, dry decks – and Villiers even finished a chapter of *Vanished Fleets*, and started on *By Way of Cape Horn*. It seemed fair they should emerge into the sunlight at last, but as Villiers might have observed, 'fair' had little to do with sailing ships.

———

Readers familiar with *By Way of Cape Horn* may have noticed that one of its most dramatic events has not yet occurred: the boy overboard on the way to the Cape. This is because it actually happened much later in the voyage, and it was not a boy who fell: it was the second mate. He was trying to commit suicide.

The episode began on 28 June, after seventy-two days at sea, when the second mate told Villiers he had been constantly worried since Walker's death, and blamed himself for the accident. His position was a lonely one in the rigid ship's hierarchy. He had little contact with those above him – the first mate was on the other watch and the captain on day duty – and since his status was higher than that of the other men on board, he had no close confidants.

The following day he walked to the foc's'l and told the men he had given them his last job aboard as second mate, and they should come with him to the officers' mess room (where foc's'l hands were rarely permitted). Curious and perturbed, they followed him; and there, with the captain, he broke down:

Poor devil, all day and all the long night watches when he has only his thoughts for company on the exposed and lonely poop, he has thought of Walker ... He sobbed, and cried, and held his head; he said that he would have jumped overboard long since if he had not wished to see his mother in Finland again ... it is not to be wondered at that a sensitive and fine man such as he should have broken down. But it is all pretty ghastly.

He was taken to his cabin to rest. At four in the afternoon he came out, apparently quite rational. He suddenly shouted, 'Goodbye, Captain!' and leapt over the side of the ship. The mate just caught him but could not hold him and he fell into the water. The captain flung him a lifebuoy, which he grabbed, and the helmsman turned the wheel as quickly as possible to bring the ship into the wind. All hands rushed to swing out a lifeboat, manned by the mate, Villiers and four others.

The waves were high and they could not see anything from the boat. They tried to retrace the ship's track without success. When they had rowed about half a mile from *Grace Harwar* – in some genuine risk that they might never be able to get back – they suddenly found him. He was 'lying in the lifebelt, swimming and drinking salt water, and appeared quite mad'. With difficulty they got him aboard and rowed back to the ship in the gathering dusk. Later the second mate did not appear to remember what had happened and wondered why he was wet. At midnight he tried to hang himself, so they locked him in his cabin with a watch posted outside.

Everybody has been splendid; I was struck by the gentle note in all their voices – Captain's, mate's, carpenter's – when they tried to talk with the poor devil. It is tragic to think that such a fine man, a quiet, peaceful, competent, magnificent officer, should be brought to such a stage ... Again we are pitched into all the horror of Walker's death ...

In his better moments he worries himself back into insane fits; 'Will Captain not tell me what I have done?' he cried once, coming staring-eyed into the saloon while the captain and I were there this afternoon.

As if in mockery of the misery aboard, the weather was beautiful, the wind steady and good. They practised launching the lifeboat again and Villiers was able to take some magnificent films and photographs of the ship from a distance. *Grace Harwar* was still leaking, and they were at the pumps every day, with 10 to 14 inches of water in the hold. The wheat began to rot, and sickening gasses rose through the ventilators on the foredeck and poop, blistering and burning paint off the steel.

The sailors spent an exhausting two hours every day of their precious off-duty time guarding and talking with the second mate. 'I feel pretty tired sometimes, and the two hours nightly watch on the second mate is a rotten nerve strain. One finds one's heart leaping at nothing ... [sic]'.

———

They crossed the Tropic of Capricorn on 10 July, eighty-four days out. 'The sea is very warm, warmer than the air ... This is the wind! SE Trade, fresh and strong, and the old lady slipping along at her best despite the grass on her sides.' Even the second mate was starting to seem a little better. They had fresh water from soft squalls of rain, the days were lovely, and Villiers filmed and wrote. In honour of the captain's wife's name day, they 'spliced the main brace that often, that after three hours of it, if there was a strand left untouched no-one was in a fit state to discover it'.

Then the winds faltered. Over days the crew replaced some of the sails aloft. It became hot and oppressive and the second mate started becoming depressed again. Everyone was on edge. Villiers wrote, 'Berqvist tells me he dreamt today that there were two whistles, and he saw Walker come from his old bunk in the foc's'l though he knew he was dead.'

On 19 July, Villiers finished writing *Vanished Fleets*, and the following day they crossed the Equator and held the traditional ceremony:

> ... even the victims, smeared with tar, made to drink sharks' blood mixed with white pepper, flung on their necks in a tub of water, seemed to enjoy it! There was the whole business in real deepwater fashion: Neptune, Mrs Neptune, and the court coming over the bows; meeting the skipper aft; the priest's introduction; the chase for victims in the rigging; the trial; the medical assassination, administration of medicine and foul barbering; and last the parade of the chaired victims, now initiated into the Grand Brotherhood of the Sons of the Sea.

They experienced only a few days of doldrums, then easily picked up the north-east trade winds. Their good progress was marred only by the scarcity of food: the sugar and margarine were all gone. Then they discovered that the remaining salt meat was bad, and five tins of bully-beef were all that remained. Villiers wrote that there was still 'one small pig' left to slaughter for fresh meat, so they were not too concerned. Then the potatoes and milk powder went.

The sailmaker became ill with scurvy, and some of the crew's faces became sunken and noticeably thinner. They decided to wait no longer and killed 'the last pig', but discovered it was inedible, with 'unmistakeable signs of disease'. They went hungry. (This telling is from *The Set of the Sails*, but in fact Villiers' diary reveals that they actually had another pig on board, slaughtered when they reached England, so their position was not quite as precarious as he made out.)

Still, the coal supplies were low and lamp oil for the binnacle compass light was gone. They went through periods of exhausting calms and the second mate's depression deepened. As the crew became weaker the captain decided they should serve only 'calashee watches', with no other labour beyond the basics of steering, sailing and pumping.

Villiers was perturbed that the captain would not request help from passing steamships. He was now writing articles at a great rate to support himself in England: by 5 August he had finished fourteen; six days later he had done twenty. On 14 August the second mate tried to poison himself with opium but survived. They saw a steamer and at last the captain agreed they should fly distress flags, but the steamer ignored them; Villiers was reminded of his *Bellands* voyage, and poor *Lysglimt* left behind to burn on her own.

————

On 18 August they passed a great Italian liner, 27,000-ton *Conte Biancamano*. She dipped her flag to 'our sweet old ship in her full glory', tiny beside her; and Villiers thought of the contrast between the liner's opulence and their own deprivations. That evening, 123 days out from Wallaroo, they finally got help from a steamer named *Orangeleaf*.[3]

They rowed a boat a mile in the rain to meet her, and the kindly crew passed them down preserved meat, milk powder, sacks of vegetables, sugar, tobacco, newspapers and even a large cake. *Orangeleaf* towed their small boat back in the dark to *Grace Harwar*, then departed with cheers and sirens. They quickly cooked some food: 'I took a handful of the beef and a mug of coffee to the wheel with me. It was fine to have something to eat again, and the name of *Orangeleaf* was blessed among us.'[4]

Now the final days of the voyage were easier. The sailmaker recovered from his scurvy. One day when the second mate was not around, he cut out the part of the fore lower topgallant sail that was still stained with Walker's blood despite the rains of the voyage, and sewed a new section into it.

Fifteen days after meeting *Orangeleaf*, *Grace Harwar* made port at Queenstown (Cobh) in Ireland, on 3 September 1929, 138 days out from Australia. Not surprisingly, all of the larger four-masted barques had made better times that year. The winner of the grain 'race' had been *Archibald Russell*, taking only ninety-three days for her voyage. A tug towed them through the Irish Sea to the Clyde to discharge the cargo. They arrived at Glasgow on 14 September, and the terrible voyage was over.

———

Two months after *Grace Harwar*'s arrival, on 25 November 1929, Villiers and his agent Curtis Brown signed a contract with Messrs Remarko Films Ltd, of 80–82 Wardour Street, London, for the 'making and exploitation of a film *Round Cape Horn*'. Villiers was to receive 60 per cent of profits for his exposed film and helping to prepare the story. 'Wardour Street' would come to represent everything that Villiers loathed about life ashore. His concept of what the film might be was utterly different to that of the film-makers: to him, the ship was so striking in itself they could ask for nothing more.

He wrote a 'Plan of the film Windjammers' in April 1930, little more than an outline of what had actually happened on *Grace Harwar*: they leave port, raise sails, get wet, take in sails, bury Walker, freeze at Cape Horn, get hot in the doldrums, welcome King Neptune, catch the wind, suffer hunger, make landfall. 'I tried to work in shots of the dog when I thought they'd be useful,' Villiers offers earnestly.[5]

The new Poet Laureate, ex-seaman John Masefield, was shown the raw footage and 'loved it', reported an article on 15 May by a 'Special Correspondent' – who, from the writing style, was probably Villiers himself. But what would work so well in Villiers' written accounts of the voyage had little power in his disjointed black-and-white footage, no matter how original and beautiful; and the film-makers were not interested in making a documentary. They wanted something with a storyline, and commissioned a script with stock characters such as a grizzled old salt, a Cockney humorist, a Scot, a Frenchman with a small black moustache and (perhaps less stock) a 'Swedish-speaking nigger'.

They built a scruffy, untidy set for the ship's interior scenes which made Villiers fume: he relates how he took the director to show him the fo'c'sle of *Archibald Russell* at the docks, 'a clean white house with tiers of fore-and-aft bunks, neatly arranged lockers, hooks for mugs, coats, oilskins, and so on'. The director said, to Villiers' astonishment, 'If we filmed this, the public wouldn't believe it was a sailing ship's forecastle at all.'

In a draft of *The Set of the Sails* he also recalls with bitterness the words of a film magnate watching the footage: 'Don't that ship ever get no place? For Chris' sake get her some place! Get the men ashore! Do somethin'! Twenny secons [sic] of that sea stuff is enough!'[6] The magnate was probably correct. The public wasn't much interested in more than a few minutes of sea and ship: it wanted a story.

Unfortunately the scriptwriter, humorist A.P. Herbert, didn't provide one. His idea of dramatic conflict was a struggle for musical supremacy between a mandolin player and a mouth organist, which must also have infuriated Villiers, as even that was a bizarre choice – ship's instruments were more usually fiddles and accordions.

As the film struggled to completion Remarko's interest waned. On 28 July 1930 it sold its 40 per cent share for £250 to British Instructional Films Ltd of Regent Studio, Welwyn Garden City, who finally released *Windjammer* on 19 September 1930, a year after *Grace Harwar* had arrived in England. By then the film industry was in transition from silent movies to sound. Even though *Windjammer* had the distinction of being the first British-Australian talking film ever made, exhibitors were reluctant to book a film about a bunch of hackneyed 'types' arguing about a mandolin, getting wet and going (apparently) nowhere.

Yet reviewers were kind, respectful of the original footage and Walker's tragedy, although the ship was called 'Louise Harwar' in one

ALAN VILLIERS

paper and 'Grace Harbour' in another. The *Daily Telegraph*'s film critic even selected *Windjammer* as one of the twelve best British films of the year, but Villiers always felt that he had let his friend down.

A year later, in mid-1931, he wrote to H. Bruce Woolfe, managing director of British Instructional Films, seeking some royalties for Walker's family. Woolfe coolly replied that the costs had been £5,741, the booking expenses £2,392, and the cash received so far was £912, hence there was a long way to go to recoup costs.[7] Over the next three years Villiers finally received royalties of just under £300, half of which went to Ronald Walker's family, but that was all.

———

The captain of *Grace Harwar* left sailing ships after the voyage and went into steam, as did the second mate, who recovered completely from his breakdown: he later received an award for bravery, rescuing the crew of a fishing schooner in a North Atlantic storm.

Villiers went to work for the Australian Newspapers Cable Service, in *The Times* office building in London. The ANCS sent cable summaries of news stories from British and European newspapers to Australia, New Zealand, South Africa and India:

> The raw material clattered into the office throughout most of the 24 hours over batteries of ticker-tapes and teleprinters at the rate of thousands of words an hour ... I was sometimes a roundsman, sometimes a correspondent attached to Australian Cabinet ministers who came to England, sometimes sent off on stories round Europe, and sometimes was a watchkeeper at the cable desk. The newspaper work never ceased to interest me.[8]

As always, he churned out articles for sale on any topic that suggested itself; he did several on the casting and filming of *Windjammer*. In January 1930 he signed a contract for the book that became *By Way of Cape Horn*. It appeared towards the end of the year and was a bestseller, although too late to help the film. It was perhaps the most honest of his books: his heartfelt account of trying to deal with the incomprehensible death of a friend was empathetic and touching. The second mate's breakdown and the crew's near-starvation were dramatic bonuses; what could not be conveyed on screen worked beautifully in print.

Villiers' wife, Daphne, came to England by steamer sometime in 1930 to stay with him at Goldershurst. Around the end of that year he signed contracts for *Vanished Fleets* to be published in Britain and America: for the first time in his life he had some money. The meeting at sea between *Grace Harwar* and the Italian liner *Conte Biancamano* also had remarkable consequences.

One of the passengers had been Dr Gilbert Grosvenor, president of the National Geographic Society of Washington, who invited Villiers to come to Washington in early 1931 to lecture to the Society and show the original voyage footage. On 21 January 1931 Alan and Daphne sailed to New York on the steamer *Majestic* for the lecture tour that would alter the course of their lives.

————

I had a copy of the real film. With this I gave my first film-lecture, before an audience of some 6,000 (they looked like 100,000 to me) in a huge Washington auditorium. All those people![9]

Alan and Daphne were met at the dock in New York by Milburn Kusterer, from Villiers' agency Shearwood-Smith Inc., and Herschel Brickell, a respected literary critic who worked for Villiers' American publisher Henry Holt and Company. Villiers would become good friends with both men.

The Washington lecture was a great success, and Shearwood-Smith organised a speaking tour of thirty-four other venues in the eastern United States. From February to April 1931 Villiers spoke at yacht clubs, universities, athletic clubs, schools, ship modeller clubs, museums, a seamen's mission and to fifty people at a private lecture. 'I often spent four nights out of five in long-distance trains,' he wrote.

His agency advertised, 'Mr Villiers ... gives a simple, straightforward narrative with ... the welcome virtues of naturalness and sincerity. He is an excellent speaker and leavens his story with charming humor and the lore of the sea.' Audience members responded: 'Mr Villiers' pictures are the finest I have ever seen', ' He gave us one of the most thrilling evenings of the season', 'Villiers took Boston by storm ... it was an unprecedented success', 'a great thrill from the realism and beauty of the shots ... and the delightful simplicity of Mr Villiers' story'.[10]

After a few weeks of the speaking tour he wrote a column, dated 5 March, for a London newspaper: 'Lecturing Is an Industry in U.S.A. – Audiences Keen – Will Listen to Anyone Talk About Anything'. The amusingly self-deprecating headline led into a grab-bag of jibes at women's efforts to inform themselves:[11]

> The women's clubs ... maybe having nothing better to do, meet once a week or more and have someone sent by a big New York bureau to lecture to them. They pay anything from £20 to £60 for the privilege. The more remote the subject and the less they know about it the more some of them like it.
> Goodness knows what they [women lecturers] talk about – anything will do, provided they become sufficiently emotional about it ... The audience consists mostly of tired women out shopping who drop in for a 'sit down'.
> Richard Halliburton, youthful author of adventure books ... went round the country lecturing to women's clubs and they liked him. Now his books touch the 100,000 mark and still go on selling. But women are not interested in sailing ships (for which they are not to be blamed) and I have no such luck.

Given that any lack of feminine interest in sailing ships probably arose from comments like this, it was good of Villiers not to blame them. In fact, despite his assumptions, many women found square-riggers fascinating; and with a little less misogyny and a little more business acumen Villiers might have found a greater market for himself.

His sales figures by the end of this tour in April 1931 were 4,000 for *Falmouth for Orders*, 7,000 for *By Way of Cape Horn* and 2,000 for *Vanished Fleets*; an unhappy contrast to the 100,000 books sold by the wily Halliburton, dauntless lecturer to women's clubs.

5

DAPHNE AT SEA

On 25 April 1931, Alan and Daphne left New York to return to London on the *Olympic*. He went back to his job at the Australian Newspapers Cable Service, and told the *Telegraph* on 9 June:

> I was glad to say farewell to the lecturing business; it becomes very depressing after a while, repeating, more or less, the same doggerel to gathering after gathering … [His book *Sea Dogs of Today* was soon to be released] After that, I shall have to write a good book.[1]

Writing 'a good book' would become a theme of Villiers' life, and an objective he never quite achieved to his own satisfaction. Still, the year 1931 brought him new diversions. When he was back in London, he met a friend of Herschel Brickell's, Colonel Frederick Clement C. Egerton, commonly known as 'Fritz'. Although he was twenty years older, Fritz Egerton would become one of Villiers' closest friends. He was fluent in Latin, German and French. He became a Lieutenant-Colonel during the First World War, and after the war taught at the Oxford Tutorial College.

He had married young and had four children, but fell in love with Kay, an American woman who, unusually for the time, was studying for a master's degree in economics. He divorced his wife and married Kay. He studied Chinese at the University of London in the 1920s, and for three years Fritz and Kay shared a flat with Shu Ch'ing Ch'un, who would become a well-known novelist under the name of Lao She. With Shu's help Fritz translated a classic of Chinese erotic literature, *The Golden Lotus*, into four volumes of English, with the sexy passages in Latin – a bonus for the educated.

During the early 1930s Fritz was working for George Routledge and Sons as an editor. He would be an unlikely friend for Alan Villiers: comfortable with Asians, interested in erotica, and frequently supported by Kay, who worked in the diplomatic service for many years. She too became a close friend of Villiers, despite being the kind of 'career woman' he usually disliked.

They called each other affectionately 'Boy', and spoke freely on personal matters. Villiers encouraged Fritz to go on an expedition to Africa, and Fritz helped Alan with his *Joseph Conrad* and Arabian ventures. Fritz and Kay's house, Great Bricett Hall, was Villiers' contact address when he was travelling, and two of his books to come (*Last of the Wind Ships* and *Cruise of the Conrad*) would be dedicated to Fritz.

The wonderful year of 1931 held another surprise in store. In August Villiers was visiting the docks and saw a small barque name *Plus*, carrying timber from the Baltic. To his pleasure he found that the master and part-owner was his old friend Ruben de Cloux. He had a proposition: there was a magnificent four-masted barque lying idle in a corner of the harbour at Hamburg. She had been launched as *Arrow* in 1902 and renamed *Parma* in 1911 by the famous Laeisz 'Flying P' line, but now Laeisz could no longer use her. If de Cloux bought her would Villiers like to become a shareholder?

Indeed he would! *Parma* was worth £9,000, but the Depression meant that she could probably be bought for as little as £2,000. Only Finns could own shares in a Finnish ship, so de Cloux and an Ålands syndicate bought the vessel, but Villiers and a London shipchandler named Appleby were re-sold some of de Cloux's shares. The de Cloux family ended up with 22/100ths of the shares, Gustaf Erikson had 20/100ths, and Villiers was the next largest investor with 19/100ths, for which he paid £703.

On 15 October 1931 – barely six weeks after first making their plans – they went to Hamburg to successfully bid just under £2,000 for *Parma*. She could carry around 5,000 tons of grain and de Cloux organised a charter immediately at 31 shillings a ton: they were assured of earning between £7,500 and £8,000 for the voyage. They estimated their expenses to be about £2,500: £900 on wages, £500 on food and water, £600 on ship's stores, £500 on insurance and legal matters. A single successful grain voyage would repay the price of the barque and all of her costs, and still yield a handsome profit.

Daphne sailed back to Australia in early October: Villiers does not record what she thought of the *Parma* venture, but two months later he wrote in his diary, 'Daphne will go in *Parma*, hooray!' She was to accompany him on the voyage from South Australia to England in March. Their relationship seems to have become warmer. Villiers received a Valentine's Day card from her in February 1931 and she wrote, 'I love you very much', in his diary on her birthday, 6 April. They had pet names for each other – Villiers was 'Chips' and Daphne 'Chops'.[2]

Parma sailed from Hamburg on 10 November 1931 under Captain de Cloux, towards South Australia to load her cargo of grain for Europe. A few weeks before that Villiers had departed for New York on the *Aquitania*. He planned to work in America for several months, before joining *Parma* at Port Broughton.

———

It must have seemed to Villiers that women just wouldn't give up, go away and accept their lot, but it was partly his own fault: since he had brought Jeanne Day worldwide notoriety as the stowaway on *Herzogin Cecilie* in 1928, women (and men) had written to Gustaf Erikson, wishing to experience the profundity of a great square-rigger for themselves. Typically, Gusta' was shrewd enough to see the business opportunity.

In 1931 he allowed passengers on to a few of his four-masted barques, and eventually about twenty-five women sailed on his ships in the 1930s. Some were relatives of the captain or stewardesses or stowaways, but most were ordinary passengers. Legally they had to be signed on the ship's books as crew members and, while many worked willingly aboard, they only had to do as much 'sailorising' as they wanted to.

However, in the 1930s there were also four women who trained as genuine square-rigger crew members: Ålander Lena Ringbom, Canadian Annette Brock Davis and two Britons, Dorothea Duff and Winifred Lloyd. The first of the four, seventeen-year-old Lena Ringbom, signed on as an apprentice on *Viking* in 1931 and sailed to Australia and back via the Cape of Good Hope. She desperately wanted to continue at sea but was found to be short-sighted. She was not allowed to study for officers' certificates and her sailing career came to an end.[3]

Although Villiers was perfectly aware of the female sailors, he believed that they had no place on square-riggers and simply ignored their existence. Since his books in these years almost single-handedly defined the public's view of merchant sail, his prejudice had the effect of writing these women out of history – yet at least one of them spent more time on grain ships than Villiers ever did.

———

Villiers celebrated New Year of 1932 in Times Square, New York – 'a mad sight of a mad mob with the lights glaring on them'. It would be the start of another extraordinary year for him.[4] He loved America – eating at the Automat, dining at good restaurants, going to the cinema and Broadway shows with his agent at Shearwood-Smith, Miss Nina Smith, and her friend, Miss McGuire. He gave talks at bookshops and clubs in New York, with lecture trips by steamer to Boston and train to Detroit and Chicago.

Villiers now had minor fame. He made new friends – among them Count Felix and Countess von Luckner, who had arrived in New York on their schooner, *Mopelia*. Von Luckner was famous for his First World War exploits with the disguised armed square-rigger *Seeadler*, which destroyed fourteen Allied vessels, including eleven sailing ships – although he distinguished himself by preserving the lives of all of their crews.

As well as numerous articles, Villiers was writing a book with over one hundred photographs from his voyages, called *The Sea in Ships*. He worked in Miss Smith's office at Shearwood-Smith, and Miss Smith hired a stenographer to help him with the many letters he had begun receiving. He remarked in his diary that having a secretary was 'an extraordinary and completely new experience which passes off well'. Usually when Villiers met someone he said so directly but now a hint of evasion begins – 'Had a grand yarn in Miss S. office about Mariehamn …' (the significant pause was his), 'Had a little yarn at Miss S. office', 'A yarn about Australians at Miss S's office.'

Villiers wrote 5,000 words on 'Women in Windjammers' for *McCall's Magazine* in March 1931. This was a time when women were taking on all sorts of non-traditional activities: climbing, exploring, shooting, sailing, flying; breaking records and creating headlines. Villiers' agent in America was publisher George Palmer Putnam, who had married aviatrix Amelia Earhart in 1931.

The topic 'Women in Sail' was marketable, and Villiers noted in June 1932, when he was aboard *Parma* with Daphne: '3 articles or experiences – Daphne – Betty'. The name 'Betty' was circled.[5] Also while on *Parma*, to the side of a prosaic diary entry for 23 June, he wrote something else in squiggles of shorthand: the symbols for the words 'Betty's birthday'.

———

Shorthand was the reporter's tool-in-trade before recording devices existed. Villiers had learned it at Zercho's College in Hobart, and often used it for notes of interviews and meetings. For a period in the 1930s he also used it to disguise his comments on an increasingly complex situation.

Villiers' papers are archived at the National Library of Australia, Canberra. Although he lived in Britain for most of his adult life and was famous in the United States, it was here in his country of birth he wanted his papers preserved: at the elegant library by the lake, with its glorious multi-coloured windows. There are more than a thousand folders in the Villiers Collection. He kept prolific records – voyage logs, diaries and notebooks of events, travels and expenses, yet occasional diaries are missing, probably not archived for personal reasons – for instance, there is nothing covering the year he met his second wife.

He did, though, preserve the notebook in which he first learned shorthand – doodled, touchingly, on the inside cover is a small diagram of a ship tacking.[6] He could easily have discarded the diaries with shorthand, or the Rosetta Stone of his Zercho's notebook, but he did not: by preserving them he was permitting an untold part of his life story to survive. He had nothing to be ashamed of, but Villiers was an emotional man who tried hard to hide the fact. After all, love for ships was one thing, but feelings for a woman were quite another.

———

'Betty' was Elizabeth Jacobsen, the secretary Villiers so enjoyed yarning to in Miss Smith's office. She wrote:

> ... when I was seventeen I graduated from high school and went to work as a stenographer. I met an author, Alan Villiers, through the bureau which handled his lectures, and got a job typing the manuscript of his book *Grain Race*.[7]

Betty lived in Bay Ridge with her Norwegian parents, Ingeborg and Louis. Bay Ridge is one of the boroughs of Brooklyn on the west of Long Island, a shoreline of the Narrows, the channel leading to the docks of New York. Villiers discovered Bay Ridge during this trip to America and it would become a second home to him, as loved as Goldershurst. He began to visit: 'Raining, had a pleasant afternoon at South Brooklyn looking at the hulk of a schooner near the 69th St ferry, Bay Ridge'. Among Villiers' photographs is one of *Tusitala*, a sailing ship at Brooklyn, with Betty and three friends standing near the bow.

A park followed the shoreline along Bay Ridge: 'I loved to walk there in the rain, to listen to the restless lapping of the cold sea on the harbor stones, to watch the ships sail out to unknown ports, and to hear the gulls crying in the evening,' Villiers wrote in the book he would later ghost-write on Betty's behalf, *A Girl Before the Mast*. Bay Ridge was the last place he visited before he left for Australia on 12 February, and on the voyage when they stopped in Wellington, New Zealand, he took a trip 'by trolly-car to Brooklyn – but a Brooklyn without Bay Ridge ... [sic]'.

When Villiers noted Betty's birthday during the *Parma* voyage she was just turning nineteen; he was twenty-eight. She was blonde and blue-eyed, religious, sweet-natured and pretty enough to be considered for a Hollywood film role. Yet Villiers' marriage was improving and Daphne was about to take on the hardships of a Cape Horn voyage; it was madness to even think of another woman. But he could not forget Betty.

———

In the meantime Villiers had become entangled with another wily film producer, one Walter A. Futter of WAFilms Incorporated of New York and Futter Studios of Hollywood, California, who held out the glittering prospect of a film based upon the *Parma* voyage. He would advance

Villiers the raw stock, pay return duties into the US and develop and print the film.

Something went horribly wrong, however, as it seemed to whenever Villiers signed his name to a contract, and he ended up owing money to Futter. This may be because in January 1932 he had also signed an agreement with Paramount Pictures for their 'unrestricted perpetual right to release, sell or license the exhibition of this film [footage] throughout the entire world'.

In August 1933, his agent George Palmer Putnam, who also worked for Paramount, wrote with gloomy resignation:

> Please realise that this is a pretty muddy situation. It concerns you more than it does me. You got into it first by signing that agreement with Futter. I realise you did that in perfectly good faith. But unless our lawyers are all wrong, you may have put your foot into it seriously. And certainly I would never have embarked upon this perilous adventure had I known of the content of that agreement.[8]

The 'perilous adventure' was still to come; but in February 1932 the future must have seemed enticing as Villiers made his way by train and the steamer *Makura* to Australia. The ship was also carrying several Hollywood stars to Tahiti. Villiers was now so well-known that the actor Douglas Fairbanks asked specifically to meet him. With his director Sutherland, Fairbanks came to Villiers' cabin 'for a yarn', but he 'does not care himself to go in sailing ships', wrote Villiers dismissively.

After stops at Tahiti, Raratonga and Wellington, Villiers reached Sydney on 12 March, then took the train to Melbourne. He saw friends, visited his mother and met Daphne again after nearly six months apart, 'looking very well'. Alan and Daphne left that afternoon for Adelaide by train, then reached Port Broughton via rail and hired car the following night. An Adelaide newspaper reported:

> Mrs A.J. Villiers, wife of the sailor-author who is part owner of the barque *Parma*, hopes to accompany her husband on that vessel ... 'She will have to sign on as ninth mate, or something,' said Mr Villiers today. ... Mrs Villiers is still in her early twenties. She is of medium height, with fair hair and blue eyes, and she is enthusiastic at the prospect of her trip on the tall ship.[9]

'First visit to the ship – how grand she is! … Captain de Cloux is very pleased with her, as well he might be,' Villiers wrote on 15 March 1932. Two days later they set sail: 'To sea! We sail at evening, in bright moonlight with a starry sky – no flags, no ballyhoo, no onlookers.' An American friend of Villiers, yachtsman Lambert Knight, worked as an able seaman and Bill Appleby, the son of one of *Parma*'s shareholders, Jim Appleby, was in the crew. 'Daphne and I at wheel – it is great to be going to sea again.'

This was to be Villiers' first voyage as a passenger, living aft with the captain and officers, no longer one of the working crew. Daphne and Alan were given separate small cabins just off the captain's saloon and there was probably little or no opportunity for intimacy between them. Although they had already been apart for six months, neither indicated any dislike of the continued separation.

Daphne kept a small diary. Early in the voyage she copied most of her entries directly from Alan's diary but soon she began to write her own version of the voyage. 'I am feeling very much at home,' she noted, 'sewing & mending and washing & reading. The days simply fly by and do not seem a bit dull.'[10]

They had sunshine, fogs and fair winds for two weeks as they passed through Bass Strait, the Tasman Sea and south of New Zealand, then westerly winds, rain and heavy seas began. On 5 April, nineteen days out, they were hit by a major storm, with hail and sleet and bitter cold.

The storm intensified, and later that night the situation suddenly became desperate. A series of giant waves came in over the stern and poop deck, and the ship almost lost buoyancy, turning side-on – broaching – to the waves. Tons of water smashed the skylights over the saloon. Villiers dashed off the notes:

> Now we need prayers! Broached to in a Cape Horn gale, my God! She pooped, and washed the compass away; second mate overboard and back again, fores'l gone to tatters, blowing 90. We heave her to then; how she rolls! The hatches hold.

Next day:

She lay out the night all right. It was the first time Captain de Cloux had ever hove-to in a big ship. When she broached to she gutted the galley, drowned a pig under the foc's'l head, washed away a compass, wrecked the entire mid-ships house, half drowned Moses, blew away the mizzen truck – and came damn near finishing the lot of us ... [sic]

Daphne wrote:

[L]ooking back, it does not seem real, only a nightmare, all day Tuesday it had been rolling, heavily, with hail & rain, then at about 6 the storm raged, we were just going to think about tea, when the ship gave a lurch, and Alan says to me hang on. I did, thinking that when the ship had steadied herself it would be al-right, but she did not steady and the next moment, everything in the saloon was moving, then over the poop came a sea, right into the saloon.

The version of events that Villiers wrote for *Voyage of the Parma* (American title *Grain Race*) was melodramatic but chillingly effective. Once again Opportunity had most helpfully tapped: he'd had a unique expedition for his first book, a girl stowaway for the second, a heart-breaking death for the third; and now for his fourth book, a moment as close to utter disaster as any ship might meet and yet survive.

———

Wives were much on Villiers' mind. Captain de Cloux had hurt his leg during the storm, and while they were all trying to dry out a few clothes on the stove he accidentally burned one of his hand-knitted socks. He was concerned at what his stern wife's reaction would be, and Villiers mused:

Oh wives! What a commentary! Here he is, wet through, injured, worried, tired and in pain, having saved his ship by his own superb seamanship, master of the ship, the storm, our fates: he burns a sock and is afraid of the tongue of a woman two thousand miles away.

After a few days of mopping-up they were hit with another, smaller gale. 'Looking down from aloft the deck just looked like the sea itself, not with white water washing about her but with the ship steady and the decks just flush full with <u>solid water</u>,' Villiers wrote. He did some filming – 'Alan took a movie of me today messing about with some rope,' said Daphne – but his main effort now was the new book, *Voyage of the Parma*, which he began on 14 April. On the 15th he wrote Chapter Two and the next day Chapter Three. Two days later Chapter Four was done; it was an astonishing rate of production.

Daphne was content to observe the surroundings with gentle bemusement: 'Alan tells me today that when I get back to England this time I shall have been right around the world.' After an initial bout of seasickness, she was very interested in the food: 'nice food today pea soup for lunch & salmon & chipped potatoes and batter cake, we have our meals with the Captain, 1st, 2nd, and third mates. Breakfast 8 o'clock, dinner 12 30 coffee & biscuits, 3 30, and tea at 6 30. I have had a look at the storerooms & we have loads of provisions.'

They had snow and hail and occasionally sunshine, were becalmed, then finally reached the Horn. A pig was killed and Daphne wrote: 'to my horrible amazement at tea, reclining in a place of honour on the table, was its liver, & I am afraid I made a great "faux-pas" by declining it with thanks. The "he-men" soon made short work of it.'

Villiers wrote grumpily:

> We had its fried liver for our tea, and Daphne, who, being a woman, has more superstitions than the entire crew, says it is bad to eat pig's liver, and we shall all probably be poisoned … We had it fried, with gravy and beans, bread and margarine, and tea. We live high here. Daphne thinks it is an extremely primitive life.

On the evidence of her diary, Daphne thought no such thing at all, but Villiers was perhaps looking to find fault with her: when they saw Staten Island on 24 April it reminded him of recent happy times. In *Voyage of the Parma*, he wrote: 'The other Staten Island stands at the entrance to New York harbour, on the left as you come in from Europe … South Brooklyn is on the other side, with Bay Ridge and its quiet Scandinavian section …'

Perhaps there was a mutual sense of irritation: Daphne wrote coolly on 27 April, 'Alan helped the starboard watch take in the mains'l and crojack this evening, and I am afraid to say was quite exhausted with the violent exercise, he is too fat.' (Evidently it was not only Daphne who was fond of the food.)

They were all out of sorts when he wrote, 'A bad day of bad tempers, heavy rolling, head-wind and near calm … The ship seems to be in a

bad temper herself as she bangs and frets about.' Again he was thinking about difficulties with wives. Contemplating de Cloux, he wrote:

> The Parma venture is a big thing to him, particularly because of the opposition
> of his wife – an unenterprising woman who has consistently opposed every
> idea he has had and has held him back for years. ... He is a fine man and his
> character becomes more admirable the closer it is studied.

A new day at sea and everything was better: 'Good weather, good
wind, good sea, good progress, good tempers.' He had finished
Chapter Ten and Cape Horn was behind them. Daphne wrote, 'The
time has passed amazingly quick & so far I have found heaps to occupy
my mind. This morning just as I was arising, I looked out the porthole
& there was a huge whale right alongside, it was a surprise.'

The captain gave the soot-covered cat a bath, the heating stoves were
put away and everyone had haircuts: 'to my horror, Alan appeared in
the salon with his hair shaved right off, he gave me quite a shock for
the moment but I guess I shall get used to it in time,' said Daphne.
Rain brought them five tons of fresh water, and Villiers finished an article and Chapter Thirteen. Daphne wrote on 9 May, 'The ship is a
hive of industry, messroom & pantry being painted, all the teak being
revarnished, rust being chipped off & and everyone in the ship
perfectly happy in this lovely weather.'

A day or two later they had a rainy, hard, changeable day – the newly
sewn foresail blew out and the boys had to mend it in place on the yard.
Then the fine weather returned. Daphne wrote on 13 May:

> Another beautiful day of sunshine. Alan has put in a full day sewing sails, & this
> afternoon I was helping unpick the fores'l. The sea is a lovely blue, just the
> colour of a blue-bag. The hens, the pigeon, the dog, the cat & the rabbit play on
> deck. The 3rd Mate cut my hair, & did a good job. Alan took a snap of it.

The warm south-east trade winds came, and over days they worked on
a new sail – 'I put in a full day seaming on the new fores'l, which is
rough on the fingers – especially soft fingers like mine', wrote Villiers.
'The amount of toil necessary to sew one sail is prodigious'. He was
also filming the changing of the canvas that usually took place in warm
latitudes, when the heavy Cape Horn sails were sent down and the
lighter 'Tropic rags' bent. 'I try to get as much film as I can but it is a

hard job. The de Vry works now but is awkward aloft: the Zeiss is about finished. I lose a colour filter overboard.'

The trade winds were unusually weak, their progress slower than expected. They crossed the Equator without ceremony on 23 May, then suffered four days of rain. Gradually the wind rose again; they hoped they were passing out of the doldrums. Villiers was still trying to film: 'The Old Man put in a big day on the Zeiss camera in which we find a broken spring – no wonder we had trouble then!' But the problems continued – 'I film and the camera drops in the cross-trees.' Next day: 'I film and the camera jambs.'

They were now in the Sargasso Sea. Daphne wrote, 'it is a grand sight to see the blue water and the seaweed which is the colour of gold', and Villiers, 'The boys catch the weed for crabs and little fishes, I see the smallest flying-fish that ever flew ...'. Daphne had found a new occupation: 'I have been in my glory these last few nights, as I have learnt to play a Swedish card game called 'Marias' (dam hard too) and have been making a fourth with Captain, 3rd Mate & Steward ...'.

'Calm, calm, calm! This will never do!' wrote Villiers in frustration in the middle of another four days of almost no wind. They put out the dinghy, and he filmed and photographed the ship across the glassy sea; and, lying on the oars and watching her as she drifted, he tried to articulate the passion that had brought him to *Parma*:

> She is a big, hard-working economic windjammer, sail's last effort against steam – big in hull, to carry much; small in the rig to carry it economically; fine-lined enough to sail reasonably; rigged with chain and wire for strength. But she has loveliness and grace; she follows nobly in the traditions of the best of sail, and blends perfectly into the peace of her surroundings. ... Her bow is good, and she looks an honest vessel, as indeed she is – a steady worker, an honest old deliverer of heavy cargoes, a staunch toiler of the sea world.
>
> Why is a sailing-ship so beautiful? ... Everything about her matches perfectly: her curves, her angles, her posture upon the water, the set of masts and yards, until the whole is [such] a creation of symmetrical loveliness that the mind is better for the eye's beholding.[11]

Then, on 11 June: 'At daylight a ship! Right ahead, about 15 miles. *Ponape, Pommern, Lawhill*? No: at 6 a.m. is clearly Laeisz liner: must

1. Leon Villiers in 1909, aged 36.

2. Annie Villiers in her late thirties.

3. Villiers children *circa* 1912. From left, Frank (6), baby Enid, Noel (10), Hazel (5), Alan (9), Lionel (3).

4. Alan Villiers, aged 16, late 1919 or early 1920. Note his badge in the shape of a ship's wheel.

5. Young Alan's dream: a painting of the barque *Rothesay Bay*.

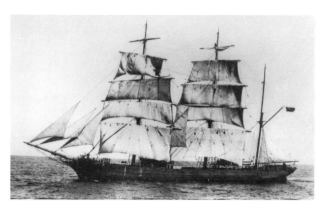

6. The less glamorous reality: a photograph of *Rothesay Bay*.

7. Four-masted steel barque *Lawhill* to the same scale as *Rothesay Bay*. Villiers fell from the fore lower topyard, i.e., the second yard up from the deck on the foremast.

8. Villiers aged 22, after the Antarctic voyage – portrait against a studio backdrop, photographed by his friend Jack Cato in 1925.

9. Daphne Harris, Villiers' first wife.

10. The stowaway, Jeanne Day, cleaning a lamp on *Herzogin Cecilie*. Her small brooch is a figure of 'Felix the Cat'.

11. Villiers is third from right, in the port watch on *Herzogin Cecilie*, early 1928.

12. *Herzogin Cecilie* officers, early 1928: from left, Bertel Jefrelius (third mate), Werner Öjst (second), Vilho Savolainen (sailmaker), Ruben de Cloux (master), Harald Lindfors (first).

13. Alan Villiers at *Herzogin Cecilie*'s wheel, 1928.

14. Programme cover for 1930 film *Windjammer*, featuring *Grace Harwar*.

15. Journalist Ronald Walker (aged 22) on *Grace Harwar, circa* April 1929.

16. *Grace Harwar's* deck in heavy weather, 1929.

17. Heavily laden *Parma*, becalmed in 1932.

18. Daphne Villiers on *Parma*, April 1932.

19. Captain Ruben de Cloux on *Parma*.

20. Publicity shot of Villiers, early 1930s.

21. With Betty Jacobsen, New York, late 1932.

22. Betty Jacobsen and Hilgard Pannes on *Parma* in early 1933.

be *Pamir*.' Scottish-built *Parma* had also been owned by Laeisz, but *Pamir*, from 1905, had the distinctive lines of a German-built ship. Now Gustaf Erikson owned her and she was *Parma*'s greatest rival in the grain race.

By noon both ships were becalmed, still about 15 miles apart, and nine of the *Parma* boys decided to row the distance to *Pamir*; Alan and Daphne went too. The row took five hours of hard work. They exchanged news with the *Pamir* crew and stayed for a meal in the cool and spacious saloon. Daphne wrote:

> Captain gave me some books, then we started on our long pull back. We left at 8.0 & and could see no sign of Parma till we had been rowing for two hours then we saw our light and rockets. We reached home at 2 A.M. After our great adventure, the boys told Alan he had a very brave wife, but I looking back think I was a little foolish to take such a risk … it was a very happy Daphne, who thanked God for seeing us safely home, that went to her bed on Parma that morning.

The calm continued for three days more and *Pamir* drifted out of sight. Villiers finished Chapter Eighteen, rewrote Chapter One and noted that he had also written twenty-two articles on the voyage.

They saw the sails of a four-master in the distance but it was not *Pamir*, and she was gone again before they could identify her. They passed the Azores, went well for a few days, and were again becalmed.

Then at last they were in the Channel, passing trawlers and a distant motor-ship ('Ugly, ugly! She looks like some futuristic Hudson ferry steamer conceived by a cubist in a drunken dream'). They arrived at Falmouth on 29 June, after 104 days from Australia. They heard that *Killoran* had taken 130 days for the voyage, *Lawhill* 121 days, *Penang* 112 and big, fast *Herzogin Cecilie* 107. *Parma* had beaten them all: but what of *Pamir*?

Finally the news came by telephone from London. *Pamir* had anchored in Queenstown at the same time as *Parma* in Falmouth. The two ships had left Australia within hours of each other but *Parma* had travelled 70 miles further to get to Falmouth. She was declared the winner of the grain race of 1932.

Villiers got a fine book – *Voyage of the Parma* – out of it. It may be the most mature of his writings on the grain ships, with fewer breathless heroics and more thoughtful history and observation, spiced up by the near-disaster in the hurricane. And the gods of drama smiled upon him once more: *Parma* may have brought them all to safety, but the terrible fate of *Melbourne* unfolded before them, providing him with a chilling postscript.

In the early morning, three days after *Parma*'s landfall, a tanker named *Seminole* arrived in Falmouth harbour with a twisted bow. Two nights before she had been outbound towards Louisiana for a cargo of oil, at the same time as a four-masted grain barque named *Melbourne*, a working vessel for forty years, had been heading towards Queenstown.

Melbourne had sailed from Port Victoria on the same day as *Parma* had left Port Broughton. Her voyage was just as hard: she had been caught in the same hurricane, and it turned out that she had been the unidentified four-master they had seen near the Azores. Her voyage time was very close to that of *Parma*: she had been at sea for 105 days when she met *Seminole* just after midnight off south-west Ireland. *Seminole* was a twin-screw tanker of 6,923 gross tons: more than two and a half times *Melbourne*'s size.

The watches on both ships had just changed over. The lookout on *Melbourne* saw the tanker's lights but knew that she would give way to their sailing vessel as required by law: but the watch on *Seminole* did not even see the barque until she was under them. *Melbourne*'s bow was ripped open and her masts brought down. She rolled onto her side and sank within minutes.

Fifteen men out of a company of twenty-six drowned, some of them with relatives among the crew of *Parma*. After sailing half-way around the world, *Melbourne* had been just six hours away from the sanctuary of port before she was lost.

———

Daphne was only one of several women on grain ships that year – the barque *Favell* also carried the wife of the captain, Sten Lille. Captain Lille wrote to Villiers on 10 August 1932, mentioning that during a gale, 'My wife, who has been sailing with me for two years, was struck down by a sea on the poop and came floating round the corner of the chart-house where I got her by the neck, and threw her down below. By the way, how did your wife stand the life on shipboard?'[12]

Daphne had stood the life very well. 'Left *Parma* today for London,' was her final diary entry on 9 July 1932, 'the boys gave me a great send off, it was quite a touching scene our parting. We arrived at Goldershurst in time for dinner, and had a wonderful reception, so ends my trip, and one I shall carry memories of all my life.'

Villiers began temporary work again at the Australian Newspapers Cable Service. His films were developed and he thought the negatives were good. His publisher, Geoffrey Bles, was 'pleased at the prospect of the new book for the Spring list'. Villiers was working long hours, writing, cutting film and visiting ships at the docks, usually with Fritz Egerton.

Parma sailed for Mariehamn with Captain de Cloux on 12 August. Her voyage had been profitable and the syndicate paid out £15 per share. Villiers earned a welcome £285, and began planning a trip to New York for mid-September. He showed the film footage to friends and thought there were 'some wonderful shots of heavy weather, fores'l blowing out and so on, and Daphne films well. I shall be able to make a good new film now, I hope.'

Fritz Egerton knew a great deal about cameras and photography, and Villiers began working on the film at Fritz's house, at 6 North Square in London, which saved him the tiring trip home to Goldershurst in the early hours. 'At night in the office, by day on the film.' He showed it at the Royal Geographical Society, and it 'goes over very well'.

There were no plans for Daphne to go to America; she was staying behind at Goldershurst. Villiers' passage to New York was booked for the *Bremen* on 24 September. He was writing articles at a great rate, sending them off, getting rejections and acceptances; *National Geographic* offered $400 for the story of *Parma* – 'this does away with financial worries in the U.S. at least until the end of the year'.

On 3 September Villiers noted in shorthand – 'Write to Betty in Bay Ridge, the secretary for me.' On 11 September, again in shorthand: 'A nice letter from Betty Jacobsen'. Lunches, writing, cameras, work at night, ship visits, showing the new film, 'clearing up business which

seems always to mount again as steadily as it is disposed of'. On 21
September he was 'Working at the Methodist Union conference for
the office, getting trodden on by sour-dialed Methodists'. At the bottom, in shorthand the exclamation – 'Betty will be my secretary!'

On 23 September was 'Chips Birthday', as written by Daphne in
Alan's diary. He added, 'a very nice present of slippers, tie and hanks
from Chops'. Next day, 'Leave Goldershurst 7.15 (Daphne has a little
cup of tea with me).' He was aboard *Bremen* by 10.30 a.m. and sailed
at noon. He could not know – and nor could she – but with that little
cup of tea his life with Daphne came to an end.

Alan Villiers arrived in New York on 29 September 1932. Lambert
Knight and Miss Smith met him; he visited Herschel Brickell, Mrs
Barbour (a literary agent), and stopped in at Miss Smith's office. The
evening was spent with Captain Jacobsen – Betty's father – at their
home, 1159 73rd Street, Bay Ridge, where he was to spend many
evenings over the next few months.

Two days later he found an apartment to live in and use as an office:
140 75th Street, Bay Ridge, a bus ride away from the Jacobsens' place.
He sketched an anchor in the margin, as he would do whenever his
ship made safe harbour. Now the secretive shorthand notes increased.

Betty began work as his secretary on 3 October – the date is circled.
The diary entry: 'To Bryant Park and a seat in the sun, a yarn and
"work" – the contemplation of the human scene – to Macy's, a grocery catalogue (God knows what we ordered), sheets, lunch, and departure for the five o'ten.' In shorthand below: 'My secretary begins
work. I hope always to have her! "I'm proud of you" she says: I hope
she always will be!'[13]

Next day, 'We work and contemplate existence – yesterday in the
sun of Bryant Park, today in the sunny quiet of the Bay Ridge apartment.' He heard that his editor Herschel Brickell and another friend
had been fired. 'I see Miss Smith, who is pessimistic and worried.
What is to be the end of it all? There are other things of which I can see
no end either ... [sic]'.

Betty brought towels and cups for the apartment, 'taking pity on my
loneliness which is very sweet of her'. He often spent evenings with

the Jacobsens. He started to call Betty 'the little girl', a nickname he would use for her only in shorthand. Sometimes he would accompany her home on the bus, where 'The little girl takes my arm'. Her genuine sweetness surprised him: 'I wonder if you really are as nice as you seem to be?'

He met George Palmer Putnam at Paramount, 'who is enthusiastic on a film of SAIL. But what about Futter? Must I go to sea again? I don't want any double-crossing ... [sic]'. But his thoughts were really on 'a happy lunch of pork chops and peas and tinned fruit salad: & tea & [taking Betty] home by bus in the rain'. In shorthand, he added: 'I'm shocked sometimes at your niceness which I would never expect in a girl. You can tell me anything, Betty.'

Villiers went to the Paramount offices and showed Putnam and his wife Amelia Earhart the footage from the *Parma* voyage. 'Putnam is very interested and suggests as a start 300 feet for Paramount gazette: I hope this goes through. May also do another voyage.' But his thoughts were on Betty: 'You're too nice to be true: I like you very much.'

He wrote often to Fritz Egerton, who 'gives deep counsel'. He worked in 'glorious sunshine', visited the Jacobsens, dined out, received a good offer from publisher Scribner's, and all the time the 'little girl' was on his mind: 'There is nothing we cannot overcome together.' But his writing was suffering: 'Do the piece for Scribner's (badly: I am going seriously off: but will come back again),' and 'the writing goes slowly, and far from well. I have lost my dash.'

George Palmer Putnam phoned and asked Villiers to see *Dinner at Eight* with him: 'I do so, first dining together at the Seymour, and he talks of a new sea film to be called perhaps "Apprentice Girl".' Villiers was to write it, and Betty play the girl. Villiers was unsure: 'I stay in working on the book and deciding about things, doing more "deciding" than making decisions.'

On 29 October he held a Halloween housewarming at his apartment. He invited a few old friends and some new ones from Bay Ridge – Raymond Reed and the Terrible Three: Betty herself and Eleanor and Marian Hansen. The party went well – 'a very pleasant evening with some wine from a flat-faced bootlegger and a supper from the Delicatessen', but something apparently went wrong. Villiers wrote bitterly in shorthand later that night, 'No woman would love you!'

The following evening Villiers went to the Jacobsens, 'where the party is continued with the Terrible Three again and Captain Jacobsen gets somewhat stewed'. To a boy who lost his father at fourteen, the happy Jacobsen family may have been as much an attraction as Betty herself.

Sometime in these few days it all came to a head. On 1 November Villiers had to go to a meeting of the Brooklyn Ship Model Makers, where 'they show me ships but I think of other things' – he continues in shorthand – 'of the lovely face smiling in tears, of a lovely girl hurt by my clumsy words ... I have told her that I love her: I can not help it: I expect it had to happen.'

Next day in his diary: 'Today is a big day – the very biggest yet'. And, in shorthand: 'She calls in the morning and I kiss her: I kiss her!' He also marked the date on the annual calendar at the front of the diary, with the shorthand, 'Kissed Betty and told her I love her.'

6

APPRENTICE GIRL

Villiers' agent George Palmer Putnam was an extraordinary man – tall, good looking and imaginative – who nurtured the best writers, critics and illustrators of his day. In 1923 he started a small literary agency outside the family publishing business. When Putnam heard that the first attempt for a woman to fly the Atlantic was being prepared and the original candidate had withdrawn, he saw an opportunity. He helped find another, who turned out to be social worker Amelia Earhart. She was thirty-one, tall, slim, fair and had been flying for eight years.

In June 1928 Amelia became the first woman to cross the Atlantic by air. She was not the pilot, although she flew the plane for some of the way. Afterwards she went on to establish numerous speed and distance flying records in her own right, loyally supported by Putnam, a superb publicist. They fell in love, and George's wife Dorothy, unhappy in the marriage herself, divorced him readily.[1] The couple wed in February 1931, and had a contented life together until Amelia disappeared in the Pacific on a round-the-world flight in 1937.

Putnam was one of the first agents to commission what he called 'fabricated books' – he would develop the idea, then find an author to write it. One of his most amusing efforts came about after 'Joan Lowell', identified by Villiers as the critic Helen Joan Wagner, wrote *Cradle of the Deep* in 1929, purporting to be her memoir of being brought up on a sailing ship by her grandfather, full of quaint adventures and crusty home-spun wisdom.

It turned out to be completely false, and humourist Corey Ford wrote a parody commissioned by Putnam – *Salt-Water Taffy or Twenty Thousand Leagues Away from the Sea* – which even today sparkles with ribald life. So if anyone was to be open to the idea of a woman working in a man's world – and being the first to sell the story to a fascinated public – it was Amelia Earhart's energetic, quick-witted husband, George Palmer Putnam.

———

Work had to go on. Villiers went to Chicago for six days to give lectures, then home to Bay Ridge for a week, then away to Indianapolis for two days and Pennsylvania for four, then Washington, to speak to the National Geographic Society. Sometimes Betty and Alan would walk together in the evenings, usually the high point of his day. In shorthand he noted, 'The little girl kisses me with her red lips.'

Yet they do not appear to have become lovers. The affair between the pious girl and the married man was innocent, and increasingly complicated by George Putnam's scheme: 'G.P. Putnam wants me to go back to sea to make "Apprentice Girl". I wonder? There are serious problems to be faced, and that would not be facing them.' Articles were written and dispatched, meetings and dinners attended, 'But the best thing is the walk in the evening, as always ... [sic]'.

A photograph of them on a roof in New York shows Betty, confident and pretty in an elegant crepe evening dress, Villiers beside her, his hair windblown, his arms crossed and his expression worried. Their bodies curve towards each other.

He called Betty 'the Little Chief': 'To the Jacobsen's for supper and the Little Chief hurries home from ... the dentist in the cold.' In shorthand, 'How fine she is! You are lovely and sweet and innocent and nice and beautiful.' Fifteen-year-old Hilgard Pannes also wanted to be an apprentice on the next voyage of *Parma*, and he and his parents met Villiers. Hilgard visited the apartment on 10 December, 'looking so fine that the Little Chief falls for him straight away. I cook him a pork chop and he still wants to go to sea.'

Next day they went 'to see Mr Putnam, at Paramount, with the Chief for "interview" – an ordeal which is very trying for her. George talks of "horseflesh" and protruding collar-bones, a share in the film and a trip round the world'. Betty's parents had not been enthusiastic about Putnam's scheme, but were relenting, reassured by the fact that Captain de Cloux's seventeen-year-old daughter Ruby would also be on board for this voyage. In shorthand, 'Only your welfare must be considered. I'm in deep enough to be hurt very much.'

After a wintry day at the beach 'where the sand is frozen and noses are red', he wrote in shorthand, 'I see ecstasy in your eyes: and I see love in hers!' On 24 December, 'The Chief helps me fix my first Xmas tree, on the round table in the corner; and in the evening to the Jacobsens for Christmas Eve where I receive presents and spend as happy a Xmas as I have ever had. There is a tree, and we have a grand Norwegian supper. I am given a lovely diary.' In shorthand: 'The best kiss in my life.'

Days passed in a rush of passport applications, birth certificates, purchasing clothes and sea kit; and 'the Chief's contracts from Mr Putnam are ready. He wants to tie her to me and not to himself – so that she cannot claim against him, I suppose … [sic]'. The contract of 31 December 1932, between 'Elizabeth Jacobsen, an infant aged nineteen years', her parents and Alan Villiers, included these clauses:[2]

> 1. Villiers employs Miss Jacobsen … and she agrees to cooperate fully in the making of a motion picture involving the grain ship background. If Villiers deems it advisable, she will ship as an apprentice seaman, but will have no obligations to perform duties other than those of assisting Villiers in every way possible in the making of the picture.
> 2. Miss Jacobsen agrees to adopt the professional name of Linda Loman, or some such name as may be mutually agreed upon by herself and Villiers. [The name they finally chose was Sonya Lind.]
> 3. Miss Jacobsen agrees to write a book of her experiences on the voyage to appear over her professional name. She agrees that all editorial decisions in connection with this book shall be made by Villiers, who will cooperate in its writing so far as may be necessary and may to him seem desirable.

———

Alan and Betty left New York on the steamer *Lurline* on 12 January 1933. They travelled via Havana and the Panama Canal to San Francisco, where Hilgard Pannes joined the ship. Then they went to Los Angeles, Honolulu, Samoa, Fiji, Auckland, and reached Sydney five weeks later. They took the train to Melbourne, then Adelaide, and joined *Parma* on 22 February at Port Victoria.

A fascinating image appears in the introduction to *The Last of the Wind Ships* (2000), a book of photographs from Villiers' grain ship voyages. It shows Alan and Betty on the deck of the *Lurline* on the way to Australia. He is annoyed perhaps, or embarrassed at being photographed; he looks quizzical, legs braced and hands jammed in his pockets. She is smartly dressed in a tweed suit, silk scarf and dainty ankle-laced high heels. Her hair is dark blonde, curly and almost jaw length under a little hat. She looks calm and pleased.

They were also photographed by the newspapers in Melbourne. One image (newspaper unknown) shows Alan and Betty walking together on 20 February, leaving Spencer Street station. They appear to be alone because Hilgard has been clipped from the photograph, although he is with them in one taken from a different angle published the same day by the *Herald*. Alan, in a smart suit and trilby, is slightly turned towards Betty with a protective air. She wears a stylish hat and pretty dress with ribbons at the waist, in some fine fabric that clings revealingly to her legs. She looks coolly at the camera.

The caption of the *Herald* photo is: 'Norwegian Actress to Play Lead in Sea Film. A Norwegian actress with a distaste for having her photograph taken passed through Melbourne today. This exceptional young lady is Miss Sonya Lind, a blonde Norwegian, who is proceeding today to Wallaroo.' It was the beginning of publicity for their 'perilous adventure', as George Palmer Putnam had called it, and the exposure was an unpleasant shock to them both.

We have no idea what Daphne in London thought of it all, but it must, at very least, have been hurtful. Captain de Cloux had said about the stowaway Jeanne Day, 'as soon as they heard of her mad escapade people would snigger and wonder whose mistress she was'. Whether or not it was true, there could be little doubt left in readers' minds whose mistress Sonya Lind was.

———

Twenty grain ships were sailing in 1933 – the largest number that ever would – and fourteen of them belonged to Gustaf Erikson. The carrying of grain ship passengers had become so routine that Erikson's English shipbrokers, H. Clarkson and Co., produced a form letter in 1932 for prospective travellers. *L'Avenir*, *Viking* and *Herzogin Cecilie* offered spare double-berthed cabins, which could take eight to ten people:

We must make it clear, however, that the vessels are not licensed for the carrying of passengers and no special provision is made for them beyond providing them with the berth and the same food as is supplied for the officers and crew ... For that reason, it might not be altogether too comfortable for ladies or young children, although some ladies have travelled by them and seemed to enjoy their experience.[3]

Herzogin Cecilie had a new captain. In 1929 Ruben de Cloux had hoped to buy some shares in her profitable syndicate but Gustaf Erikson had refused to sell him any. De Cloux then left Erikson's employ, and in 1931 set up the shareholder group that bought *Parma*. Command of *Herzogin Cecilie* had passed to a distant relative of Erikson's who had been her first mate, Sven Eriksson. The Duchess was now fitted out with a men's smoking-room and nine cabins, 'her saloon prettied with carpets and such junk', wrote Villiers scathingly.

On 21 February 1933 Alan, Betty and Hilgard travelled from Adelaide to Wallaroo, then hired a motor truck to take them the final 60 miles to Port Victoria, where they joined *Parma*. Villiers would record this passage in three documents: a diary that was far more impersonal than earlier ones,[4] the introduction to *Last of the Wind Ships* (1934), and the ghosted 'memoirs' of Betty Jacobsen in *A Girl Before the Mast*. None of them explains what really happened on the voyage.

Parma sailed on 1 March 1933. Ruby de Cloux and Betty berthed in small cabins off the captain's saloon. There would be no possibility of the closeness she and Villiers had shared in New York, and he could only watch her from a distance: 'At 4 bells in the first night watch we tack ship, with all hands, and afterwards Betty curls up asleep on the chartroom floor.'

He was bitter about the book he was to ghost-write for 'Sonya Lind': 'nothing but cold prostitution of whatever talent I may have, which isn't much ... and it is entirely foreign to Betty's nature to be party to what is an arrant falsehood ... Sometimes I am very worried about this whole enterprise – very much so – but what is there to do but go on?'

Five weeks after embarking he noted: 'Betty is very despondent all day.' Betty was clearly not a true apprentice, expected to battle sails in any weather, but with Ruby de Cloux, she worked away at the endless scraping, cleaning and painting jobs that actually took up the larger part of any square-rig sailor's time. She became annoyed that every mealtime conversation was about ships – 'I will hate them when I get home,' she says.

Villiers also found the process of filming as difficult as ever: the second-last camera was broken within five weeks, with 12,000 feet of film not yet exposed. He became increasingly morose. In late April: 'This voyage ... will be nothing but a photographic and literary tragedy ... and it may well be in more ways than one.' In early May: 'I hate the film like a personal enemy, and that book is just false enough to annoy me and not false enough to sell.' He was deeply unhappy about more than the film.

———

Villiers tried desperately to make a story out the trip, but unfortunately, this time, the gods of drama had left him high and dry: *Parma*'s passage was embarrassingly devoid of incident. There were few storms and fewer anecdotes that hadn't already been touched upon in previous books. A stowaway did emerge from the hold – Englishman Stewart Maybury – but boringly, became a useful member of the crew.

There was so little going on that the tedious Moses, from *Voyage of the Parma*, got called into service again – a small, whinging Nazi sympathiser who somehow seems to have charmed Villiers. Moses collected guns, loathed the French and was a 'young follower of Herr Hitler'. He was lazy, rude to the captain, snooped among private letters, exploded flares in the heads and tortured *Parma*'s cat, hens and pigs. When he finally left the ship in Copenhagen he stole, among other things, the ship's binoculars. Such an offence against the integrity of a vessel would normally appall Villiers but here he depicted Moses as no more than a mischievous child.

In 1933 Nazism was just another political movement, and anti-Semitism so widespread, that for Villiers to perceive the ugliness of Moses' attitudes would be asking him to recognise a threat to which many were blind. But a confronting aspect of Villiers' writings in the 1930s is that he seems to have found an outlet for his own loathing of the urban world in dislike of 'the Jews'. That the blond north European square-rigger crews he admired fitted the Aryan stereotype simply reinforced his bias.

Ironically, he himself was far from any Aryan ideal – swarthy, inclined to tubbiness and prematurely balding. Perhaps there was an element of self-hatred, both in what he admired and what he despised. And like so many others of the 1930s, he could not have imagined that such carelessly voiced prejudices would lead to the deaths of millions of people within a decade.

———

Villiers gained something on this *Parma* voyage he had never had before: a glimpse of the masculine world of the sea through a woman's eyes, those of a woman he loved. Since his youth he had disliked 'girls'. He believed they disliked him equally and had painful memories of being scorned, overlooked and unloved. His marriage was 'not a conspicuous success' and the sea had become his refuge. The 'boys' he so identified with had similar youthful insecurities, and some of his criticisms, such as that regarding the captain's niece on *Bellands* – 'she was by no means popular, though I don't suppose that troubled her' – or the stowaway – 'nobody asked her to come' – have the air of eight-year-olds in a tree-house complaining about girls wanting to join their club.

Although he had sailed with women, Jeanne Day had offended his sense of the heroic and Daphne was the wife he longed to leave; from neither had he derived – or wanted to derive – the slightest understanding of a shipboard world from their perspective. Betty was different. In the book he ghosted for her, *A Girl Before the Mast*, he starts to acknowledge how painful it was to be on the outside, to be deliberately excluded from sharing in the joyful experience of sailing ships. He wrote as 'Betty':

> I find myself with an unfair disadvantage to make up. Given the same chance of development, and not being told all her life 'You can't do that; you're a girl,' the girl might give a better account of herself too. I know many sissies, and they aren't all of my sex. I'm no sissie and I'm not going to be treated like one here.

Even kindly Captain de Cloux joked more than once that he 'had twenty-eight souls on board, and two women'. 'Betty' wrote,

> I can always feel a deep resentment and hostility to the presence of girls on board, even though one of them is the captain's daughter, and the resentment is not openly expressed. I always feel that if anything goes wrong they will blame us.

'She' overhears two of the boys loudly:

> ... suggesting going down to slack up the tops'l sheet that I was sitting on, and then I would probably have been killed. On calmer reflection I decided they did not mean it for a moment and would never have done such a thing, but at the time I felt angry.
>
> It is not nice to have remarks like that made about you. It is not nice to be among a group of boys – tied up among them, unable to get away from them for five minutes until the ship reaches port – who profess the utmost scorn for you and all your sex.

'Betty' does not mention Villiers at all, except in the prologue and early in the voyage, when 'Mr Villiers' is pictured swearing in four languages when he rips his trousers on a belaying pin. It is as if, after a single attempt at jocularity, Villiers cannot bear to portray himself through the imagined Betty's eyes, as they slowly drift apart.

There is bitterness, too. When the mate remarks that 'love is a quality only imagined by women', 'Betty' responds, 'My experience has been that it is the other way round. Perhaps both sexes are equally deluded in that respect, or perhaps such a quality does exist. I do not know.' Nonetheless, by the end of the book Villiers seems to have come to an understanding of his own emotional needs that is both new and prophetic, when 'Betty' writes:

> But I hope that life will yield a little more to me – a great love, perhaps, that will leave me kinder and more human, and will fill my old age with sweetness. Somehow I feel that, deep as it may be, devotion to these ships and the sea is not and cannot be so fine a thing as a full human devotion.

——

Parma made fabulous time, romping home in mostly glorious weather in a record eighty-three days, beating every other grain ship with contemptuous ease. She arrived at Falmouth on 23 May 1933, in what was said to be the fastest square-rigger cargo passage of the century. Coming second was her old rival *Pamir*, at ninety-two days. *Herzogin Cecilie* took all of 115 days. Her captain Sven Eriksson blamed her slowness on her age 'with lamentations'; Villiers dryly observed, 'but age does not warp the lines of a steel hull nor reduce her rigging and *Herzogin Cecilie* is still the best ship of them all. But there is a lot in luck, and a lot in handling.'

While *Parma* waited in Falmouth for her orders, Villiers, Betty and Ruby went for a day to London. Villiers' prejudices may have eased a little towards women but not towards Jews. One of his fellow share-holders in *Parma* was Appleby, a shipchandler, who discussed 'pisi-ness' (business) and spoke with familiarity to the women, calling them 'Ruby and Bet'. Villiers was furious: 'The Jewboy at sea, all right! Damn him and his "pisiness"! The dull pursuit of foul money is an aim high enough for him.'

As his relationship with Betty was slipping away from him Villiers was certainly going through an agonising time, but that does not ex-plain his prejudice leading him, some months later, to make a bizarre assertion in *Last of the Wind Ships*. There he claimed that young sailors 'come from all countries and all races, except the Jewish: a Jew in a square-rigger's half-deck has always been unknown.' Dis-regarding the proximity of London's immigrant-crowded East End to its busy docklands, this extraordinary statement is not even supported by his own experience – on *Parma*'s 1932 voyage with Daphne, Appleby's Jewish son had joined them as a working crew member.

———

Parma sailed to Hull to discharge, reaching there on 7 June 1933. Betty and Villiers took the train to London the next day. She went to stay with Fritz and Kay Egerton at 6 North Square, and Alan (presum-ably) went back to Goldershurst and Daphne. His diary for 9 to 27 June is a single long impersonal summary of that time, revealing very little. He states that Daphne sailed on 24 June to see her mother in Hobart. Since she had waited patiently for Alan in London for nine months, it seems more likely that he told her what had happened in their time apart, and Daphne left him.

On 27 June Betty and Villiers took the train back to Hull so she could legally sign off the ship's articles. That evening she returned by herself to London. On 30 June *Parma* sailed from Hull towards Mariehamn with Villiers on board – he still had 6,000 feet of film left and hoped to get some footage of Baltic ships on the way. He wrote: 'Betty sails from Liverpool for New York via Queenstown and Boston tomorrow. Daphne is in Toulon today on her way to Australia. And here I am between Hull and the Baltic … it is cold, and grey, and depressing here again. I feel like saying "Damn the sea!"'

As they were sailing along the Gotland coast he noted, 'I write hard all day and manufacture 8000 words in the name of Sonya Lind. Poor Betty! The tripe comes easily. I sometimes wonder whether a facility in the production of narrative of that kind is my only talent. I am inclined to think it is.'

What had happened between them? Betty would later become a good family friend, and a few easygoing letters between them from the 1940s and 1950s remain among Villiers' papers. But from the emotionally turbulent period of the 1930s there is only a single letter of hers still preserved, headed 'Bay Ridge February 19th' (probably 1938).[5] In it she writes:

> Your letter sounded very blue. I suppose you do get lonesome sometimes, but isn't that better than being constantly surrounded by people with whom you have nothing in common, some of whom you actually dislike? …
>
> It has its disadvantages of course, but on the whole I think you are better off. The trouble with you is that you are too warm-hearted & unselfish and really need someone to lavish your affections on … [sic]
>
> The only danger is that you might one day mistake such affection for love – I think you have in the past, and I think you are now in danger of doing it again. Am I right?[6]

This suggests that she saw his feelings for her as the yearning of a lonely man; and her cool assessment indicates that by the end of the *Parma* voyage it was no more than affection she felt for him. The unpleasant falsity of the 'Sonya Lind' situation, the attractions of boys her own age, and the knowledge that Villiers was an older married man years away from any potential divorce had probably made it very clear to nice, wise Betty that any relationship had no future.

———

There was yet a final loss to come that year; a painful disillusionment in Mariehamn, the home of Villiers' beloved square-riggers. Despite his autobiography reporting a conversation with Gusta' in the Ålands in the late 1920s, it did not take place then. This time was actually his first visit, and the account is fascinating. *Parma* arrived at her port of registry on 12 July 1933: 'we anchored under the lee of a low, rocky island. Nearby the point of a larger island ran into the grey sea; all around were islands, and pine trees, and square-rigged ships lying with unbent sails at anchor.'

Mariehamn was small, 'even smaller than I expected. The main street is a piece of thinned-out forest with a gravel path through it. Along the side of this forest are the houses of the shipowners (Erikson, Lundqvist, Anderson, Troberg); and butting proudly into its centre is Troberg's church built from the profits of worn-out ships and sailors' blood.' He records his intense guilt at the low wages handed out to the hard-working seamen from the ship he partly owned. On 16 July he decided:

> I would rather like to sell my share of Parma. I have met the other shareholders, and with the exception of August Gustafsson, my God they are mean. A Jew would starve here in Åland and a Scot commit suicide. ... I rather think now I don't like Ålanders so much: at least their bad qualities are very apparent. They are intensely narrow-minded and their dissection of one another is merciless and often bitter. I begin to understand – well, lots of things ... [sic][7]

He was also deeply saddened at meeting Ruben de Cloux's son Åke for the first time, a sailor who had been struck by polio. 'The Old Man cannot bear to talk of his son's paralysis, which is readily understood. Mrs de Cloux is all right, in her way; but she seems to hold the idea that wives, merely because of wifehood, hold proprietory rights in their husband's souls.'

The President of Finland came to visit the Åland Islands for the first time in history. There was a big celebration on board *Herzogin Cecilie* but, spitefully, de Cloux was not invited: his success with *Parma* had made him a threat to the other Åland shipowners. Villiers commented, 'Gustaf the mean shipowner ... would send a mental case in his ships for 10/- a day, regardless of the consequences for the captain. Six of his captains are now leaving – Penang, Pommern, Passat, Pamir, Olivebank and A. Russell.'

Now that *Parma* was a success there was a jealous outcry in Mariehamn that foreigners – Villiers and Appleby – had shares in an Ålands vessel. It was enough. Villiers was nearly thirty years old and had given half of his life to the square-riggers. He returned to London and decided to sell his shares in *Parma*.

In October 1933, as the grain ships were leaving for Australia for the next season, Villiers wrote in his diary, 'The "Parma" has three American apprentices and three passengers: a girl who came from Montreal was sent to join "l'Avenir".' The girl who joined *L'Avenir* was twenty-three-year-old Annette Brock Davis, the second of the female square-rig sailors of the 1930s.

Annette apprenticed on a voyage to Australia and back via Cape Horn, and six decades afterwards wryly described her experiences in the marvellous *My Year Before the Mast*. Although she eventually found acceptance as a competent sailor, along the way she had to cope serenely with intimidation, vile tricks, near-rape and threats of murder. Grain-ship society could be brutal to an outsider, and Annette's memoirs add a vivid counterbalance to Villiers' more partisan portrayals.

Villiers worked for the Australian News Cable Service through what was a hot, sleepless English summer. He had planned to return to America at the beginning of October 1933, but in September his throat appears to have been operated upon – 'delayed in a nursing home where my allegedly infected larynx had been torn about on Sept 23 [Villiers' thirtieth birthday]. Apart from that nothing has happened in London except that Colonel Egerton has made me into a limited liability company. Putnam came to Paris but I did not see him. He suggested that I should go over but I didn't.'

The conflict between the different contracts signed with Wally Futter and George Palmer Putnam blew up. On 9 August 1933 Putnam dictated a letter to Villiers in Betty's presence:

About Betty's book. She feels strongly, and I agree with her, that the best thing to do is to get the manuscript over here as quickly as possible. She has been working a bit with a chap in my office who seems to be very helpful. She thinks that probably she and he together can add just a little something to the material which will help it. Somehow I feel that you have written too much of this material, which is so essentially all your own, to be able to do it with the girl angle. What's more, I don't think you should be bothered with it. You have plenty of other troubles and it is important for you to get at your own writing work. P.S. As I said at the beginning of this letter, Betty has heard every word of it and at its conclusion tells me that she and I are in agreement.[8]

No matter how difficult the 'girl angle', it must have been painful to let the book go to a chap in Putnam's office to add 'just a little something'. It must have been even more painful to be told that Betty wanted it so. It is hard to tell what was added to Villiers' manuscript, which, at his standard rate of production, would have been completed soon after the end of the voyage. Throughout, the language is clearly reminiscent of his usual style, apart from the occasional, rather forced 'Gee!' and reveries about chocolate sundaes.

George Putnam and Amelia Earhart's annual Christmas card normally pictured an aeroplane, but in 1933, the year of *Parma* and 'Apprentice Girl', it had a model of an old sailing vessel instead, with the message, 'This is the Merchant Sailing Ship, George and Amelia ... although no models ourselves at least we're still afloat, hopeful that in 1934 your ship may come in ... [sic]'.9

———

On 7 October 1933, Villiers sailed from London to America, and settled again in Bay Ridge, where he wrote *Last of the Wind Ships*, which aches with sadness. He depicts the hectic bustle of the 'speed-mad' world and the 'twenty doomed wind ships' soon to pass from it. 'Poor ship! Poor ships!'

In harrowing contrast to his usual portrayals of sturdy boys bringing home great Cape Horners, he wrote of the death of an apprentice, which had occurred in late 1933 on *Parma*'s outward passage for the 1934 season: 'the body of a sailor drifted up on the coast of France floating in a lifebuoy marked "*Parma*, Mariehamn". The body had been in the sea a month; there was no flesh on the face and there could be no identification. It had been about five feet four inches high; quite young.' Captain Ruben de Cloux wrote to Villiers in early 1934, naming the dead boy as Birger Ekström from Mariehamn.

De Cloux also described the loss of the barque *Plus*, on which he had been master in 1931. *Plus* had sunk near Mariehamn on 13 December 1933, with the death of thirteen out of seventeen men. He wrote sardonically, 'If the Plus crew had not dropped the anchor, they would have had time to run the vessel aground and no lives would have been lost. But for a disaster to happen, one has to help it along.' He ended, 'I see from your letter that you have started writing two books.

If I were to try to guess what they were to be about, I would guess a dramatic love story.'[10]

He could not have been more wrong. *Last of the Wind Ships* portrays a bizarre, claustrophobic version of Villiers' life in New York during the previous year: he is trapped in 'crowds and traffic lights and gaudy shops, and concrete skyscrapers and chewed cigar-ends flung into the gutters ... and Broadway, that garish, horrible thoroughfare of the hardest-faced women on earth'. The recasting of his memories of joyful days with Betty into such gloom suggests deep depression.

Betty herself is barely mentioned. She makes the briefest of appearances as a nice young girl who came along to be an apprentice with Ruby de Cloux, 'But she went home instead, and so did Ruby, too – and that was a better place.' Better for whom? There is not the slightest hint of their plans for a film, a book or the 'Norwegian actress' Sonya Lind. Towards the end of *Last of the Wind Ships*, Villiers writes:

> It is Christmas Eve now, 1933, and I am here in New York. At the bottom of the street the *Tusitala* swings to wind and tide; through the Narrows the hurrying liners churn the waters, while along the stone embankment beyond the Shore Road the wheeling gulls cry in the rain.

Just one year before, Villiers had spent as happy a Christmas as he had ever had. Now he laments in winter for 'the twenty doomed wind ships in the ocean far from here, quietly sailing'. The fate of the wind ships was tragic indeed, but he was mourning for far more than that.

7

AN EXQUISITE
MOMENT

Alan Villiers was a stoic, stubborn man, but again he yearned to sail away. He began searching for a vessel to live on; to go wherever he wished, no longer tied to the land by hopes of love. He kept a notebook labelled *The Log of the Schooner 'Aimless' (at present mythical) Being Suggestions, Ideas and Information As Such Occur Or Are Found*, in which he listed over a dozen possibilities in America, England and Denmark, but one by one he crossed them out.

At the bottom of the list was *Georg Stage* and a price, £1,450; and in June 1934 on the Copenhagen waterfront he saw the exquisite little Danish training ship for the first time. She was 'of the real old frigate type, gloriously proportioned hull, with a seat in the water like a sea bird; tall symmetrical masts and tapering yards, all painted a light golden colour, and a long jib-boom projecting far beyond the sweet grace of her cutwater and the bronze figurehead.'

Villiers wrote in *Cruise of the Conrad* that he was shocked to overhear someone saying that *Georg Stage* had been superseded and was soon to be broken up, although the ship's presence on his list suggests he already knew she was for sale. In any case, he dashed to a broker and 'bought the lovely little ship that afternoon'. He took possession of *Georg Stage* two months later. She cost £1,571, most of the capital he had built up from books and lecturing. He renamed her *Joseph Conrad* after the writer who had captained the barque *Otago*, the hulk he had often contemplated in Hobart during his years as a reporter.

Joseph Conrad would carry Villiers into an extraordinary new phase of his life. He would sail around the world in the old-fashioned frigate, just as Europe was stumbling headlong into a very modern war. But perhaps he should have paid a little more attention to the words of the great writer himself in *The Shadow-Line*:

> A ship! My ship! She was mine, more absolutely mine for possession and care than anything in the world; an object of responsibility and devotion. ... A sudden passion of anxious impatience rushed through my veins and gave me such a sense of the intensity of existence as I have never felt before or since. ...
>
> I had an exquisite moment. It was unique also.

———

Captain de Cloux put the four-masted barque *Parma* up for sale, planning to buy himself a small steamer and stick to quieter Baltic waters in the future. Villiers had hoped to get £1,000 for selling back his shares but de Cloux would offer only what Villiers had originally paid – £703 – although the ship they had bought for less than £2,000 three years before was now on the market (Villiers heard) for £15,000. It was another disappointment, adding to his disillusionment with the once-idealised Ålanders.

To command *Joseph Conrad* for the passage from Copenhagen to England, Villiers found an old shipmate, now Captain Wicksteed, he had known since they were boys together on *Bellands*. 'In the evening yarning with Godfrey Wicksteed in the cabin, about old days in the *Bellands* and the strangeness of being here, after everything.'[1] Mrs Wicksteed and a friend, Herbert Ward, sailed with them too, as did Fritz and Kay Egerton – 'Fritz comes in the evening from Stockholm with a Leica lenz [sic] a foot wide, a new hat, and a great joy at beholding the little vessel.' 'Kay comes from London, looking very well, and falls in love with the ship as does everybody.'

Kielland Brandt, a designer, and Bruce Rogers, an eminent American typographer who had made several passages in Erikson ships, also travelled with them: Rogers painted the ship's name in gold on the bows and stern. Colonel T.E. Lawrence – Lawrence of Arabia – was a friend of Rogers' and hoped to sail on *Joseph Conrad*, but to Villiers' great disappointment the plan fell through.

As crew, there were the Germans from *Parma*, Karl Sperling and Horst de Wolff, as bosun and sailmaker, and Enno ter Hell as second mate. The Ålanders Olaf Bjorkholm and Knut Villhelmes joined as first mate and steward, and two Danes who had sailed on *Georg Stage*, Hans Petersen and Jan Junker, decided to stay with the ship.

Several of the working passengers were 'haw-haw yachtsmen' – upper-class English boating enthusiasts who Villiers thought might find the reality of a square-rigger more than they had bargained for, including two army chaps he called Major Major and Major Minor; Stewart Maybury, the stowaway from the 1933 *Parma* voyage; the Reverend Matthews, who 'has the largest repertoire of smoking room stories on board'; and Dr Dunlop, who, 'true to all sea tradition ... is the only person on board who is ill'.

———

They sailed on 3 September 1934 in calm weather. The yachtsmen 'who have played at seafaring for years' took time to adjust. 'Major Minor strikes twelve bells for six, explaining apologetically when bawled out that he had counted six lots of two. Barber, reporting a light, said he thought it was moving so it probably was a lighthouse. The Parson, aft trying to buy grog, raises hell at the ship's prices.'

Villiers took photos of *Joseph Conrad* from the motorboat – 'wandering gracefully and slowly along, going quietly from her old Denmark where over 52 years she has trained 4000 boys: now at last she is free to set off round the world'. Next day they were out into the open sea, heading for Harwich in fine warm weather. The following night brought a severe electrical storm with heavy rain, and discontent among the haw-haw crew. Villiers savagely mocked one complaint:

> After all, one is not an ordinary seaman. Such persons, like one's servants, delight in menial tasks: but a gentleman should (I gather) choose what he should and should not do aboard a vessel. ... I wonder what these sods thought they were coming to. The Mate says the only one worth a bang is the parson, and he'll be dam glad when he is back in his pulpit.

After nine days some had had enough. Four passengers took the motor boat to a nearby trawler and asked to be taken into Grimsby. The trawlers had just left port and had no intention of returning, so all the runaways got was a basket of fish. On 13 September *Joseph Conrad* reached Harwich, and the following day, 'our yachting bums leave, neglecting to say goodbye, thankyous or anything else, overlooking paying for their tobacco, and singing chanteys out of tune on the pier. They are good land sailors, damn them!'

———

Villiers had decided to take *Joseph Conrad* on an 'ambling circumnavigation by way of Good Hope and the Horn, the East Indies and the South Seas; and to ship all the young fellows who cared to come and there was room for'. He did not plan it for profit: 'I would make no films, advertise nothing, perform no stunts, engage in no radio programs ... It was my firm belief that such a voyage as this could not fail to be of incalculable benefit to any young fellow who had the guts to go and to stay'.

However, writing immediately after the voyage in *Cruise of the Conrad*, he dwelt more upon the satisfaction of the task itself: 'But I could keep a form of art alive upon an earth which had grown, it thought, beyond the need for it; and I could sail for the sailing's sake, for the sake of the health and the life and the clean wind and all the joy of being there.' His rationale was true enough, but it also evaded the deeper truth that he went to sea on *Joseph Conrad* because he could not have a life ashore with Betty.

Many of the crew who had sailed from Denmark stayed, but it was difficult to find more. Sixteen-year-old Hilgard Pannes from the 1933 *Parma* voyage came from America to join as an ordinary seaman. Villiers' brother Frank came aboard in Harwich as a leading seaman and quickly settled in with the European crew: 'He speaks Norwegian very well. So he should, as this is the first British ship he has been in and he has been ten years at sea.'

Villiers was worried at the overall lack of experience of the other candidates. He finally employed Swedish Nils Nilsen as second mate, Finn Usko Österman as carpenter, and Britons Eric McConnel as third mate, W. Arthur Catchpole as cook and Douglas Ratcliffe as seaman. Money was an enormous problem. Villiers' English publisher Geoffrey Bles and his agent Michael Joseph would not help finance the expedition. 'Mr Bles will not answer his telephone, and Mr Joseph has given the cat that was to be mine away. I think it is time I left that partnership.'

He put small advertisements in the paper but had very few candidates for cadet positions. So he followed up with a more emphatic appeal: 'Mr A. J. Villiers, having acquired a full-rigged ship ideal for the purpose, invites YOUTH and YOUNG MEN of sound physique who would appreciate two years of thorough TRAINING in SQUARE-RIG on a two-year circumnavigation of the globe. Reasonable premium.'

On 17 September *Joseph Conrad* was towed to a buoy off Ipswich, and carpenters began installing cabins in the after 'tweendecks. Reporters came to interview Villiers and photograph the ship, and publicise his search for cadets for the voyage. A stream of candidates began to turn up, most highly unsuitable, thought Villiers. Then two fourteen-year-olds from Ipswich came aboard timidly and asked for jobs – Jim Fuller and Stanley Goodchild, nicknamed respectively 'Hardcase' and 'Stormalong'.

Villiers wrote, 'They look decent boys: we shall see if England may not be better represented by these than by the haw-haw gang from Copenhagen and the pale specimens who come nightly to psycho-analyse their desires to go to sea in my cabin and are never seen near the ship again.' To Villiers males were either 'boys' or 'men'. Boys had to undergo some sort of trial – war, injury, Cape Horn – to become men. To question this assumption implied weakness, perhaps even homosexuality.

The publicity spread far and wide. On one day 700 letters turned up at Great Bricett Hall, Fritz and Kay's home and Villiers' mailing address, 'and most depressing reading, the lot of them. ... None has been to sea: none was any use. Six hundred of them want to be "anything or cook". The widespread idea that to be a ship's cook is an unskilled job is completely erroneous.' He ended gloomily, 'I am 31 today – getting old.'

The search for cadets continued: 'It would be easy enough to assemble a shipload of drones. And it seemed to me that women might be had by the liner-load: but in them I was not interested. There are some problems better left ashore,' he declared loftily. Finally eight were selected – Harcourt, Evershed, Twynam, Devlin, Horsfall, Leech, Tapper – all British – plus an American, Hunt.

During the stay in England Villiers managed to scrape together nearly £2,000 from fares, advances and the little remaining of his own funds, but had to spend £1,600 on supplies, repairs, insurance, fuel, charts, advances, canvas and so on, in what seemed an endless list of demands. The new cabins in the 'tweendecks were for the paying passengers – the voyage could not have taken place without them. The passengers were signed on as seamen or cadets, and there were eight of them also –Wilson, an Army man; Tilbury, an accountant; Conley, a small-goods merchant; Ward, who had sailed from Copenhagen; Dyer, a sixty-two-year-old American lawyer, and a young British flyer, Le Grice.

And the other two paying passengers? They are not mentioned in the pages of *Cruise of the Conrad*, or the ship's official Log Book, or in anything Villiers wrote for publication about the voyage. They were the female cadets, American Elsie Jansen, twenty-seven, and Briton Christine Baker, twenty-one. Women might be a problem better left ashore, but Villiers simply could not afford to do that.

———

Villiers knew Elsie Jansen from Bay Ridge. The *Melbourne Herald* on 11 January 1936 reported him saying that she had built up a business she called Tramp Trips, arranging voyages on merchant steamers for people who did not want to go on passenger liners. '"She has made an amazing success of it," Mr Villiers said, "She is a remarkable looking girl too, very tall and handsome".' He got on well with Elsie, and in later years her agency organised some of his travel.

His relationship with Christine Baker was less easy. Both women had been Sea Rangers, senior Girl Guides involved in maritime activities. Christine wrote an article about her experiences for *The Marine Magazine* of 15 August 1936, saying that, as Elsie's hair was dark and hers reddish, they were known as 'Tar' and 'Oakum' on board *Joseph Conrad*. Villiers usually referred to Christine, crossly, as 'the Redhead'.

The month spent fitting out the ship was difficult. 'I live only for the day when we may sail down the Orwell away from the man-made problems, to face some of the God-made ones.' *Joseph Conrad* carried no cargo so was not a merchant vessel; she had to be formally registered as a yacht, 'though I abominate the word', Villiers wrote.

A Board of Trade surveyor inspected the ship and 'saw the officers' certificates: fortunately he did not ask for mine. I had none.' (As an Australian, Villiers could not become certified on Finnish ships.) 'But I was merely following in the best tradition of the sea ... most of the great trade routes of the world were opened up and sailed for centuries by men who held no kind of certificate.' It was time to go before any more awkward questions were asked. *Joseph Conrad* sailed from Harwich on 22 October 1934.

———

The voyage, which would take two years, would be an unparalleled achievement. Each passage between major ports was a sailing experience as long and intense as any single grain ship voyage. There were eight legs:

October 1934 – December 1934, Ipswich to New York
January 1935 – March 1935, New York to Rio de Janeiro
April 1935 – July 1935, Rio de Janeiro to Bali
July 1935 – October 1935, Bali to the Trobriands
October 1935 – December 1935, Trobriands to Australia
January 1936 – March 1936, Australia to Samarai
March 1936 – July 1936, Samarai to Tahiti
July 1936 – October 1936, Tahiti to New York

It would be an experience of unremitting pressure. Alone, Villiers performed the tasks that would today consume the resources of a ship's master, doctor, accountant, teacher, human resources manager, film technician, publicist and more. To his sorrow, friends who had spoken for years of coming with him, such as Fritz, did not.

It took eight days to beat the ship down the Channel against a series of westerly gales, 'the boys, green with seasickness, learning more in one bitter week than they would in a month of trade wind Sundays'. Christine Baker was ill for ten days: 'a deputation from the others asking that I put into Plymouth to land to save her life. I did not go there: and it must be said in her favour that she would not have landed there if I had put in.'

George Conley, the smallgoods merchant, was scathing about Christine: 'She had the over-accented, shrill manner of speaking that is not uncommon in the crowds of suburban girls who flock night and morning to clerical work in London.' He was kinder to Elsie: 'She came of seafaring stock, was a cheerful, companionable soul, warm natured and quietly philosophical, strong yet feminine.'[2]

Entries in Villiers' diary became irregular: 'a master's job, I find, leaves little leisure ... there is little peace in it, particularly for one so congenitally incompetent as myself'. On 5 November they were hit by 'a sudden furious squall of thunder and lightning and hail: I heard nothing but suddenly saw a mess of headstays and headsails where they had no business to be.' The end of the jib boom had broken away.

But it was people more than the ship that harried him. 'Mr Dyer wants to be put ashore at Madeira. Conley mixes ill with the old Etonians. The women are a damned nuisance, cluttering up the charthouse. The Yank has too much bounce: Ward is fed up with being on watch: Tilbury has a poisoned finger, two boils and a stye on his left eye.'

A few days later they successfully re-rigged the jib boom, shortened by 5 feet for greater strength, but the human problems continued. 'The boys want bunks instead of hammocks: the steward's port leaks; Ward tells Conley off: Evershed falls over daily in the scuppers: and the blasted women are forever sprawling in the charthouse ... and Mr Dyer, morosely reading 1001 pages of humour assembled by one Wodehouse, does not smile.'

On 11 November they reached Madeira, about 400 miles west of Morocco. Villiers was worried about his navigational skills as his positions sometimes varied from those of the mate. 'Thank God I was right: we have made a perfect landfall at Porto Santo – the first landfall I ever made. There is a great satisfaction in it.'

They stopped only to take Mr Dyer ashore, then sailed again that evening. Tiredness was wearing Villiers down: 'The women are a damned nuisance ... I feel myself drawn more and more towards the so-called "old" view of woman and her place ... Elsie Jansen says the Redhead gushes too much. She certainly does. She's writing a book too – about what God knows.'

Christine Baker, blissfully oblivious of Villiers' disapproval, reported (gushingly) in *The Marine Magazine* that:

> Between us, we two girls supplied that chafing gear. How I hated it. No-one else seemed to make any, but of course someone has to do it. ... Various odd jobs helped to vary the monotony of chafing gear – helping to serve splices, cleaning brass on Sundays, painting – and of course, overhauling buntlines. These jobs were like islands in a sea of chafing gear.[3]

Villiers wrote, 'We have some curious humans here ... but Stormalong and Hardcase, the two little poor boys from Ipswich, are without doubt the best representatives of England on board.' He was depressed by the radio broadcasts they could sometimes pick up. 'A queer picture of 1934! Here we are, westward bound in the tracks of Columbus for San Salvador ... and our civilisation shouts through the Trade Wind air of the effects of a laxative upon the bowels of a child ...'. His gloom deepened on 21 November when the winds became unreliable and he wrote that 'the carpenter is afraid he has syphilis'.

———

'The Redhead wench asks if the girls may have the lifeboat to "play with" tomorrow. Play with? They certainly may not!' wrote Villiers indignantly. 'There will be no more of women aboard this ship at sea. But I would be doing this pair an injustice if I only condemned them. They are not so bad: they could be a lot worse.'

It became hotter, the trade winds fell away, and they found themselves in the doldrums. The wind came back and they had days of good running – 'This was worth waiting for!' Despite the good sailing the human complications multiplied: 'I saw the Second Mate with his arm around the Redhead on the poop. I suppose it had to be: but by Heaven there will be no more women! ... The other one [Elsie Jansen] is not so bad, but she takes up a lot of the Mate's time – not her fault I suppose. And I wish she knew the carpenter was syphilitic: I can hardly tell her.' (At a time when syphilis could be fatal this was rather an odd attitude for a master responsible for everyone on board.) On 6 December, the radio brought him

> alarming news of Europe and of Japan and of this and that – the more alarming is the news the better pleased do they appear ... The whole nightly shouting, importuning, wailing, moaning, gnashing, cringing brings home forcibly the complete and utter impotence of individuality – except so far as one may live one's life at peace with God, if that can be achieved. And if it can be achieved then that is everything.

Villiers' religious faith was greater now (and would remain strong all of his life), and it seemed to offer him comfort in coming to grips with the extraordinary task he had taken on. 'It is sometimes strange to reflect that I own this ship, and command her: but I am not boastful for either of these blessings – held only through the grace of the Lord and continued only as long as I may be worthy. What worries me is that I rather think I never was. But I can try ... [sic]'.

One morning brought dark masses of clouds to the west and north-west, and a troubled calm: 'I had read ... of such conditions indicating a blow and began to shorten down – just in time! It came suddenly, with ferocity, and the old lady lay right over. It was all hands then to get her down to storm canvas, but in an hour the worst had gone ...'.

Passenger George Conley complained that Villiers deliberately insisted upon cultivating a 'hard-case' atmosphere, more suited to desperate Cape Horn voyages than this one. He seems to have had little understanding of the discipline needed to keep a ship safe, especially in emergencies. Problems continued with the ship and the people:

> I told the Redhead off today ... told her she was impairing the efficiency of the starboard watch and threatening the spirit and even the safety of the ship. She took it meekly, but I hope it went deep. It is inevitable, this sex stuff ... The mental condition of the Second Mate of late has been deplorable ... Elsie Jansen says there won't be an end to the troubles in this ship when the women go. There will never be an end to human troubles anywhere.

———

On 14 December Villiers wrote wryly, 'Our painting and cleaning ship continue with intolerable sloth. I think we had better come into Nassau – if we ever get there – under the flag of Greece.' They finally reached Nassau late on 16 December, after a worrying time trying to find an anchorage in the dark. 'Nassau is the hell of an expensive place, but there is a great satisfaction at being here, in having the crossing successfully made – 55 [days] from Dover, entirely under sail.'

Third Mate McConnel flew to New York on personal business, and three of the passengers, Ward, Wilson and Conley, left the ship at Nassau.[4] 'I gather that Messrs Wilson, Ward and Conley were somewhat critical of me,' Villiers wrote in his diary. 'I did not run the ship properly, they said ... I sometimes wonder how far my critics would get, in the same circumstances – running an old ship with a scratch crew, several token (yes, I may as well be truthful) merely because they produced some funds, too old to be "disciplined", too wealthy to be controlled, too developed to be changed, not really wanting to be sailors. The only way to hold them – the whole gang – is, well, by a

kind of individual, quiet but pretty strong appeal to character ...
I suppose this is a kind of Australian attitude ...'.

The strain of his lonely position in command of the ship was beginning to be felt. 'The Mate is very drunk. I am afraid my experience
here shows that I cannot ever leave this ship to my subordinates. I must
look after her myself all the time. The second mate is incompetent ...
And Frank – he is asleep on a bar-room floor. A great fellow at sea, indeed; but I'm afraid he cannot be a very trustworthy second lieutenant
in the ports.'

They sailed from Nassau on 19 December for New York. They
made good time briefly, then the wind dropped and came around
against them. Frustration with the slow progress and the passengers
grew, but eased again days later when the winds returned and
Christmas approached. Christine Baker wrote, 'The carpenter and
sailmaker made a tree, and it was decorated with tinsel made from
strips cut from the silver paper wrapping in cigarette tins, tin stars and
coloured pictures of fruit ... and on the fly a little flag for every nation-
ality represented on board – there were seven.'

It was a more sombre time for Villiers. He wrote in his diary:

> It is Christmas Eve. Christmas to such as me becomes an occasion for remem-
> bering what was, and for thinking of what might have been – with our family I
> mean. It is all – well, rather tragic, in a way: Frank here, and me here, a capital-
> ist (of sorts): and Noel God knows where and Lionel struggling with his
> school-teaching and his degree: and Enid married to a rat, bearing under-
> nourished babies every year: and Hazel married to some farmer – and Father,
> who thought so much of us all and sacrificed so much for us and everyone, dead
> these 16 years in Coburg clay. And Mother – she is a pretty good character. I
> think it would be decent of me to spend next Christmas with the ship in
> Melbourne, if she would like it.
>
> At midnight I see Hardcase asleep in his hammock, with Stormalong in his
> hammock alongside, well-fed and tired and sleeping soundly, like two babes. I
> think of the trust in me that they may sleep so; and I hope to God that I may
> always be worthy of that trust.

On Boxing Day they were off Cape Hatteras and were struck by a
freezing gale which stayed with them. Four days later they were near
Long Island in terrible visibility, with ice heavy on the deck. They
took a pilot on board – 'a decent bird – enjoyed the beating about, the

experience being new to him: but to us it is an old story somewhat staled by endless repetition in bitter cold.'

On 30 December: 'The anchor is down at last, 70 days out from Harwich of which 67 have been spent at sea. We have sailed 7014 miles, and the engine was used only going into and out of Nassau Harbour ... It is my first passage in command: I think the Lord has been more than kind to me.'

On New Year's Eve the ship was towed to the Quarantine station, where a man asked them if the *Conrad* was a British naval ship: 'with the nondescript crew all round and Elsie Jansen and the redhead Baker hanging all over the rail. They must have a queer idea of British naval vessels.' The quarantine men came on board: 'a circumstance which proves unfortunate for the liquor locker. Customs, medicos, immigration and whatnot are on board: and the only good they do is to keep the newspaper men off.'

The Englishman Le Grice, much liked by Villiers, had to leave for England as soon as they arrived in New York. Elsie and Christine also departed the ship. 'We arrived in New York on New Year's Eve and went up to Times Square to see 1935 safely started,' wrote the irrepressible Christine, leaving the turmoil of *Joseph Conrad* blithely in her wake. She took a small flat with Elsie, worked at her travel agency for a few months, then left for Singapore on the Norwegian tanker *Corneville*: by the end of the voyage she had a discharge as able seaman and had married the mate.

———

In New York on New Year's Eve 1934, a tug towed *Joseph Conrad* to an anchorage on the Bay Ridge Flats. 'We lie in about 25 feet of water: the Pilot says it is good holding-ground. If we drag, he says, we will have to drag uphill. It is the lighter and schooner anchorage ... there is ice along our sides.' Visitors came out to the ship, among them Betty Jacobsen and Ray Reed, but Villiers wrote nothing on how he felt about seeing Betty again after nearly a year.

On New Year's Day many of the crew were given leave and hit the town. Hilgard took two sailors to stay with his parents and most of the cadets visited friends of Villiers. Ordinary seaman Ratcliffe was appointed watchman; Frank Villiers, leading seaman, was left in charge.

Alan went ashore in the afternoon to see the Jacobsens, and then to his friends Norma and Hershel Brickell at their Park Avenue apartment.

That evening, as it was a holiday, no boatmen were around to take him back to the ship. Instead he took a ferry to Staten Island: he could see *Joseph Conrad*'s lights in the distance and all seemed well. He checked into a small hotel, and next morning went by ferry to Bay Ridge to find a boat to take him out.

On the ferry he overheard someone say, 'Did you hear about the school-ship? She is on the rocks full of water and all the crew are in hospital frozen to death.' Perhaps the Lord had not been as kind as Villiers had imagined.

> [H]ow the ferry crawled! … I had to stand there and calmly wait. It was some time before I saw the ship. She is so small, and there were steamers and lighters in the way. Then I saw her: she did not look so bad at first glance … Then I saw that she was resting on the rocks and she was full of water 'midships right enough …

He ran to *Joseph Conrad* as soon as the ferry berthed nearby. A crowd had gathered to watch, and aeroplanes overhead were taking photographs. It was bitterly cold, the park covered with snow and ice. To his great relief he found that no one at all was hurt.

Frank told him that the ship had been struck by a fierce squall at about three in the morning, and the watchman had suddenly realised that the ship was driving, not dragging, towards the lights ashore: that is, her anchor chain had broken and the ship was at the mercy of the wind – had the anchor still been attached they would have felt it catching on the sea floor. The Bay Ridge Channel was only 800 feet wide and they just had time to rouse the sleeping crew before the ship struck a pile of rocks beneath the harbour wall. It was very lucky that most of the cadets were ashore, as their compartment filled rapidly with water.

When the tide fell, *Joseph Conrad* began to capsize into the harbour. They stopped her with wires to fences and trees, then used lorries to pull the ship upright. Two tugs tried to drag her off at high water but Villiers felt her grinding on the rocks and stopped the attempt. They installed a pump to remove some of the water.

Villiers sent most of the cadets away to stay with relatives or with Betty's friends, the Hansens at 71 Mackay Place; 'the ship's cat, which was cold and shivering, to the Lunden's, on 75th St, and my private papers, sextant and chronometer and a few things I sent to the Jacobsen's … There was of course a good chance that the ship would be lost.' The crew were lodged at a hotel where the mate and carpenter proceeded to get drunk. Villiers spent the night 'wretchedly' in the galley on board, trying to keep warm.

> [S]o ended the first day on the rocks. It was pretty rotten, and I had a sheaf of congratulatory cablegrams in my pocket, from England, on having successfully made the west-ward crossing … [sic] Sometimes I felt like Bede Egerton [Fritz's son], a year or two ago, when he saw his young wife, dead in childbirth, lowered into her grave. 'It didn't last very long,' he said … [sic].

———

Next morning Villiers signed a 'no-cure-no-pay' salvage contract, and a hard-hat diver started patching holes in the ship's side with blankets and mattresses. A large floating crane brought drainage pumps and a salvage steamer, *Resolute*, arrived. When the pumps were unloaded and the diver had patched the worst of the holes *Resolute* began to heave on the ship.

The floating crane was tied up to *Joseph Conrad* but 'the gale howled down a vicious squall', and the steamer could not hold the combined mass of the ship and crane against the wind. All three vessels drove helplessly the short distance towards the 69th Street pier.

The men on *Resolute* smashed axes through the towlines to free themselves. The floating crane crushed two motorboats, while its derrick arm twanged down *Joseph Conrad*'s mizzen rigging 'like a giant finger on a keyboard'. The ship itself crashed again and again against the pier. The rail on the port side was torn away, the forward bulwarks stove in, rigging chain-plates were torn out, dead-eyes and lanyards ripped to pieces, davits wrenched and skids adrift, and it looked like the 'largely unsupported rigging would come down any moment'. The diver's repairs failed, the powerful pumps stopped dead, and 'the water poured in 'midships, filling her to the deck again'.

There was no possibility of now reaching the dry-dock; the only chance was to get her to the shelter of wharves directly across the river. Unfortunately, *Resolute* began towing before they had properly cast off, and the ship was damaged further as the moorings snapped. One of them struck Jan Junker in the leg, and he had to be rushed off to hospital.

The *Resolute* now went at full speed and we swept along, with the cold harbour water rushing through the hawsepipes and gurgling up every scupper-hole. I did not see how she could remain afloat ... the spray, driving over us, touched everything to ice: the other tug dared not pass a line for fear of being pulled over when we went.

She steamed close alongside aft, with her searchlight going ready to pick us out of the water at any moment. I had all hands – those who were still aboard – stand by on the foc's'l head and monkey poop, <u>away</u> from the rigging, so that when she went no one might be dragged down ... They could all swim. I un-buttoned my coat and looked at the black water, in which loose ice-floes from the upper Hudson were drifting.

After the long, agonising tow they finally reached the shelter of Pier 6 on Staten Island, and tied up out of the wind at three in the morning.

Next day the diver again patched the side of the ship, the pumps were fixed, and temporary lanyards rigged to hold the masts up. That evening the ship was towed to a dry-dock. When the water was pumped out they could see she had a big hole under the engine room, as well as damage above the waterline from the collision with the pier. The bill would be $1,550 for the original stranding and $1,400 for the collision damage, but Villiers believed that insurance would cover most of it. The ship spent a week in dry-dock then two weeks in the ship-yard.

Now the strain on the crew began to tell, and several were drinking too much. 'Tilbury, for whose sanity at the best of times I had fears, became quite insane when intoxicated and fell in the harbour. It was quite a job to get him out, more insane than ever: he then wanted to fight the Second Mate – a somewhat foolish proceeding.' The crew were put up at the Y.M.C.A: 'having arranged a decent rate there for shipwrecked sailors [I] saw them promptly doll themselves out in their uniforms and get drunk as quickly as possible', Villiers wrote bitterly.

A few of the cadets and crew demanded to be sent home to Britain: Villiers was happy to pay for them to go. The third mate, McConnel, never returned to the ship after Nassau, and the pugnacious Tilbury (a placid accountant before joining *Joseph Conrad*) signed on as fourth cook in a steamer. Villiers felt that the only people he could trust were

Hilgard, Stormalong, Hardcase and the German and Danish crew members. He decided not to make an eastward circumnavigation as he had originally planned, but instead go westwards – Africa, south-east Asia, Australia, the Pacific – with Cape Horn on the final leg of the voyage.

The cost of the accident in New York seemed to be covered by an advance from Scribner's for a book on the voyage, the anticipated insurance on the ship damage, and payments from seven new American cadets. Despite the many bills, *Joseph Conrad* was well provisioned; Villiers did not stint on food or equipment, or even dental work needed by Stormalong. The ship was generously treated by a few helpful people – salvage and tug crews, surveyors and insurance representatives, and 'Mr Amos Carver ... the grandest shipchandler in the whole world'.

Villiers again felt abandoned by some old, unnamed friends, although one old friend did a fine thing: designer Bruce Rogers carved a magnificent likeness of the writer Joseph Conrad as a figurehead for the ship. Scribner's organised a small unveiling ceremony in pale sunlight and freezing cold, with a speech by the British Consul-General. Villiers lectured, wrote articles, answered letters, cables and telephones, talked to callers and shook 'the hands of Danes who had been boys in the ship, of whom at least a hundred must have been aboard during our stay'. He could hardly sleep or eat, and felt 'driven almost to distraction'.

Finally, on the afternoon of 31 January – a month after their triumphant arrival in New York – 'with the Hudson full of ice and twenty-seven souls on board', a tug towed *Joseph Conrad* away from her berth. She set her frozen sails beneath the Statue of Liberty and started out for Rio de Janeiro.

———

As they sailed further from New York the ice began to melt. Villiers wrote philosophically, 'Looking back, on the whole, my experiences in New York were mainly beneficial – inasmuch as their principal effect was to produce evidence in favour of the innate decency of the human race: or some members of it, anyhow. Every now and then one needs a little evidence, to go on.' But he was far from unscathed. He wrote:

Last night, in the middle watch, I had a dreadful nightmare about a fellow who took a ship on a voyage without sufficient funds and awoke in a sweat to find that the fellow was myself. The nightmare gave me quite a shock and I could not sleep again. I find my rest now very much disturbed by visions in which the ship and myself are in all manner of troubles ... Those rocks ground pretty hard – and pretty deep.

On 6 February they were reducing sail, when 'we were caught aback in a heavy NE gale ... and came pretty near again to – well, losing the ship. Only this time it would have been missing with all hands.' They took in more sail and slowly, agonisingly, turned the ship's bows away from the wind. Afterwards below, 'the new boys [were] pretty quiet. I thought how easily they all might have been at the bottom of the sea'.

The new cadets were Sturges, Griswold, Hopper, Miller, Lindsay and Lane, while Adamson was 'making the voyage for his health'. Villiers thought they were 'a good bunch'. Among the cadets, though, he especially appreciated Hilgard and the 'little poor boys from Ipswich'.

I like having those two young devils along: I am rather alone now – very much so, sometimes. Hilgard is my best friend: he is rather like what a son ought to be but seldom is. Storm and Hardcase are kind of sons too. I like to see old Storm happy round the decks, grinning with his fixed-up teeth, with Betty Jacobsen's rubber shoes on, Betty Gibson's striped yachting jumper ... he is such a kid; and his accent is so weird. But some of his yarns are scarcely fit for drawing-rooms.

The weather became warmer. They tacked back and forward, the ship ghosted along in the calm: 'she still glides, almost imperceptibly, though the sea is like glass and there is hardly a flap to the sails'. Then towards the end of February the trade winds came, puffing squalls and showers.

Sometimes I get to thinking about this life. It is, of course, a glorious interlude – to all these boys, and to anyone: but to pretend that it is a natural life would be foolish ... one becomes so accustomed to the company of the sea, and is at home there, that one is not again ever really at home in the society of human beings.

Villiers pondered the crew. 'Have I said anywhere that the second mate is a different man with that Redhead gone? ... These Americans, by the way, are good fellows: the only one who isn't much good is ... a drunkard, spoiled boy, seducer, wastrel. Yet of course he is not bad (no one is) – only just as bad as he knows how to be.'

They were now about 3,300 miles from New York, and had about 2,800 to go before Rio, but it did not matter – the nights brought 'the black sky, gold-studded, and the black sails quietly rolling and the sound of the seaspray swept aside, protesting softly ... And the snatches of accordion music and laughter from the 'tweendecks'.

Joseph Conrad crossed the Line on 9 March 1935, thirty-six days and 4,283 miles away from New York. 'Neptune came aboard, in the person of Frank, aided by Horst, Karl, Hilgard and the Cook – a small gang to handle the multitude of the uninitiated: but it went very well.' However, despite the beauty of the voyage, the grounding of the ship still affected Villiers deeply. He wrote on 16 March:

> Sometimes – often indeed – the misery of that near-wreck in New York will come back upon me suddenly here, like going down the ... tweendeck companion 'midships today. I suddenly saw the place full of dirty water again, cold and depressing, afloat with the wretched jetsam of the boys' destroyed clothes, and sodden biscuits here and there, and oil from the engine increasing the dirt and depression.

He continued, with horrifying imagery, 'Somehow the ship will never be quite the same again: she is like a wife, I suppose, who has been nearly dead and then survived a terrible operation: or a grand dog that has been vivisected, and then put back in its skin again.'

His spirits were low. He wrote two articles 'of the utmost indifference'. He saw birds blown out to sea by the wind: 'It is tragic to watch them beaten down in the sea. Once down they never rise again: and they all go down.' The next day his diary notes simply, 'Unsettled, overcast, variable, morose'. They caught two sharks and slaughtered them in a 'welter of threshing tails and spilled gore'. Ugliness was all around: and discord too.

The mate, who was poor at handling the men, stepped into a quarrel between Frank Villiers and Dave Hunt, and punched Hunt. Villiers wrote, 'He said he was "stopping" the fight, but I think rather with the idea of getting a crack at Dave under safe conditions. I do not think much of the Mate's actions but unfortunately I was not on deck at the time. Dave vows to "get him" in Rio: I rather hope he does.'

On 29 March they slowly approached Rio and hove-to overnight outside the harbour: *Joseph Conrad* had covered the 5,980 miles from New York in fifty-seven days. The wind rose next morning, and they entered Rio harbour elegantly under sail.

8

THERE CANNOT BE TWO VOYAGES SUCH AS THIS

Up to this point, the accounts in *Cruise of the Conrad* and Villiers' diary reflect each other closely, apart from the matter of the female cadets Christine and Elsie, and some of Villiers' more cutting observations on his fellow voyagers. In fact, he goes out of his way in *Cruise of the Conrad* to treat generously even those he felt had let him down.

Incidents that involve the ship itself are faithfully recorded in both diary and book: what departs from the book after Rio, however, is much that concerned the real lives of the crew. The books that Villiers wrote were his livelihood: he was a naturally reticent man, one who lived and wrote in prudish times. It was not that human life itself was any different then but its acceptable portrayals were.

It is hardly surprising, then, that Villiers' personal diary and his 1937 book of the voyage would diverge significantly. In real life he worried about the physical and moral health of the young men of the *Conrad*. He lectured them on the dangers of venereal diseases, and when they ignored him he paid for (and grumpily administered) their medical treatment. In the book, embarrassing events and awkward people are simply omitted, while the voyage takes on the bland and rosy hues of a travelogue for children; and as it veers further away from reality, life seeps quietly out of it.

Yet the diary hums: Villiers criticises, laughs, scolds, enjoys, frets and ponders the long voyage in *Joseph Conrad*, from the bliss of first ownership to the misery of final loss. He often said that he wished he could write better books. He did, but they weren't the ones that got published.

————

They spent a week in Rio, setting up the rigging for the Cape of Good Hope passage, knocking barnacles off the hull, cleaning and taking on provisions. Villiers did not trust the shipchandler, and spent very little time away from *Joseph Conrad*, although the crew had leave. Villiers wrote dryly, 'most of the Scandinavians spend it whoring, the carpenter being delighted with what he describes as the best street of whores he has yet found. A great place, Rio, he says the number of whores in this estimable thoroughfare, wherever it is, starting at 300, increases to the 10th power daily, until now there are 3,000,000. Maybe there are.'[1]

They sailed on 6 April 1935, the weather continuing warm and mild. Villiers spent some days pleasurably imagining and drawing sketches of his ideal ship, a barque with a good diesel engine: 'she could go to many places now barred to her.' The winds finally rose and *Joseph Conrad* started making 11 knots. 'How beautifully she runs! She really is a masterpiece of design ... she picks her hurrying path as if she were an intelligent thing created of the Lord.'

Everyday life continued. 'The carpenter whiles away the afternoon reminiscing to his cronies about whores, with particular emphasis and satisfaction as to the cattle market of Rio de Janeiro. There is something unnatural about a life which so distorts an important natural function: but he does not seem to mind.'

They reached Cape Town on 7 May; sailing the 3,516 miles from Rio in thirty-one fairly uneventful days. Villiers learned that insurance on the accident in New York would cover only the initial stranding expenses, and not the extra from the collision at the pier: it was a blow to his plans. 'I am a good thousand pounds behind the sum necessary for the completion of the voyage.' During the week in South Africa only a single cadet, Carmichael, joined them. They sailed out of Cape Town on 14 May.

————

Shipboard life continued, both sublime and ridiculous. 'The moon is brilliant and the night most beautiful, with an undulating progress and noiseless peace and quiet ... [sic]'. The following day, 'The Mate has crabs and Petersen is still troubled by a dose from Rio.'

Villiers much disliked his role as ship's doctor by default, and wished desperately that an experienced medical man would want to ship with them – 'it would be a weight off my mind in more ways than one. But here he is not – neither he, nor any other person to occupy the spare cabins.'

He was re-reading Joseph Conrad's book *The Nigger of the Narcissus* and thinking about his own writing and sailing:

> But he depresses me: he says everything that I would like to say, everything to which I could possibly think my way, so much better than I could, and so perfectly and so finally, that I cannot again feel justified in taking up my pen. And yet? ... There's always a story: there is always a little further groping after meaning to be done.
>
> But most of all I can see Conrad walking the poop of his square-rigged ships and thinking, thinking (it is so evident in his books) ... And I get to thinking of my own responsibilities here, and that I really do own this vessel, that there aloft are my sails that brought me here, that they blow out in grace and beauty through the quiet night, driving this little ship gently along, because – because, well, I want them to.
>
> There would not be a square-rigged ship running her Easting down now between Good Hope and Australia if I had not found this one about to meet an ignoble end in Copenhagen: there would not be a square-rigged ship under the British flag.
>
> And here am I, a foc's'l hand, a drifter, an opportunist, almost. It is strange: this is not even a dream ship to me. I never dared to dream of having such a ship or of making such a voyage.

———

The first gale hit them on 26 May, and young Stormalong accidentally let the wheel come up. The sea smashed through the skylight into the saloon and water came into the charthouse and down the companion-way. 'It was not his fault, he is too small', wrote Villiers. Gale after gale struck the ship but she flew along: 1,200 miles in a single week. Although *Joseph Conrad* was only about 100 feet at the waterline she was a good size for those seas, fitting nicely between the wave crests.

The crew worked well during the gales, but the long period of pressure brought disagreements – a fight over jam, complaints about burnt soup – still, 'the run was exhilarating and the whole experience good for the salt of one's soul'. Not far from the coast of Australia the ship was turned northwards into warmer waters – 'the clouds are queer, the sunrise bloodred, and there is sand in the air. We passed today less than 100 miles from the western extremity of Australia.'

Navigation and ship handling lessons for the cadets were going well, but Villiers observed, 'By the way, now I know that teaching is a pretty difficult profession.' He noticed weed on the hull and was angry to realise that the expensive anti-fouling paint he had bought from the Rio shipchandler had not been the real thing: 'There is no limit to the mean knavery of white men for the sake of some paltry graft.'

On 30 June *Joseph Conrad* entered the Bali Strait, between the islands of Java and Bali, which narrowed from 28 miles wide at the entrance to 1 mile wide at the far end, with reefs and rips and a strong tidal race. The wind behind them was good and Villiers decided to go through the Strait with the ebb tide that night – he knew there were good navigational lights. By the evening, sheer mountains towered above them in haze. Night fell and there was no moon.

> [I]n about twenty minutes of quiet sailing the rush begins! We seem caught upon the crest of a giant tide: it blows strong and with everything set but the mainsail, we snore along. She's controllable ... now the land looms up high, tremendous, threatening, seemingly almost upon us ... The foam boils at the old prow: the wake races phosphorescent astern ...
>
> I con from the foc's'l head – but it is easy. The Lord is kind. And the Strait is so well lit ... I loved her then, looking aft from the foc's'l head, at the black sails and all the old tried grace of her gently running now in the night through the waters of the Java Sea, for the first time in her so long and so honourable life.

In forty-nine days from Cape Town *Joseph Conrad* had covered 6,500 miles. They anchored on 2 July at Boeleleng, where Villiers had hoped to find an untouched paradise and instead found a 1930s tourist trap. Bali was getting 2,000 visitors a month, a local manager for KPM, the Dutch steamship line, told him proudly.

> It's the tourist liners that have done it. Ashore in the evening I see Buleleng is a Chinese town wherein the Balinese work, the Chinese trade, and the Dutch take the profits. In a little Chinese restaurant an aged Malay comes selling

photographs of Balinese breasts, having discovered, I suppose, what is expected of him: and the streets are full of motorcars and shops. Unspoiled!

He spent the next day wandering around the town. 'The Balinese music – I hear an orchestra at a Chinese wedding, between the firing of the fireworks – is weirdly beautiful too: somehow it seems more to mean something, to express something, than so much of western music.'

The harbourmaster, who was amazed they had sailed Bali Strait by night, demanded 100 guilders for the privilege of visiting a Dutch port – about £14 – then when Villiers questioned him about applying for a rebate from the Governor, suddenly discovered he meant 30 guilders instead. When he returned to the ship, the cook 'reports that harlots here cost one guilder – very good. The other connoisseurs seem satisfied. Two female runners from one house, I hear, were out last night after I'd gone ashore, nor was their visit quite in vain.'

At a Balinese performance he watched 'a man who danced superbly with his fingers and little girls sedate and lovely ... they dance for religion, for sorrow, and for joy'. The audience was made up of 'useless Europeans ... a divorcee, a thick-jowelled moron with beatle brows, half a dozen pale undistinguished tourists, a woman with a large behind, three Dutch all with large behinds, a pale youth with great discontent heavy on his characterless features ... artificial, stunted, half-morbid, half-alive'.

> One gathers abiding impressions of Bali's intense fertility, of the even tenor of its life: and from the trip there rushes a bewildering array of memories which elude the pen. What can I say of stone figures and temple walls ... of the terraced fields and the lovely scenery into which the grace of the Balinese fit so perfectly?
>
> I return to the ship, glad to be back and to find her safe at the calm anchorage, to find the Mate and the steward taking [a cadet] to a whore-house to add to his experience. Good God! ... [Three other cadets] discovering themselves venereally diseased go ashore to seek attention.

They stayed eight days, working on *Joseph Conrad*, swimming, fishing and sailing. 'In the evening with Frank and Hilgard for a very pleasant walk along country roads and over fields ... I am reminded ... that the shore life may have some compensations too. But I have tried it once. No, no, this will do.'

———

Joseph Conrad sailed for Singapore at daylight on 10 July. 'Day after day the south-east monsoon blew us quietly along, with beautiful dawns and the whole long days tranquil and superb.'

In his diary he notes, 'I ... work upon the cut feet, the infected hands, and the venereal young gentlemen.' The ship crossed the Equator again, 'without ceremony, except that Carmichael is dipped. I write an indifferent article, teach navigation, navigate the ship, and so forth.' The medical problems escalated when Miller cut his foot badly on a knife and Carmichael gashed a big vein on his thumb. 'I fix them both with tarred oakum and a tourniquet: and teach navigation, and lecture the assembled youth once more on the foolishness and seriousness of VD.'

The lights of Singapore Strait came into view. They had a close brush with reefs near Lima Island then continued to Singapore itself on 19 July, covering 917 miles in nine days. 'Then I get the mail, and learn that of the £1500 I lost in New York the insurance is paying £143-2-5d: and I cannot give away an article in England. And the piece I wrote about our wreck in Bay Ridge Mrs Barbour has sold to the Brooklyn Eagle for $20. But Scribners, thank heaven, are pleased with the indifferent stuff I sent to them.'

According to *Cruise of the Conrad*, they had an uneventful time in Singapore: Villiers found it a fine port, with a 'very good hospital'. He enjoyed Chinese food, made good friends among the pilots and the Merchant Service Guild, had the compass readjusted and 'shipped two young people to come with us to Sydney (and they fitted in very well)'. Naturally, there was a little more to it than that. The night they left Singapore, 31 July, Villiers wrote in his diary:

This port ... has cost me £1000. [One venereal cadet] was told his case was well in hand. Then he probably went on the razzle again ... I spoke to him until I was sick of it: I cannot lead these fellows by the hand ashore and there is no-one else to do it.

Then one night he was suddenly taken with swollen testicles and pain so much he could scarcely walk. He was taken to the hospital and there he will stay for the next three months ... I could not clear the ship until I ... deposited funds ... for the whole of his hospital expenses and his fare to the United States.

I fired the second mate. This really was necessary for the sake of the ship ... I had to pay his fare to London ... he wasn't a bad fellow but he was no second mate: I cannot carry fools ... I have made Petersen second mate. He shapes very well.

And the 'two young people' coming on the ship to Sydney? Villiers wrote:

I found two passengers, a cold little sandy runt almost 28 and his hawk-nosed wife, painfully artificial: I fear we are going to get to know them very well and I for one feel that I could do without that privilege ... But they have paid in £240 to the pool for the five-month passage to Sydney and that almost paid for the provisions ... Now I am tired, and I have about £100 to see me to Australia and that is all the money I have.

———

From Singapore they sailed north-east through the China Sea, then east into the Sulu Sea between Borneo and the Philippines. Villiers had now carried the responsibility of the ship for nearly a year without a break. He had to give two of the cadets hypodermic injections prescribed in Singapore every four days. In early August he found another was infected, 'but he says he has been with no woman though he admits he was at the whore-house in Bali ... I told him he is making medical history.' The following day: 'And now ... the sixth from Bali. He had gonorrhea, I'm afraid.'

They visited a small island, and met an officious gentleman who thought they might be pirates. They ran into doldrums and beat backwards and forwards. On 21 August *Joseph Conrad* reached Tawi Tawi, a little cluster of islands between the Sulu and Celebes Seas. They landed at Bongao, a 'pleasant, sleepy place of palms and beaches and a ricketty wharf', with a church, residences and shops. They visited the Moro people at Malasa – for centuries boat builders and more recently pirates – and watched little girl dancers like those in Bali, but not as skilled, Villiers felt.

In late August came a startling reminder of the world they had left behind: 'Back on board there is talk of war: it has come over the radio from Manila – Italy and England, or something. Italy and England? It's too mad to be believable, but it might be true, none the less.'

It was time to move on. The night before they left Tawi Tawi, the chief of the Moro visited the ship late at night with musicians, an interpreter and his twelve-year-old daughter – he wanted the boy Stormalong to stay behind and marry her.

> As soon as he awakened sufficiently to take it in Storm brusquely refused, saying the Captain had told him to keep away from women, and at the first opportunity he ran down and hid himself in the hold … he rather thought it might have been a decoy to eat him. Prince Stormalong, White King of Malasa! What a career to turn down – and the little Princess was not bad-looking either. Hardcase asks ruefully why couldn't she have chosen him?

———

The ship made very slow progress through the Celebes Sea, but by 2 September had left it behind and entered the Pacific – 'a real ocean swell at last'. But at night on the radio, 'I hear that Europe's spew of perverts still shriek of war.'

They steadily sailed eastwards through the waters above New Guinea, then turned southwards, sailing 2,200 miles in three weeks, 'which passed much more pleasantly than I had ever expected'. The ship badly needed careening, so Villiers decided to put into Nissan Atoll, between New Ireland and Bougainville. With some difficulty they scraped through the narrow entrance to the lagoon, then heaved the ship over with tackles to trees on the beach and cleaned the hull.

Villiers was perturbed by the general ill-health of the local Melanesians, many of whom had ulcers, scurf and elephantiasis. It rained almost constantly the eight days they were there, and the lagoon seemed to be full of lethal sea-life. He was happy to motor carefully out of the entrance and away.

They had hoped to sail south-easterly towards the Solomon Islands but met headwinds and contrary currents. After more than a week, the ship had been pushed so far south-west instead that it was within sight of the Trobriand Islands, so Villiers decided to land for a few days. He enjoyed the stay enormously: the local people were 'clean, muscular, well-built and most attractive in appearance and behaviour'. They wore red flowers or feathers in their 'great mops of fuzzy hair', the grass skirts of the women 'swung seductively on their rounded forms', and their villages were clean, pleasant and prosperous.

Fritz Egerton had introduced Villiers to the fascinating ideas of Professor Malinowski, the pioneering ethnologist who had studied the life of the Trobrianders, with their relaxed view of sexuality and their skillful use of sailing craft. When they left on 17 October, Villiers wrote, 'I want to go back to the Trobriands. I am satisfied with this voyage now. I feel that I have found the place I wanted to.'

But even on an idyllic South Sea island the world intruded. 'Tonight the radio speaks of 8000 Ethiopians killed and joy in Italy and warships in the Mediterranean: and the trade wind blows quietly in the Trobriand trees.'

———

They reached Tulagi in the Solomon Islands fifteen days after leaving the Trobriands. It had 'a club, golf course, wireless station, Chinatown, gaol, government house, British flag and all the rest ... frankly and plainly a headquarters for white living'. The *Joseph Conrad* was received warmly, and the boys played cricket and went swimming and horse-riding. After a week they went on to Guadalcanal for another few days of sightseeing, where they adopted two kittens for the ship, a ginger one they called Joseph, and a grey and white, Conrad.

They sailed on 11 November but the winds were against them for days; so Villiers decided to stop at a tiny island off the south-east of the Solomons, Owa Raha. There they met a German trader who had sailed on *Parma* twenty years before, and an elderly black American who had worked on brutal Yankee clippers, who were both delighted to see a square-rigger.

Villiers watched a performance of the Tree Men at Owa Raha, and was astonished by the hours-long dance, telling the island's history with 'great energy and considerable grace'. The Tree Men were clay-covered grotesques, the earliest inhabitants of the islands. They battled and mingled with invaders, lived tranquilly, fought off the Spanish, then saw the coming of the traders and missionaries – and died horribly from their diseases: 'here the chanting grew low, and the shrub-clad ones stood still a while, a long while.'

'All the leading parts ... were taken by two men in great bull masks; their work was magnificent.' They showed the white men, the church schools, the breakdown of customs, and now, even the tourists: 'in a satiric finale the two extraordinarily capable performers did the dance of the queer strangers taking photographs.' Villiers held a party that night on the ship for everyone, with more dancing, and chanty-singing from the elderly sailors, and food and fireworks and cheering. When *Joseph Conrad* sailed next morning, on 21 November 1935, everyone came out in boats and canoes to wave green branches of friendship, and 'the sun shone and the whole Pacific world was smiling'.

———

This was perhaps the high point of the whole voyage, a little over halfway through. Just one day out of Owa Raha they were struck by a virulent form of malaria. Villiers had experienced malaria occasionally for some years, ever since his 1922 voyage on *Erriba* to French Somaliland, but this was far worse – delirium, fever, vomiting, chills, jaundice, fatigue and severe pain.

The initial attack lasted for a week and a half, then recurred at intervals for several days at a time. From this time on, Villiers' usual resilience was sapped by illness, and the financial and human problems would sometimes overwhelm him. He was too ill to enjoy the ship's wonderful progress – they covered 1,500 miles in twelve days.

Finally, on 9 December they sailed through Sydney Heads, 'with the ferries blowing a welcome on their syrens [sic] and, even at that early hour, launches around and aeroplanes overhead'. Villiers was more famous than he realised – weighed down by his many concerns he did not appreciate how much his books were enjoyed, or how many armchair sailors loved photos of *Joseph Conrad* against the sunset, or anecdotes about hurricanes, or the dusky princess who wanted to marry little Stormalong.

He was sick and exhausted and it was raining. He had an argument with the Customs man about the origin of a few bags of semolina. 'So it goes. We have arrived. We have sailed here from England, by devious routes and through some perils: and there is shouting and clamour and weak cheering and Customs forms ... I still feel a little fever myself and I would like some sleep.'

They stayed for nine days, anchored at Double Bay in Sydney Harbour. Hundreds of people visited the ship, including the Governor-General designate Lord Gowrie, artist Norman Lindsay, 'shiploving ancients' from famous clippers, Lady Snowden, the entire wardroom of HMAS *Canberra*, a Danish professor of music, and 'Sir John Butters, the Minister for Something-or-other of New South Wales'. Villiers lunched at the Wentworth with Prime Minister Joseph Lyons, who had known his father Leon.

Maritime artist Oswald Brett, then fifteen, recalls meeting Villiers for the first time on *Joseph Conrad* on 13 December, 'but didn't dare speak to him – he was instructing the Finnish mate to not let visitors go below. The next day I was aboard with [maritime artist] John Allcot when we were entertained in the saloon by Alan. Quite a contrast to my previous day's visit!'[2]

Some people asked to go with the ship but were reluctant to pay the costs. Villiers was already bitter about the attitudes of some of the 'college boys' he felt he was subsidising, and did not want to take on any more cadets.

> Yet why, I asked, should I add unnecessarily to my responsibilities? ... The boys are poor crew – wasteful, complaining, unreliable, fundamentally disloyal. They have no real interest either in the ship or in the sea: seeking escape and not finding it, they suffer the voyage from port to port ... in vain quest of band-aids of adventure and romance ...

The seven weeks in Australia were to be a painful, introspective time:

> It has been strange, to come back here like this, owner and master of the smallest full-rigged ship, dropped in for a visit on a voyage around the world ... yet I do not feel that I have made very good: that, if ever it comes, is still before me ...
>
> And what have I? A ship – a ship, and a life that seems to other people, not thinking very deeply about it ... rather enviable. Yet my financial problems are such that all ports are nightmares: and my wife, I am informed, is to sue me for divorce. Well, well ... [sic]

They sailed out of Sydney Harbour to cheering on 18 December, aeroplanes above, launches following, and ferries listing as their passengers rushed to the side to watch *Joseph Conrad* under full sail. The artist Norman Lindsay wrote to Villiers, 'I must thank you for the glorious spectacle of the Conrad's departure ... She was pure beauty: I've never seen anything so lovely ... I am tremendously in your debt for this rare experience.'[3]

The way to Melbourne was 'the most difficult short passage of the whole voyage'. Malaria recurred among four of the crew for several days, and 'the malaria patients creep about the decks, pale and haggard-eyed'. By the evening of 30 December *Joseph Conrad* was outside Port Phillip, a pilot on board to take the ship through the narrow, dangerous rip at the flood tide.

> Now I have the malaria myself, damn it: and I am very worried, having got to this infernal place, as to how I am going to get out. A year ago tonight we came to New York and I had the same curious feeling – almost of impending disaster. ... It came: by God it came.

At midnight they passed through the Rip, then late next day moored safely by the Gellibrand Pier at Williamstown, where Villiers had joined his first four-master, *Bellands*, almost fifteen years before.

―――

A month later Villiers wrote of this time in Melbourne, 'My alarm at coming into Melbourne was well-founded enough. In Brooklyn the rocks – and here the whole voyage came near to foundering in Collins Street.' In the section of *Cruise of the Conrad* dealing with Melbourne he describes the stay with gentle wit, but in the diary his worries cut deeper. Money was the obvious pressure: he had only £30 when they arrived. He cabled Fritz to send him funds but it took weeks to come through.

He was contemplating laying-up *Joseph Conrad* for six months and 'getting out' of Melbourne, when a promoter asked him to take a small group back to the South Seas to check out a potential gold mine. He was suspicious, but they offered him £2,000 and he started to consider the possibility. He met the prospector, Harold Slocombe, who had discovered the gold (on Sudest Island off south-east Papua) but

Villiers observed, 'I should not personally care to entrust him with the gold in a country dental business – nor feel sure that he would find it, either.'

Villiers was made a director in the gold-mining company, although it had neither funds nor legal existence. Shares were offered to the public, with much publicity generated by *Joseph Conrad*'s link to the expedition, probably the reason for involving Villiers in the first place. No one subscribed to the share offering, perhaps more concerned with the sudden death that week of the King of England.

Then a group of brokers from Collins Street took over. They said, quite reasonably, they could send the expedition on a steamer for £300, but Villiers pointed out the benefit of using the ship, 'which by this time had been ballyhooed in the press ad nauseum', and argued them up to £1,000. They responded with an offer of £400 up front, the rest later. Daphne's lawyers wanted over £200 for her allowance and divorce expenses, so a desperate Villiers accepted the deal.

He was ill-tempered with fever and worry. On board 'my own cadets began to turn on me'. Some spoke of leaving the ship – afraid, Villiers thought bitterly, of malaria and the Cape Horn passage yet to come. A few decided to think it over on the next leg of the journey, but one left them in Melbourne. Villiers also wanted to leave behind one of the cadets who now had secondary syphilis but could not afford to pay for his treatment and repatriation. He had to learn how to give the boy injections at the ghastly venereal clinic.

At the same time, as in Sydney, 'the half-forgotten chapters of the melancholy past are all re-opened – school days, sea days, newspaper days, factory days', and Villiers struggled with the visibility the ship had brought him. He gave speeches, was photographed, attended luncheons, signed autographs, received honorary memberships and dealt with a near-endless stream of visitors and letters every day.

Despite the great publicity *Joseph Conrad* received, however, no new cadets or passengers wanted to sail with them from Melbourne. One relief, however, was that competent Jim Evans had joined them as able seaman. Another was that on the passage with the gold prospectors they would stop at Auckland to pick up – at last! – three paying passengers. Villiers had only £30 in his pocket when they left Melbourne – the same amount he had arrived with – but he calculated that the remaining fee from the gold expedition and the fares from the passengers would give him just enough funds to complete the voyage.

———

Joseph Conrad sailed from Melbourne for Auckland on 30 January 1936. Four 'gold men' were on board, including the prospector Slocombe whose personal habits irritated Villiers intensely. The run was uneventful, and they arrived at Auckland on 21 February.

Three of the American cadets decided to leave there. Villiers, suffering through another bout of fever, was unhappy they were giving up; particularly since another who had been with him since England was also going with them. But he was relieved to find a replacement for the original first mate. The new man was an Australian named Gordon Chapman, who had been a seaman on barques, an officer on steamships, and was now studying for his Master's Certificate. And at the last minute, to his surprise, five promising young New Zealand cadets signed on – Crawford, Henley, McDougall, Vickerstaff and Ussher.

The three passengers also boarded at Auckland: one was Harold Sowerby, the brother of the man who had been on the Singapore to Sydney leg, and the other two were Americans: a divorced writer, Mrs M.A. Lindsley, and her daughter Leonora. Once again finance had forced Villiers to take women on *Joseph Conrad*, and once again he resented it:

> I must take these extraneous humans, women and all, or I could not be here myself. To keep the ship and to keep her going, almost any sacrifice is justified.
> The Lindsleys are all right, but the daughter needs discipline. I am not going to give it to her: I have enough troubles here. She is seated on the chartroom table now smoking a pipe: she is about 18 and can drink whisky and soda with any man. She will get none here.

They sailed for the Louisiades on 27 February 1936. It went easily enough at first, though it was the cyclone season. The passengers soon began to grate upon Villiers. On 6 March: 'Mrs Lindsley wants to go to Noumea. It is, she says, on our way. It is not.'

Next day, 'Mrs Lindsley still speaks of Noumea, and I discover she has the support of the teeth-sucking swollen-gut Slocombe. I hope that bastard knows more about gold than he knows of all else.'

On 8 March, 'I am feverish again ... The Lindsley gramophone blares Cuban rumbas on the main hatch: I wonder why all Americans have this gramophone mind and what in the name of God is pictured in their heads when they hear the fool noise. Nothing?'

After two weeks at sea he is outraged:

> Mrs Lindsley wants tea in the morning and quinine for the unattractive Leonora, and has [the cadet] syphilis like Griswold told her and Mr Slocombe says he has? He has, I say: she chanced to glance in the saloon this morning as I was about to jab the starboard cheek of that youth's backside with a hypodermic full of Metarsenobillon ... I am of course obliged to the admirable Griswold and the tooth-sucking bull-doser Slocombe for their attention to this detail ...

Luckily the weather distracted him with a rapidly falling barometer and ominous swirling clouds on the horizon. The ship flew before the gale over two or three days and made great progress, but two of the masts were damaged. They made their way towards Samarai, the administrative centre of the Louisiades, anchoring at midnight on 25 March.

The gold men left there, and cadet Vickerstaff went prospecting. Villiers was ill and exhausted, and devastated to hear that some of the cadets and passengers 'were being utterly disloyal to the ship – deriding everything'. The main critic was the 'tooth-sucking theatrical bastard Slocombe':

> He gave the impression that the ship was a floating hell, unfit to be lived in or sailed: that I was a sadistic dope-fiend (he had often seen me with a hypodermic in the saloon), depressed and dejected with the whole enterprise and taking out my spite on the boys ...
>
> I wish to God I could get some faith in human beings. Poor spawn! What fools we are! ... For what is lacking in themselves they turn on me ... I have fever ... Where is the practical Christianity anywhere? Nightly the radio blares of inevitable, approaching annihilating war. Well let it annihilate, even if it reaches here ... [sic]

And this probably hurt too: 'I read in a newspaper one day in Samarai that I had been divorced – desertion, the Judge said ... [sic]'. Villiers' older brother Noel wrote, 'I do not wish to put my foot in it but perhaps you would like to know that the divorce did not get any unpleasant publicity, even The Truth treated you very well, in fact except for a hue and cry headline in the Melb Sun it was very sympathetic. Every paper made it plain that you had maintained her and that there were no other women in it.' In the depths of Villiers' professional woes it must have been doubly bruising to know that his private life was newspaper fodder.

———

They sailed from Samarai for Tahiti on 31 March. Villiers recovered his equilibrium and decided to use the engine to visit some of the Louisiade islands, which fascinated him. But almost immediately the engine broke down. It was too dangerous to stay within the archipelago: disappointingly, they had to make for the open Coral Sea. They anchored inside the reef of Wari Island, and bartered tobacco with grass-skirted natives for oranges, lemons and coconuts. At night there was a singalong of native songs and mission hymns on the beach.

Early next morning the wind was good and the tide rushing out through the lagoon entrance. Cadets in a lifeboat towed the ship to help with steering, and Villiers watched for reefs from aloft. But as they approached the entrance the waves pushed the *Conrad* sideways and she slid aground. They tried to haul the ship off with a kedge anchor, then,

> ... without warning she lifted clear and, caught in the tide and unmanageable with the sails, swung clear round with her stern against a coral outcrop and her bows up on some more. This second situation was infinitely worse than the first. We were now, instead of being inside the lagoon, lying on the point of the reef outside it, and in the breakers ...

They took out a heavy anchor, dropped it and hauled at the capstan. The surf lifted the ship and she suddenly slid off the coral just after midday. Villiers wrote that 'the instant the ship is lost I am insolvent'. How could he conceivably get the boys home again or even feed them, without the well-stocked ship?

The euphoria of success lasted only a few days, then several of the boys resigned from the senior navigation class, 'not wishing to be bothered with Rules of the Road and signalling and "that stuff". They can go: I wish they would all resign.'

It transpires in the blasted kindergarten navigation class that the studious Miss Lindsley, never having done any mathematics in her life, does not know the multiplication table ... her mother is damned little better. 'Why,' she laments, 'Leonora can't even score at bridge!'

The wind and waves were against them and the Great Barrier Reef was a constant danger. They beat the ship back and forth for a month, working their way through the Coral Sea and down the coast of Queensland. Once out of the Barrier Reef they set off eastwards towards Lord Howe Island, reaching there on 11 May.

For a day at Lord Howe they had a brief respite of fresh food and a friendly welcome with the Kirby family, 'and I met some readers – here! – and some had my books: and I wished that I had written them well and not hurriedly and slapdash and carelessly, as I have ... [sic]'. They sailed in the evening, and next day, 'The fair Leonora complains that the scones at the Kirby's were not hot ... and the boys name the pig after her but afterwards are sorry, feeling they have been too harsh on the pig.'

Villiers had hoped to sail eastwards from Lord Howe to Tahiti, but again the wind was against them, pushing them so far south they had to pass through New Zealand's Cook Strait to get to the Pacific Ocean. On 22 May the ginger tomcat Joseph lost his grip when leaping on to the rail and fell into the sea. Villiers had the ship hove-to, and Hilgard and Karl Sperling rowed in the dinghy to look for him. After twenty minutes of searching, to everyone's surprise they found him swimming feebly, and brought him back to be dried out in the galley.

Villiers' fever returned. A gale descended on them that lasted for eight days. They had to heave-to three times simply to try to ride out the worst of it. Slowly they made their way towards Tahiti, and finally anchored at Papeete on 18 June 1936.

———

Tahiti brought Villiers renewed awareness of his loneliness, but it brought him a new contentment too. First there were the disappointments. Conley, who had sailed with them to Nassau, had published a series of snide, critical articles; ex-cadet Vickerstaff had dissuaded a new cadet from joining them; Mr Sowerby was not now coming on the

Cape Horn leg so his fare was lost, and Mrs Lindsley, who 'had not, she said, had anything like the voyage that she had come for (this is true enough!)', refused to pay Villiers the $300 she still owed him.

> I am happy in the achievement of my two great aims, to preserve the ship and her people, and conduct the both in safety about the world ... But in the ports it slips from me. In the ports I am alone ... Here all problems of falseness and false standards raise, that have no place at sea: and I face them utterly alone ...
>
> But oh God, how long? For the ports fling my insufficiency in my face. This is no full life: this is no living! The sea is my escape – my terrible and grim escape, even as it was to me as a child and walked the docks, bewildered ... I cannot for ever hold this ship against the wind. I will have to give in: I will have to give in – some time ... But not now ... The voyage will – must go on. For without the successful achievement of this voyage I shall be nothing ...
>
> I am not bitter and I am not sad though there is so much to embitter and to sadden: but I wish sometimes that I could see in human eyes what shines ... in my own mind, deep in, and allows me to go on. Faith, ideals, determination: with whom to share them?

The discontented cadets went away at last, along with the irritating passengers. The crew repaired the damaged masts. They remained for two weeks in Papeete, and the famous magic of Tahiti began to work on Villiers. He found the officials obliging, and the port was:

> ... a good one, inexpensive, clean, interesting ... every day there were schooners, white-painted, rakish vessels with mellow-sounding native names ... and the graceful wahines and the pretty half-castes, all beflowered, passing in the cool of the evening ... the loveliness of Tahitian hills, the gardens of bold mountains with their heads almost always in the clouds ... To lift up one's eyes and look around in Tahiti – even its port – how beautiful!

Villiers made friends, including a Tahitian woman named Hinano: 'I rather liked Hinano ... Aye, I liked Hinano – rather much. Strange? But understandable enough, in all the circumstances ...'. Sadly for Villiers their time together was brief. She asked to go with him on *Joseph Conrad*, 'but I would not take her ... from flowered island and light laughter to the cold sea and the misery of Cape Horn! No, no: it might kill her'.

They sailed from Tahiti on 2 July. Villiers wrote, 'I find myself for the first time looking back upon the land with regrets – disquieted, not so sure of the realities of this seafaring life ... If I had not had this ship to sail I might have stayed a while in Tahiti: I might have found there – other things … [sic] But I had to go.'

———

Villiers had drawn upon the very last of his funds in Tahiti. 'I get worried almost sick sometimes wondering how I am going to meet my liabilities after this voyage.' Now they were on the final great passage – from Tahiti via Cape Horn to New York. They would not stop; there were no malcontents, no passengers, no women. All on board were experienced sailors, and they began preparing *Joseph Conrad* for the midwinter Cape Horn passage: there was a kind of peace in the finality of it.

Twenty-five days out of Tahiti they were hit by a long violent storm, then they made easier progress in gloomy weather. Villiers knew they had rounded Cape Horn on 8 August from 'the obvious ground swell of greying soundings by the Horn bank, a swell that stayed all day and is now gone, its coming and its going as noticeable as name-boards on a street'. It was done, almost an anti-climax: Cape Horn was over.

The days grew steadily warmer, and in the kinder weather the crew chipped and painted and repaired the ship. They crossed the Equator for the fourth time on 15 September. The grey and white cat, Conrad, started having fits and had to be shot.

Villiers began writing the book that became *Cruise of the Conrad* but thought it was 'pretty rotten'. He was ill again with fever. He rewrote much of the book but still disliked it. On 23 September they caught the trade winds and Villiers turned thirty-three – it was the third birthday he had spent aboard *Joseph Conrad*.

The last easy days of the voyage passed dreamily: 'There was no noise but the roll of foam, as the rolling cutwater slowly ploughed its way. The sidelights shone on the studding sails full of the fresh soft air of the gentle trade.' The air grew cold; the lights of New York could be seen red on the clouds from 100 miles away.

On 10 October 1936 they sailed into the examination anchorage off Staten Island, after travelling 57,800 miles in 555 days at sea. Next morning Villiers wrote the final entry in his *Joseph Conrad* diary: 'The voyage is over. Now I have only to get in. And sell the ship I suppose: there cannot be two voyages such as this.'

9

ADRIFT IN ARABIA

About the time *Joseph Conrad* was almost lost at Wari Island, *Herzogin Cecilie*, still the most famous square-rigger in the world, was also facing great peril. On 17 October 1935 she had sailed from Copenhagen to Port Lincoln. It was a honeymoon voyage for Captain Sven Eriksson and his new wife, Pamela Bourne, an adventurous journalist.

Herzogin Cecilie suffered two accidents even before she got out of the Baltic. She slightly damaged the stern of a ferry that carelessly crossed her path, and later that night in a gale she collided with a German trawler, *Rastede*, moving off without a look-out. A steamer towed *Rastede* to safety but she was badly damaged. Gustaf Erikson was furious.[1]

The Duchess loaded wheat in Port Lincoln and sailed on 27 January 1936, just as Villiers was preparing to leave Melbourne with the gold expedition for Samarai. *Herzogin Cecilie* made a fast passage of eighty-six days to Falmouth, but on arrival was arrested because of the *Rastede* collision, with a writ tied dramatically to the mast. Shipbrokers Clarkson's went guarantor for £2,500 and the barque was released.

She left for Ipswich the next night to unload her cargo, sailing in heavy fog. Somehow a navigational error was made, and the current was probably stronger than they realised. At about 4.00 a.m. on 25 April, *Herzogin Cecilie* collided with the Ham Stone at Soar Mill Cove near Salcombe, Devon.[2]

Her crew furled the sails, started the pumps and sent up distress flares. After a time the ship lifted free and started drifting towards the cliffs beyond the Ham Stone. They let go the anchors, but at about 50 yards from land went solidly aground. The Salcombe lifeboat came and took off many of the crew. A salvage tug refused to try to rescue *Herzogin Cecilie* – there was so little value in a square-rigger and its rapidly saturating cargo that they would never have recovered their costs.

Gusta' wrote, complaining, 'My wife has taken the sorrowful news especially badly. Her nerves are broken and she is now in bed, since H.C. was everything to her.' *Herzogin Cecilie* was everything to Pamela and Sven too, and the few others who fought desperately to save her. They unloaded enough rotting grain for tugs to pull her off the rocks on 19 June and tow her to Starehole Bay, which was supposed to be well protected from storms. It wasn't.

A gale swept in on 16 July; Elis Karlsson wrote, 'we stood listening to rivets snapping with reports like pistol-shots; the ship was working heavily in the swell and had reached rock. Staunchions between the decks bent and buckled. It was the end.'[3]

The Duchess was worldwide news for months in 1936. The reasons for her stranding were always a little mysterious, but it was true that the whole area was notorious for wrecks: some from human error, some from an unusually difficult coastline.

Sven never went back to sail. Pamela had just become pregnant when the ship ran aground, and they worked on the family farm in the Ålands throughout the Second World War. Afterwards they went to South Africa to farm, where Sven died in 1954, and Pamela wrote *The Duchess*, an extraordinary and beautiful memoir.

Herzogin Cecilie's mate Elis Karlsson fought in the British army during the war, then went to Southern Rhodesia and became a boat builder. Villiers and Karlsson had met in the 1930s, and in 1961 Villiers wrote a generous foreword for Karlsson's beautiful book *Mother Sea*. Villiers was curious about his personal opinion on *Herzogin Cecilie*'s loss, and Karlsson responded:

> Sven Eriksson – from my point of view as mate I must admit that I could find no fault with him as an efficient captain, except in one thing. On several occasions I saw him taking risks when approaching land that I personally would never have taken. But so did de Cloux, once, when we went ashore on the coast of Jutland … But – and you might agree with me from your own observations – in one respect we Ålanders showed neglect: we did not use the lead enough. Here I share the blame with Eriksson in the case of the loss of H.C. If I had insisted, I am sure he would not have forbidden me to use the lead.[4]

The unforgiving elements and a chain of small errors brought *Herzogin Cecilie* to the Ham Stone, but of the few precautions her crew might have taken in the fog, they neglected to use the one that might have told them they were close to land.

———

Since the terrible sinking of *Melbourne* in June 1932, roughly one grain ship a year had been lost to the breaker's yard. *Beatrice*, central to *Falmouth for Orders*, went for scrap metal in 1932. *Favell* was broken up in 1934; *Grace Harwar*, forever linked to Ronald Walker, in 1935; and *Mozart*, the only four-masted barquentine still in existence, went that year too. The pace of destruction accelerated in 1936 after *Herzogin Cecilie* was stranded, when both *Parma* and *Ponape* were broken up.

Parma's last great race was her record-breaking eighty-three days in 1933. Then Villiers sold his share in her, Ruben de Cloux stepped down as captain, and *Parma*'s luck changed. An apprentice was lost in the English Channel, a sailor died in a fall from the rigging, and her grain passages were slow. At Glasgow on 31 July 1936 she struck a dock and damaged her hull. The cost of repairs was nearly £500 and *Parma* was not insured. She was sent for scrap in August 1936.

The other ship broken up that year, *Ponape*, seems to have carried some rather unusual people, including the third of the female square-rigger sailors of the 1930s, Dorothea Duff. Dorothea had already learned to fly, travelled to Tibet, and hunted sharks off Sydney Heads before she worked two passages on *Ponape* in 1935 and another on *Killoran* in 1936. After square-riggers, she took to racing cars and Blackshirt politics, and was eventually interned as a British Fascist during the Second World War.

But the oddest person to sail on *Ponape* – perhaps on any grain ship – was a little girl stowaway. Five-year-old Nancie Lawson ran away from home in September 1935. She somehow got herself aboard *Ponape* and hid, until she was discovered three days out on the passage to Australia. Captain Carl Granith and the crew were especially kind to her, and she sailed with them to Port Lincoln and home again, on *Ponape*'s final voyage. The sailors made her warm clothes, Granith gave her school-lessons every day, and she was allowed to 'help' the cook.[5]

Grain ship society had matured since the 1920s. Boys wanting a life at sea now went into steam, so most sailing-ship crews were aging family men. Their world had become gentler, more at ease with women and children, but that was a side Villiers did not portray.

The fourth female square-rigger sailor, Oxfordshire teacher Winifred Lloyd, first went to sea as a passenger in the mid-1930s on *Herzogin Cecilie* and *Viking*. In 1936 she joined *Olivebank* as a stewardess, learned sailmaking and never looked back. She spent the next two years as a sailmaker on *Olivebank*, then moved to *Penang* for another two years. Winifred eventually made ten passages on square-riggers, eight of them as a crew member.

Villiers worked just four times on grain-ships. He made a living out of a female-free, 'boys' own adventure' version of a sailor's life, but found contentment himself only in marriage. Winifred Lloyd, however, experienced a true sailor's life – and death.

In late 1936 Villiers sold *Joseph Conrad* to a spoilt twenty-five-year-old millionaire, Huntington Hartford, who wrote a ghastly article about the 'boat' for *Esquire* magazine in October 1938. In 'Gone Without the Wind' he described his conversion of the working vessel to a rich man's toy with coy references to swaggering pirates, plank-walking and gold doubloons. It must have broken Villiers' heart.

Villiers took an apartment in Bay Ridge and worked on *Cruise of the Conrad*. He was now a divorced man and it seems he still had hopes for his relationship with Betty. In November 1936, a month after *Joseph Conrad* had returned, Fritz Egerton wrote to him:

> You are as cryptic as ever about the most vital thing. I hate to bring it up too. But what is happening about Betty? You can't go on as you are going on … either you're going to marry her or you aren't. I like Betty very much indeed, as you know quite well, but that doesn't make me feel that you ought to marry her. I don't think you ought to marry anybody unless you are prepared to change your whole mode of life, and there doesn't seem to be any indication of that.[6]

Villiers told his wife Nancie in later years that he had proposed to Betty, but she turned him down, fearing that she could not keep up with his adventurous life.[7] That probably happened about this time, because Fritz wrote in December 1936:

I hope there isn't any bitterness in your mind about her. She realises, because she has simple common sense, that it would not be wise for the pair of you to marry ... I can't help feeling that one or the other of you would have had to sacrifice too much of his (or her) individuality to be happy.

Fritz's letters offer fascinating insights into Villiers' personality. He wrote, 'Sometimes you aren't really quite reasonable in your demands upon the rank and file of human beings. You have been brought up in hardship of one kind and another, and you've remained a great deal of child in spite of it. That's part of the quality of you, and perhaps why some of us are so fond of you.'

It had been over two years since they had seen each other, so Fritz came from England to stay with Villiers at Bay Ridge in late 1936. In January 1937 Fritz wrote:

I'm afraid loneliness is always going to be with you ... It seems to arise from some sort of internal conflict of whose nature you aren't actually conscious ... You complicate matters by having the hell of an inferiority complex about yourself ... I can sympathise with you perhaps more fully than anyone else I know could do ... The knowledge (or even the thought) that someone has let you down, gets you like a knife.

A great deal, I think, may depend upon 'Cruise of the Conrad'. You know that book ought to be absolutely first class, and it isn't quite ... You can do it and you never do. There is always a perfectly good excuse ... You were nearing New York; you were without funds; you had all the anxieties of the ship, and you were writing a chapter a day. The situation was hopeless for the best book of your life, and this ought to have been it ... Can't you see that I believe pas-sionately in your power to write it?[8]

In early 1937 Villiers became interested in learning to fly, and Fritz was worried: 'I'm not awfully happy about this flying of yours. You're not in the right frame of mind for it. I don't want anything to happen to you, you old scout, and you don't care half enough whether anything does.' Villiers was indeed low. He wrote back to Fritz, 'I have half a mind to come to England in June now – previously, to be quite frank, I didn't give a damn where I went. And I don't very much now.'

Fritz, who was then fifty-two and yearning to travel and write, started organising a year-long expedition to the French Cameroons in Africa. Originally Villiers and Fritz's wife, Kay, were to come too, but Villiers wanted to return to the Trobriand Islands, and Kay was in the running for a long-denied promotion at the US Consulate. The gregarious Fritz wrote to Villiers, 'Now that I have decided to go without Kay I can't get up enthusiasm for Africa or anywhere else … It's the tremendous loneliness I'm most afraid of.' But his plans had gone too far to cancel.

Villiers had become involved with a divorced air hostess named Rita – probably Rita Rozelle, a hostess with American Airlines and minor starlet, who was photographed with him in 1937.[9] Fritz was worried that Villiers was rushing into the relationship: 'you and your blinking air hostesses: you <u>dare</u> go and get yourself tied up again and I'll run all round the earth to unty [sic] you. You work bloody hard; you don't spare yourself in any way, and YET you don't knuckle down to the one real problem which is that of saving your own soul alive for yourself and by yourself.'

In April 1937, *Cruise of the Conrad* was published and became a major success for Villiers. He dedicated it 'To FRITZ, who had more to do with all this than I had'. At the same time Fritz himself glumly boarded a steamer for Douala, and Betty Jacobsen married Ray Reed, her old friend from Bay Ridge.

———◆———

On the ship to Douala, Fritz heard that Kay had been unexpectedly called to America for a diplomatic meeting. He wrote to Villiers, 'I got a terrible shock when I found out how close she had been to travelling on the *Hindenburg*. What about Mr and Mrs Pannes? I have seen no newspapers at all. I do hope they were saved.' On 6 May the airship *Hindenburg* had exploded into flames as it was docking with its mooring mast in New Jersey. On board were Emma and John Pannes, the parents of young Hilgard; they both died. Villiers had always liked Hilgard, and when he published *The Making of a Sailor* the following year, he dedicated it to him. (The name was unfortunately misspelt 'Hilgrade' by a careless editor.)

To his own surprise, Fritz enjoyed his travels alone in the Cameroons, but by August 1937 he had had enough and came home to start writing his book *African Majesty*. When Amelia Earhart's plane disappeared over the Pacific in July during a round-the-world flight, Fritz wrote, 'Boy, I don't think that travel through the air is any sort of

23. The western harbour at Mariehamn, 1933 – *L'Avenir* to the left, *Archibald Russell* to the right. Note the size of the bowsprit compared to the people.

24. *Joseph Conrad*, the last British square-rigger, on her round the world voyage, 1934 to 1936.

25. Christine Baker, 'the Redhead', and 'Hardcase' on *Joseph Conrad* in late 1934.

26. On *Joseph Conrad*, late 1934. Villiers with 'Stormalong' (Stanley Goodchild, left) and 'Hardcase' (Jim Fuller), the 'two little poor boys from Ipswich'.

27. Elsie Jansen and Christine Baker using sailmakers' leather 'palms', late 1934.

28. *Joseph Conrad* aground on rocks, New York, 1 January 1935.

29. *Joseph Conrad*'s dramatic figurehead, carved by typographer Bruce Rogers in 1935.

30. Alan Villiers, strain showing on his face, 1936.

31. Crew aloft on *Joseph Conrad*.

32. Pamela and Sven Eriksson, in *Herzogin Cecilie*'s beautiful saloon, *circa* 1935.

33. Magnificent *Herzogin Cecilie* aground at Soar Mill Cove, with fatal Ham Stone in the background, 25 April 1936.

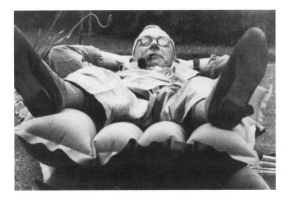

34. Villiers' close friend Fritz Egerton in 1937: a postcard Fritz made while preparing for his African expedition.

35. *L'Avenir*, renamed *Admiral Karpfanger*, and lost in 1938.

36. Erikson four-masted barque *Olivebank*, sunk by a mine in September 1939.

37. The large ocean-going boom *Bayan* (*Triumph of Righteousness*), on which Villiers sailed from Aden to Zanzibar and the Persian Gulf in 1939.

38. The bench at the stern of the Arabian boom *Bayan*, where Villiers lived for six months in 1939.

39. A relaxed Villiers at the end of his year with the Arabs, 1939 – the men are probably friends from the al-Hamad family. He wrote on the back, 'That's me with the cutlery.'

40. Nancie and Alan, 1940.

41. Last moments of *Penang*, 8 December 1940.

42. Alan Villiers, mid-1940s.

43. Examples of LCI(L) – Landing Craft Infantry (Large). Both of these vessels were in squadrons commanded by Villiers at different times.

mode of transport for you or anybody else I love', but Villiers still wanted to fly. On 9 September 1937 a seagull smashed into his cockpit, and the plane crashed from about 100 feet. He received only minor head and face wounds, but it was a mark of his fame that the accident was reported in newspapers all over the world. To the relief of his friends, he gave up flying soon afterwards.

Villiers and Rita visited the Egertons at this time, who became uneasy about the relationship. Earlier in the year, Fritz had written sympathetically, 'you're fed up to the teeth because you have no mate. You would like to carry her off and marry her just like that', but by November 1937 he was blunter:

> [Y]ou must not think of marrying. This affair was to be a trial ... let it stay at that ... You know, and she knows, she caught you on the rebound from Betty. I know further that she succeeded in – what shall we call it? – loosening you up ... but what about the years ahead? It won't do, boy. She is, as you say yourself, hardboiled and inclined to be expensive.

Kay wrote in the same letter, 'I can see a lot of good points about Rita – but I don't think she is the one for you.' In any case, Rita and Villiers were already drifting apart, and the relationship was over by the end of 1937.

The Making of a Sailor was published in January 1938. It was illustrated with photographs of *Joseph Conrad* and *Georg Stage*, and in it Villiers argued for the value of sail-training in developing character among boys. Unfortunately, March 1938 brought the appalling loss of another training ship full of cadets.

The four-master *L'Avenir* had been sold by Erikson for £10,000 in June 1937 to the Hamburg-America Line. She was renamed *Admiral Karpfanger*, given a modern radio transmitter and carefully refitted as a school ship. She carried a crew of twenty-seven, plus thirty-three boys aged fifteen to eighteen.

On her first voyage as *Admiral Karpfanger* in late 1937 she went out to Port Germain to load grain, and on 8 February 1938 she sailed for Europe. Her captain was ordered to report the ship's position at least once a fortnight and on 1 March reported that all was well, and the ship was at 51S and 172E. This was roughly 930 miles south-east of Wellington, New Zealand, with another 3,730 miles or so to go before the Horn.

Admiral Karpfanger acknowledged receipt of a radio message sent on 12 March. On the 15th she should have reported her position as usual, but did not. No concern was felt at first because generator trouble had been reported, but time passed. Steamers searched for the ship, then they searched for wreckage; both without success.

Villiers wrote about the disappearance in his 1956 book *Posted Missing*, attributing it to the icebergs reported at the time from other vessels, but modern work suggests that an unstable condition may have caused the ship's loss.[10] Wreckage identified to be from *Admiral Karpfanger* was eventually found on islands at the tip of Cape Horn.

—

The *Cruise of the Conrad* became a much-loved book – wherever Villiers went, he was asked about the ginger cat, Joseph, that fell over-board – 'I gave it away in Philadelphia', he would say deadpan, 'The last I heard it was living with a nervous breakdown. It doesn't like Philadelphia.' In December 1937, Hilgard Pannes, Karl Sperling and Alan Villiers were awarded medals from the American Humane Society for their rescue of Joseph.

By early 1938 he was considering crewing in a yacht race to Tahiti, and Fritz teased him that he was hoping 'to see a certain unsophisti-cated maiden in unsophisticated surroundings'. Villiers had recently written to Hinano, but when she eventually bothered to reply – many months later – as 'Helene', it was clear she had become rather more so-phisticated than he might have preferred, and they did not meet again.

Villiers was also working as the company photographer for Schedule Transport Flights of American Airlines. For a time he was close to Betty's friend Eleanor Hansen from Bay Ridge. Twenty-year-old Eleanor worked as Fritz's secretary over the summer at Great Bricett Hall, then went on to visit Germany and Norway, while Villiers stayed at Bricett.

Villiers began writing a novel in collaboration with Fritz, based on Scotsman Malcolm Robertson, who fought for Peruvian and Chilean independence in the early 1800s. He said in a letter to Fritz later that year, 'I find dialogue difficult and do it badly ... I'm afraid I haven't much patience with fiction. Not enough patience to do a good job, I mean ... it isn't the Robertson story that has worried me, for it is essentially a splendid story. It is my own inadequacy that bothers me.' The book was never finished.

He was almost thirty-five, and adrift. It was now nearly two years since the painful end of the *Joseph Conrad* venture, and he had found himself lost in the modern world. His square-rigger days were over and the family life he had hoped one day to enjoy was as far from his reach as ever. Then 'one day at Bricett this summer, when I was working indifferently on the novel about Robertson ... Fritz came in and said why don't you sail an Arab dhow to New York?'[11]

———

'Dhow' is a general term for the large, fast trading vessels of the Red Sea, Persian Gulf and Indian Ocean. They are lateen-rigged: that is, with great triangular sails set on long curved yards, dipping low at the bow and pointing high at the stern. By August 1938 Villiers had made plans to go to Aden in early October. He would learn all about Arab craft there, then buy a dhow. With the good winds in December he would sail it up the Red Sea, through the Mediterranean and then to New York via the Gulf Stream and West Indies.

Villiers thought he would need a crew of about seven. Young Hardcase wanted to sign on, and twenty-year-old Hilgard Pannes, now an archaeology student, offered to be second mate. 'Then Czecho-Slovakia blew up ... and there could be no thought of dhows or anything as peaceful, necessary and desirable whatever.' Villiers set his impressions of the fateful events of September 1938 against the serenity of Great Bricett Hall:

As Hitler's voice, hoarse and powerful and menacing, came through the loud-speaker of the radio in the still drawing-room with its quiet Buddhas and its fat books, its altar of the Colonel's brasses and its fragile Chinese prints, one looked outside at the trees and the clouds and the ploughed fields and thought By God, only man is vile.

There followed a grim week ... of Chamberlain to Godesberg, Chamberlain to Munich, Chamberlain to Bechtesgaden, Chamberlain in the House of Commons; zig heil zig heil zig heil!! from a million fleshy throats ready for hell;

> Hitler and Goering and Goebbels and von Ribbentrop; ... the fleet mobilised
> and the Admiralty crowded with young officers and old officers – aye, and my-
> self along at the Admiralty ... and ready enough too.[12]

Villiers wrote for information on joining the Royal Naval Volunteer
Reserve, but things went quiet again in early October after the signing
of the short-lived 'peace in our time' agreement, which permitted
Germany to take over one-third of Czechoslovakia. Now he no longer
knew if he could catch the monsoon winds in time, but he had already
signed a contract for a book to be called *Voyage in an Arab Dhow* and
had to go.

He sent £100 to Tasmania, his annual alimony 'for my former wife,
poor soul, who is so much better off there than she would be with me',
then he and Hilgard left London on 18 October. On the train to Dover
Villiers was irritated by the voices of a group of 'flutter-fingered
English pansies ... contrast these flavoured cissies with the noble
Fritz! I wonder sometimes what the Germans think of them. I would
pack them off to the Air Force station at Aden or in the Persian Gulf',
he grumbled, 'and let them do fatigue for six months.'

Villiers and Hilgard took a steamer across the Channel and the train
from Paris to Marseilles. There they boarded *Le Conte de Lisle*, which
reached Aden on 31 October.

———

The president of the Royal Geographical Society had given Villiers a
letter to Harold Ingrams, the British Resident Adviser to the Sultan of
Hadhramaut, which was a region of the Aden Protectorate near the
strategic entrance to the Red Sea. Ingrams introduced Villiers through
a chain of people to the Abdul-Latif al-Hamad family of Kuwait, who
had business interests in 'every port small and large on both sides of
the Red Sea and down the coast of Africa as far as Arab ships could
sail'.[13]

During Villiers' year in Arabia, from late 1938 to late 1939, the two
younger brothers of the family, Ali and Abdulla, would become particular friends. It was Ali Abdul-Latif who gave Villiers his chance to sail
on Arabian ships. He was in charge of the company's Aden office, 'a
tall, slightly built young man dressed in a well-made linen suit', who

was surprised at Villiers' interest, but offered him a voyage on their zarook *Sheikh Mansur*, to Gizan in the Red Sea.

Sheikh Mansur 'leaked as if she loved it ... she was dreadfully small,
horribly overloaded, and she stank frightfully'. Villiers and Hilgard
Pannes joined the zarook on 8 November and spent eight days aboard
as they sailed to Gizan, about one-quarter of the way along the eastern
coast of the Red Sea. Hilgard found the passage interesting at first,
then dull, and disliked the food.

For Villiers, it was an intense period of initiation into Arab culture.
The time of year was Ramadan, when 'the faithful may neither eat nor
drink from before dawn until after sunset. If you are with the faithful,
it is mannerly to behave as they do.' Most Westerners of the time
would probably have had little but contempt for the manners of 'the
faithful', yet Villiers' writings throughout this period, while sometimes privately exasperated, were usually thoughtful and tolerant: it
was the start of a happier time in his life.

> The sailors were all good friends. Their simplicity and their direct free hon-
> esty, their utter lack of hypocrisy and all shams, the calm unhurried philosophy
> of their simple lives, were very appealing. They fasted, prayed, washed in
> the sea water, did such work as was necessary, and cheerfully ate their frugal
> meals ...
>
> Such as their little ship was, they loved her. To them she had no imperfec-
> tions. In a little while, living so closely with that spirit on board, I began to be
> almost ashamed that I had first thought her so lowly.

After they arrived in Gizan, Villiers and Hilgard had to stay a week as
there was no transport out. They both became ill and bad-tempered
with dysentery. Hilgard was now twenty-one and had known Villiers
for five years, on *Parma* and *Joseph Conrad*. His early hero-worship
had become a little more critical as he grew up, and although they always remained friends, their world views had somewhat diverged.

'I asked Master Pannes what he thought about his beloved prole-
tariat as they banged his gear furiously about, but he gave no answer,'
Villiers had written during the passage to Aden. At Gizan one man was
particularly hard to deal with, wrote Hilgard, and 'Villiers, with his
usual anti-semitism, labelled him a Jew. I thought that was most unfair
and showed a great deal of juvenile rationalisation.'[14]

Though they could barely move for illness, Hilgard and Villiers managed to board a small steamer named *El Amin*, and went further up the Red Sea to Jiddah and Port Sudan. They finally got back to Aden at the beginning of December 1938.

———

It amused Ali Abdul-Latif that Villiers was up for further punishment. He arranged for him to meet Nejdi, the nakhoda (captain) of a deep-sea dhow that was just about to sail to Zanzibar. Ali bin Nasir al-Nejdi was 'the best young nakhoda from Kuwait ... a small, slight man, with a very strong face which the ravages of smallpox had not spoiled'.

Villiers had seen nakhodas around the port: 'lithe and straight ... handsome, too, in their own way: they have the expression and the eyes of men long accustomed to the sea. ... Two wander hand in hand, for in this queer burnt-out land the women are rigidly suppressed and much of the natural affection he might feel towards women in gentler circumstances the Arab man often gives to another man.'[15] He made no judgements of 'pansies' here.

The traditional large dhow was called a baggala, with a high, five-windowed carved stern, curved stem and horned figurehead. Baggalas were rare by Villiers' time – the most common dhows by then were sambuks, with high square windowless sterns and low curved stems; and booms, which were double-ended (pointed at bow and stern), with straight stemposts 'built out into a sort of planked bowsprit'.

Nejdi's vessel was a boom named *Bayan*, which Villiers translated as 'Triumph of Righteousness' but which actually implied 'clarity' or 'manifestation', as of a majestic vessel visible from afar.[16] Her capacity was around 150 tons: in the local metric there was stowage space for 2,500 packages of dates. *Bayan*'s voyage would take six months, longer than Hilgard could spare, so he stayed behind to travel in southern Arabia for two months instead.

Villiers joined the boom on the evening of 9 December 1938, and set off in the early hours of the following day. They sailed along the coast of southern Arabia towards Mukhalla, the main town of the Hadhramaut region. He was pleased to be allocated 'six feet of the navigator's bench' at the starboard stern. It was less than 3 feet wide, with a carpet to sleep on and a view of almost all that was happening on board.

He settled quickly in to the ship's routine of three simple meals a day and five sessions of prayers. 'None of them prayed hurriedly: they always spent a few moments first in silent meditation, in this discard of their worldly thoughts. I watched them with some envious interest, for I did not find my own worldly thoughts so easy to dismiss.'

Villiers gradually got to know the crew of about twenty-seven men, although he joked that at first he thought half were called Mohamed and the other half Abdulla, as he found it difficult to hear the subtle differences between names such Mohamed, Hamed, Ahmed, Hamoud or Mamoud. He learned a little Arabic and taught a little English, and treated the ulcerated legs of the sailors.

> They were mostly a silent lot and were always quiet except when there was work afoot, when always a continuous chanting would go on. Sometimes there would not be a voice raised on those decks for hours. It was a new kind of sea-faring to me, and I was most astonished at the effortless smoothness of the ship's routine, the harmony of the big crew, and the pleasant agreement with which they worked together.

———

After a few days at sea, Villiers became ill with a blinding eye infection and a painfully swollen knee. In *Sons of Sinbad* ('Sindbad' in the British edition), Villiers ascribed the knee problem to an accident: 'Something, I believe, carried away from aloft, and it must have struck me.' But he wrote in his journal for 12 December 1938, two days after leaving Aden and before he collapsed:

> By the way, this deck's hard and wet to sleep on with heavy dew every night. I have already a bad infection in the left eye, and last night my left knee pained so that I could not sleep. I do not know what is wrong with it, but it is hard to walk ... [sic] My left eye is discharging badly, as it has never done before.[17]

This entry suggests that his knee might have become infected by some tropical bug or inflamed through dampness, rather than struck by anything. It had been his left thigh that was hurt in the fall on *Lawhill* seventeen years before, so perhaps the old injury had flared up again. Whatever the cause, he was extremely ill.

An old man named Yusef Shirazi tended to him. On 18 December Villiers found he could open his eyes and sit up, and Yusef and others helped him up to the deck. 'My eyes were still misty and my head swam, but the air was heavenly. ... The littered decks looked clear and clean and beautiful, in the shadow of the sail, and the brown crew looked like gowned young gods.'

He found that even though his eyes had improved, 'I am still much bothered by my left knee. I cannot understand what is wrong with that, but it is still greatly swollen and very painful.' The crew treated him with kindness:

> It was embarrassing to be so lamed ... I lay on a carpet on my place on the tran-som bench, and night and morning as the sailors came aft with their greetings each of them would gently add something about the mercy of Allah on my ills. They were sincere and well-meant condolences, and I felt better for them.

They arrived at Mukhalla on the evening of 21 December. A young Indian doctor came out to the ship to see Villiers, 'who appears capable and prescribes vigorously'. He went to stay with Harold Ingrams, the British Resident. 'I am taken to the Residency where, my gear sent for and quietly brought, I am established. I did not care to go when I was so lame and generally helpless, but I was damned glad to be taken.'

He had a peaceful Christmas with the Ingrams family, and rejoined *Bayan* on the night of 28 December, to discover it seemingly full to the brim with passengers. 'I had to walk upon six Beduin, a Seyyid, and a lesser Hadhrami sheik to reach the place where I slept,' he noted wryly in his diary.

A day later they arrived at Shihr, further along the Hadhrami coast. The Na'ib of Shihr invited Villiers to stay at his palace, a large building overlooking the town. The doctor came to the palace to put hot belladonna plasters on Villiers' knee, and a few days later it felt 'considerably better'. When he returned to the ship he noticed a fleet of little boats leaving the shore, bringing a horde of Beduin out to join them. He wrote in *Sons of Sinbad*,

> I saw that they kept passing up queer long bundles swathed in black, one after the other, which were immediately passed with some deference into the blackness underneath the poop. ... Bints! Yusef said as he rushed by, bints. Women! ... Poor devils! I wondered how fifteen or twenty women were going to survive a voyage cooped up in that foul and loathsome den.

Bayan sailed from Shihr on 3 January 1939, then turned southwards for Africa; the first stop was Haifun, near the tip of Italian Somaliland. From his bench Villiers observed the crowded ship. He described the passengers vividly, critically, thoughtfully. The hard-working crew danced and chanted through their tasks as dedicated as any Cape Horners, and even the discordant musician Ismael impressed him with a fearless rescue of a child fallen overboard, just before they reached Haifun.

> I had visions of a succession of pleasant ports up African rivers and in roman-tic bays ... Now we had come to our first port and it was nothing but a semi-circle of dull sand, the beach covered with sheep dung and the entrails of fish, the centre of the scene a very modern saltworks.

They moored in the heat at Haifun for almost two weeks. Villiers would visit a beautiful Persian baggala, which reminded him of his childhood dreams:

> I could see again all the wondrous ships of my pre-maritime youth, when all the sea was wonderful and every ship an ark of grand adventure. How different had the reality been! Yet here on board this ancient Arab dhow lying at that stifling anchorage ... it was easy to dream again of the sea there never was, knowing so well the sea there is.

Only the crew were permitted off *Bayan*, enthusiastically smuggling ashore anything they could carry. Villiers was entirely on the side of the smugglers: 'the complex and unworkable system of hide-bound regulations by which we seek to control our world, and their world too, was a bad joke ... They are wandering seafarers doing their best to make a living, and they find that hard enough.'

He was touched, too, by the death of a girl, a fifteen-year-old on the way to be married in Zanzibar. 'Her face was uncovered, now that she was dead. I looked at it and saw, to my surprise, that she had been lovely ...'. Yusef told him that the girl was named Amira and he be-lieved she had been murdered.

A few days later *Bayan* left Haifun at last, heading towards Mogadishu. 'The constantly cramped quarters, the crowds, the wretched food, the exposure to the elements, the day-long burning sun and the night-long heavy dews, if they continued to be disadvantages, were far offset by the interest of being there …'. Villiers noted in his diary for 18 January: 'Eleven years ago today I sailed AB in the "Herzogin Cecilie" from Port Lincoln to write "Falmouth for Orders". But I never thought of Arab dhows … [sic]'.

———

Bayan arrived at Mogadishu on 22 January, to find that the Italian authorities would not permit the passengers to land. Eventually they relented, and more smuggling took place on a grand scale: 'I watched our Persian carpets go ashore, and did not see them come back.' They stayed at Mogadishu for a hot twelve days.

Finally the women stuck in the stifling great cabin had had enough. The hatchway banged open and they rushed out and complained bitterly to the shocked Nejdi. 'They were all Bedu and they wore the slitted veil of the desert; their flashing eyes gleamed dangerously, and now and then three or four of them broke into a supporting chorus of the stout one's harangue.'

The unprecedented mutiny worked: *Bayan* sailed at dawn. They arrived at Lamu in northern Kenya three days later. Villiers found it 'a wild and picturesque scene, and Lamu Roads was such a place as I had dreamed of when first I had heard of this African voyage. … The narrow streets of the old Arab town teem with life and the whole place is enchanting … The tall flat-roofed houses lean towards each other, with their upper windows open, welcoming.'

After a week they sailed for Mombasa, which Villiers liked as much as Lamu. There was a big party on *Bayan*: the men danced, 'shaking their bodies and looking tremendously pleased', and on the final beat, 'would jump high and turn round, yell, and go off laughing to sit down … there seemed to be no order in these proceedings and I soon gave up the attempt to look for any.'

Bayan left Mombasa and arrived at Zanzibar the following day. Villiers admired the ship's mooring: as she raced between the crowded dhows, sailors jumped in the water and carried lines which they tied to the other ships to slow *Bayan*. 'Nejdi, using these checks brilliantly, and very rapidly, eased his big vessel through the gap …'.

In Zanzibar unlicensed nakhodas had to be examined for competency. When asked what lights a dhow should carry, one young applicant replied 'none', as, among other drawbacks, they were a temptation to swordfish to ram the vessel. 'This seemed to me, even as it was passed on by the interpreter', mused Villiers, 'a fatally incorrect answer', but the applicant got through. 'If masters' licences could be handed out like that in Zanzibar I felt inclined to sit for one myself, for it was about time I had one. So I sat, and passed too, and was duly certified by the Sultan's government as fit to act as nakhoda of deep-sea dhows.'[18]

On 3 March *Bayan* sailed for the delta of the Rufiji River, 100 miles further south, to take on a cargo of mangrove poles. Villiers wrote, 'In this awful place, this gloomy, wretched delta of the swift Rufiji, we spent a month. It was the worst month of the voyage.' At Salale a British forestry officer directed dhows to remote areas upstream to load mangrove poles, where gangs of Swahili men were recruited to chop the trees. But for all of the officially checked logs that were loaded, the crew illicitly stowed as many again, deeper in the ship.

Villiers got to know the sailors better during this time. He put brief notes in his diary against their names – ages, years at sea, children, marriages and comments such as: 'a good chap [his most frequent judgement], indifferent helmsman, always smiling, addicted to hashish, looks very Persian, somewhat embarrassingly covetous, a bit whiney, very active aloft, ex-pearldiver, the only one I definitely dislike'. He wrote without censoriousness that Ismael the musician:

> shows me a photograph of a young boy with whom he is in 'love', in Mogadishu: these strange affairs are curiously common among many of the Arabs, but I gather they are unusual among the Kuweiti. I gather however that the serang goes in for boys. ... The Suri make no pretenses about their preferences, and the 'bebes' [prostitutes] don't get much business out of them in Zanzibar.

Villiers helped with what medical treatment he could, for fevers, wounds, boils, parasites and skin infections. It was an exhausting time, but after they had left Salale on 30 March, he was pleased he had gone. 'We were good friends before that Rufiji loading: after it we were shipmates.'

———

They returned to Zanzibar for two weeks, then sailed for the Persian Gulf in company with other dhows. After three and a half weeks they reached Muscat, which had no market for the mangrove poles, so they left for Kuwait. During another quiet period of slow sailing, Villiers discovered there was still much he had not even suspected about the crew. On 15 May 1939 he wrote in his diary:

> Do I mean to say I have been here five and a half months (pretty near) and have just now discovered how the ship is really worked? Well I do. There was no way, when all squat on the deck or atop the cargo with their cloaks wrapped round them, of knowing that half were on watch, and half were not ...
>
> Well, there <u>are</u> watches – clear-cut and definite. M'hamed the serang [bosun] has charge of one ... the serang's mate has charge of the other ... Ten sailors are on watch at night always, ready for an instant call ... The word Ki-yaw! brings them all up ... But for this manoeuver, which for months looked like a noisy scrum, is extremely well organised.[19]

Villiers wondered how he could not have noticed such a simple thing before: 'It is of course difficult to discover things here: my vast ignorance of Arabic is a handicap ... The Arab simply does not understand anyone being interested in ships as ships and sailors as sailors ...'. His relationship with Nejdi had been difficult at first. He admired his sailing but was dismissive of his navigation abilities, although other Arabs had substantial skill in that area.[20] Later he wrote in a draft of *Sons of Sinbad*:

> Nejdi too was a harsh, hard man: Nejdi was an arrogant, intolerant, licentious little scoundrel, I suppose, by most of our standards ... [yet] Nejdi was the soundest and most complete character of them all, and I learned before long to admire him greatly.[21]

They stopped at Bahrain on 23 May. It was very hot but Villiers liked talking with nakhodas, walking in the bazaar, and swimming in the Persian baths, 'with the scent from the flowers and the fruit blossoms blowing over it and the cooling breeze from the seas'. He met the master of one of only three surviving Kuwaiti baggalas – *Salam-te*, nicknamed 'Cat'. 'I still toyed with the idea of perhaps saving a baggala by a transatlantic voyage: the Cat looked ideal for the purpose.'

They easily sold the mangrove log cargo in Bahrain, as building was booming as a result of the developing oil fields. Villiers went to visit Awali, an oil facility, where he enjoyed a few days of air-conditioning and gave several lectures. *Bayan* sailed on 4 June and came into Kuwait harbour two nights later, the sailors singing and drumming all the way to the anchorage.

Over six months Villiers had sailed perhaps 5,000 miles to Africa and back on the deep-sea dhow *Bayan*, on a trading voyage unchanged for centuries. He was the first European to do so; and now at the end of the 1930s, with the world about to change forever, he was the only one who ever would.

10

AIRCRAFTWOMAN
WILLS

Villiers spent from June to October 1939 in Kuwait, one-third of his total time in Arabia. His portrayals of the people of the desert port, just before oil irrevocably changed their world, are as significant as his memories of sailing on their ships. *Sons of Sinbad* is dense with detail and perhaps less easily accessible than his square-rigger books, yet its portraits of men that Villiers privately found alien, exasperating and occasionally unlikeable, are generous. He was a great admirer of Lawrence of Arabia, who had come so close to sailing on *Joseph Conrad*, which may have predisposed him towards Arabic culture.

He went to stay with the Abdul-Latif al-Hamad family at Dimner, outside Kuwait, in a walled house by the beach of Kuwait Bay. 'Here we lived the life of the well-to-do Arab, and lunched on succulent fish and dined on sheep day after day. We bathed in the dawns and the sunsets, and slept through the hot noon hours.' Villiers still hoped to sail a baggala across the Atlantic, and Ali and Abdulla Abdul-Latif were also interested in the idea. They discussed a partnership to buy the baggala *Cat*, with Nejdi as nakhoda.

On 16 June he went with Ali and Abdulla by car to Basra in Iraq, a trip of about four hours. Ali was going to Iraq to marry a second wife. Basra was less religiously strict than Kuwait, and Villiers noted with amusement: 'a beer with Ali, who says his brothers must not know'; and the following day: 'a beer with Abdulla, who says his brothers must not know'.

When they drove back to Kuwait Villiers had his first chance to board the *Cat*: she stank of fish oil, which he loathed. Nejdi had backed out of the plan, and Villiers wrote, 'I begin to wonder about the baggala idea which is so full of catches ... I could otherwise be back in New York and London next spring, and be down in the summer to Australia for the "Coral Seas" – with the baggala there is no NY before next May, if then.' On 30 June: 'Decide to give up, at any rate for now, the idea of sailing a baggala to New York.'

———

Villiers set a picture of the good life against the terrible poverty of those, like Yusef Shirazi, who barely survived. Yusef had tended to Villiers when he was so ill on *Bayan*, and at the time Villiers thought he was an elderly man, calling him 'the greyhaired, tired old reprobate': later he was appalled to find out he was only forty-five, less than a decade older than Villiers himself.

The Kuwaiti pearling industry had been in a slump for some years owing to the Japanese factory-ships fishing for pearlshell in Australian waters, not, as Villiers thought, from the success of Japanese cultured pearls. (He seems to have been under the fairly common misapprehension that the industry was based on pearls, rather than oyster shell, which even in 1939 was worth a lucrative £90 per ton.[1]) Yusef was responsible for the debts of a dead brother, and had to go diving to pay them off: it seemed 'iniquitous' to Villiers. He wanted to see more of the lives of the divers, so went with a pearl-buyer on a brief voyage from 2 to 12 August 1939.

The vessels were overcrowded and the divers laboured incessantly, chilled by the constant immersion with no protective suit or air – ten dives on, ten off, each of them up to ninety seconds underwater, for 120 dives a day, ten days at a time. He met his friend Yusef and was horrified: 'His face was strained and gaunt ... his feet and hands were lacerated ... his stomach was hollow ... his legs were thin, worn almost to the bone ... judged by any standard I know, compared with any form of maritime hardship I have experienced, or seen, or read about, pearling in the Persian Gulf can be terrible indeed.'

Back in Kuwait, the waterfront, barely changed over centuries, fascinated Villiers: 'Ships were being built, paid, caulked, repaired, launched, floated off, rigged, danced to, and sung about.'

He walked and photographed almost every day. He bought pearls, carpets and coffee pots, daggers, incense burners, sandals, head cloths, a sword, a carved wooden chest, silver for Kay, robes for Fritz and a sapphire for Eleanor Hansen, who was handling his business affairs while he was away.

Now he had decided against buying the baggala, he began to plan his future. It was at this stage he came up with the idea of a study of Eastern sailing craft over some years, rather than at the start of the Arabian venture, as he says in *Sons of Sinbad*. He had hopes of returning to the Coral Sea in 1940 and Arabia in 1941.

On 23 August he spent another quiet day 'round the waterfront with camera and notebook … completing my detailed survey and count of ships, whereof there are 170 now lying in the port'. On the same day in Moscow the Russo–German Pact was signed. It allowed the Nazis to attack Poland without fear of Soviet reprisal; and the world began mobilising for war.

———

Days of tension and rumour passed. On 1 September 1939 Germany invaded Poland. On 3 September Britain, France, Canada, Australia and New Zealand declared war on Germany. Villiers had an idea for an intelligence role involving native vessels, which he submitted to the Admiralty. A frustrating month followed. He waited. He gave away belongings. He wrote essays on the economics of Arab sailing and half a dozen articles, and thought about his book on dhows. On 22 September he decided, 'I shall call the book (when I can write it) "The Sons of Sinbad".' The following day was his birthday: 'Gosh, 36! It doesn't seem long ago since that appeared a hoary old age … [sic]'.

Finally he heard from the Admiralty. There was 'no immediate prospect of using the idea, and so I can go home'. He packed and said his farewells in a hurry, 'and in the evening walk for a last time round the waterfront in the moonlight looking at the graceful hulls of the pearlers'.

He took a steamer from Basra on 14 October to Aden. 'I watch belenes, canoes, baggalas, booms, and get to thinking of the related forms of all these ships, and how all sailing might very well have started from this river.' But he noted dryly in the margin, 'Ramadhan starts: thank God I've left.'

At Aden, Villiers collected the gear he had left there before he shipped on *Bayan*, and on 29 October boarded the Italian liner *Leonardo da Vinci*, bound for Genoa. They reached there on 10 November, where Villiers boarded the *Conte de Savoia* for New York. He planned to store his films, documents and gear in America, write a book as quickly as possible, then return to Britain to do what he could for the war effort.

His year away in Arabia had left him ignorant of the reality of life under Nazism. He noticed that the third-class section of *Conte de Savoia* carried many Jews and political dissidents from Germany and Austria. They told him they were 'worried that the Allied patrol will take them off', as had happened on other ships. Yet even when he heard that a number of passengers had been taken away in the middle of the night at Gibraltar, it did not occur to him to wonder what lay ahead of them, or what had already descended upon so many that they would flee from their homes to an unknown world.

He wrote, without the thoughtfulness he had shown to the Arabs, 'None of the Jews, as I have noticed before, look particularly like victims of persecution. They are mainly fat youths, loud-mouths, obnoxious persons who complain about being shepherded into labour battalions. What, I should work! And so they are coming to America.'

Until the liberation of the concentration camps in 1945, when the trajectory from forced labour to industrial genocide became as clear to the world as it was to its victims, like so many others Villiers would barely comprehend the wellsprings of the war that would soon engulf more than six years of his life.

———

While Villiers was in Arabia, the 1939 grain fleet sailed for the final time. Erikson's *Moshulu* won, with a passage amusingly immortalised by Eric Newby in *The Last Grain Race*.[2] Thirteen barques arrived in Britain just as war was breaking out. Although Finland was neutral her vessels were still affected: lack of crew left *Archibald Russell* and *Pamir* stranded, while *Pommern*, *Viking*, *Passat* and *Winterhude* were taken home to Mariehamn to be laid up.

Just before war was declared, *Olivebank* also left for Mariehamn. The little girl stowaway Nancie Lawson, now nine, just missed out on being a guest of Captain Carl Granith on the passage as she was late getting to the dock. On 8 September 1939, when roughly halfway between England and Denmark, the lookout on *Olivebank* sighted a mine ahead. The crew turned the ship but there were mines all around, and suddenly there was a great explosion. *Olivebank* listed to port and began to sink: there was not even time to launch a boat. Of the twenty-one sailors on board, fourteen died, including Captain Granith. Amazingly, *Olivebank* sank upright, with the tip of her long foremast just out of the water. The seven surviving crewmen clung to it for forty-eight long hours until a Danish fishing cutter rescued them.[3]

Neutrality could not protect *Olivebank*; nor would it protect Finland. The Nazis and Soviets had signed a secret pact in August 1939, and non-aligned Finland was attacked by the USSR on 30 November. The confident Soviets invaded with marching bands and singing soldiers, but the Finns, with only two-fifths of the enemy forces, fought them off in the extraordinary 'Winter War'.

The Finns understood the snow. They wore white, attacked on skis, destroyed field kitchens, and sniped at the starving invaders when they huddled miserably around campfires. The USSR lost five times as many men as the Finns, and desperately offered an armistice. The Finns had little ammunition left and the Swedes and Germans pressured them to sign. They did so on 12 March 1940, ceding 10 per cent of their territory to the Soviet Union; but for the time being, 'gallant little Finland' and her ships remained independent.

———

The *Conte de Savoia* docked at New York on 23 November 1939. Villiers went to stay with Eleanor Hansen and her family in Bay Ridge and worked on *Sons of Sinbad*. In January 1940 he left his files, voyage logs and journals with the Hansens, gave Betty Jacobsen Reed a much-loved John Allcot painting of *Joseph Conrad*, then took a liner to England, arriving in February 1940.

He stayed with Fritz and Kay at Bricett. He was still working on *Sons of Sinbad* and found it hard going – 'somehow there always seems one reason or another why one cannot do one's best work. I am beginning to suspect the truth – that one is simply incapable of it,' he wrote in discouragement to his brother Noel on 24 February.

Joining the Royal Naval Volunteer Reserve (RNVR) took longer than Villiers had expected. He finished his book, and on 10 April was interviewed on the radio. Finally, on 25 April the Admiralty asked him to attend a Selection Board, and on 30 May he was sent to HMS *Hornet*, the Royal Navy Torpedo School at Portsmouth. Between those two events the greatest turning point of his life occurred: he had dinner with Nancie Wills.

Nancie was born on 29 July 1915 in Tasmania but grew up in the Melbourne suburb of Camberwell. She led an outdoor life – canoeing, horse-riding and swimming. In January 1936 her uncle took Nancie and her cousin to hear Alan Villiers lecture when *Joseph Conrad* was in Melbourne.[4] Nancie was then twenty years old, dark-haired and slim, with beautiful cheekbones and intense brown eyes. She enjoyed Villiers' lecture greatly, and found a picture in a magazine – the one of him in a studio mountainscape looking sensitive and determined – and stuck it up on her bedroom wall. She met him very briefly as she hoped to become a passenger on *Joseph Conrad* for the leg to New Zealand, but in the end did not go.

In 1937 she made plans with her good friend Phyllis Downe (later Warren) to travel to Britain and Europe, at the time an adventurous prospect for two young Australian women. They studied German and French, and worked as secretaries to get the money to go to London on the *Orion* in March 1939. Coincidentally, their ship passed through Arabian waters at the same time as Villiers was sailing on *Bayan*.

Phyll wrote *Wind on the Heath* about her time with Nancie in Britain.[5] Phyll and Nancie arrived at London in May 1939 for what would become the famous summer – the glorious summer – before the war began: and from the day they landed they loved it all. They took long cycling tours into the country almost every weekend, staying at hostels, revelling in landscapes, old churches, near-empty roads and excellent weather. The happy young women seemed to evoke friendliness from everyone they met.

They rented a comfortable bedsitter in Notting Hill Gate, with gardens, clean linen and breakfast served by a maid, for only 25 shillings a week. London itself was a revelation, with opera, ballet and plays that they could never have seen in Australia. On the ship they had met eighty-year-old Axel Munthe, the distinguished Swedish author of *The Story of San Michele*, and one of their friends became his assistant. He warned them not to go to Germany, so they stayed in Britain, Phyll working as a secretary at Australia House, and Nancie with Munthe's publisher, John Murray.

In September 1939 the war began. Poland was invaded and the spoils divided between Germany and the Soviet Union. In Britain, children were evacuated from London, gas masks were distributed and air-raid sirens heard for the first time. But they were false alarms; nothing about the war seemed real. Christmas 1939 came like a fairy-tale, with frost and holly and carols and log fires, and then to top it all off it began to snow and snow.

The winter became the coldest in fifty years but still Nancie and Phyll were happy. They saw John Gielgud, Sybil Thorndike and Michael Redgrave on the stage. They joined the Linguists' Club, and did canteen work at the Australian Women's Voluntary Service. In March 1940 they spent Easter in a beautiful part of Wales, and as spring arrived they began cycling and sightseeing again.

On 9 April 1940 the Nazis invaded Denmark and Norway; and on 10 April Nancie listened to the BBC on the radio – 'something like *In Town Tonight*', she recalls. She heard Alan Villiers being interviewed, and on impulse decided to renew their acquaintance. She wrote him a note, he wrote back, and they arranged to meet after work outside John Murray on 7 May. She joked that she thought he was going to take her to a coffee shop, but instead he took her to a posh restaurant – the sort of place he usually loathed – for the first and only time in their lives.

Nancie was twenty-four, Alan thirty-six. They fell in love.

On 10 May the Germans invaded France, Belgium, Luxembourg and the Netherlands. Three weeks later Temporary Lieutenant Villiers RNVR joined HMS *Hornet* at Portsmouth, for several weeks of training. The irony must have stung: to meet the love of his life at last, at such a time of separations. Nancie and Alan became officially engaged on 29 July, Nancie's twenty-fifth birthday, less than four months after her fateful note; then she joined the Women's Auxiliary Air Force (WAAF). She would have preferred the Women's Royal Naval Service

(WRENS) but they had no vacancies, so she became Aircraftwoman Wills instead.

On 26 May 1940, the Germans cornered 225,000 British soldiers and 121,000 French and Belgian troops near Dunkirk. Their successful rescue with boats of all varieties took place over ten extraordinary days. Until that point, small fast craft to defend coastal regions had not been high on the priorities of the Admiralty, but after Dunkirk the Royal Navy embarked on a crash programme to develop 'little ships' for the Coastal Forces. Coastal Forces vessels laid and swept minefields, escorted convoys and rescued downed aircrews. They fought German boats, raided occupied ports, picked up people rescued by the Resistance, and landed commandos and special agents in Europe.

In June 1940 Villiers was posted to a Coastal Forces ship, *Aberdonian*, based at Chatham, near the southern Thames estuary. *Aberdonian* was 1,648 tons and had been built in 1909. She had served as a hospital ship in the First World War, then was converted at around the time Villiers joined her. But she was hardly what he'd expected:

> The ludicrous Aberdonian was an alleged advanced striking base for MTB's [Motor Torpedo Boats], which, while I was under the galling misfortune of serving in her, never saw any operational MTB's, advanced nowhere save to Fort William, and struck nothing but quays, buoys, boats, and dock-walls.[6]

In September 1940 Villiers managed to spend two months on *Deodar*, a minesweeping and anti-submarine trawler. *Deodar* was escorting convoys around 'Hell's Corner', the Channel from the Thames estuary to Portsmouth. Villiers wrote,

> I greatly enjoyed the Deodar's small part in the war … It was a good life, of real use: though while I was there we were not really attacked enough for my liking … We were shelled very heartily for some hours from the German-occupied French coast each time we passed Dover: we swept up enemy mines; we had some spasmodic air attacks; we heard E-boats, but saw none. This was Sept.–October 1940, while the Battle of Britain was at its height, and we saw a lot of that.

Coastal Forces ran more than thirty establishments around Britain, one of which was Fort William, near the famous peak of Ben Nevis in

Scotland. It was as far from the open sea as a maritime base might be, and it was to Fort William that *Aberdonian* was sent when Villiers rejoined her.

> She became a forgotten ship in Loch Linnhe, and did nothing. She arrived there in November 1940, remained a year, and – beyond maddening her officers, losing some anchors, sending off various members of the fed-up ship's company to cells (they had my sympathy), and consuming vast quantities of liquor and the King's stores – did exactly nothing.
>
> This was very, very far from my ideas of my own usefulness in the war, and it was galling beyond words to be unable, despite all efforts, to get out of her. … I thought up schemes for the confusion of merchant-raiders (with sail) and of Focke-Wulf Kuriers (with an A.A. tramp-decoy) and sent them off to their Lordships who were not much impressed …

Moshulu had had the misfortune to arrive in Norway on 9 April 1940 – the day before the Nazis invaded – so was duly confiscated and used as accommodation. *Pamir* and *Lawhill* began carrying cargo between South Africa, New Zealand and Australia, and *Killoran*, the last three-master ever to be launched from a British shipyard, sailed from Buenos Aires in June 1940 with maize and sugar for the Canary Islands. Unfortunately, on her way to Las Palmas in full sail, she came to the attention of the German merchant raider *Widder*, an armed, disguised cargo vessel.

On 10 August 1940 *Widder* fired two shots across *Killoran*'s bows, and ordered her to heave-to. *Killoran* was flying a neutral flag and sailing between two neutral countries, but the captain saw in the ship's papers that her agents, as always, were the British company Clarkson's. He decided that the cargo was destined for the enemy, and the ship was legitimate prey. *Killoran*'s crew were taken aboard *Widder*, then time-bombs placed in her bow, stern and sides. They exploded at 15.36 hours, and the barque sank within three minutes. Her fragments lie at 33.06'N, 24.19'W, in the darkness of three miles down. Her master and crew were imprisoned on *Widder* for six weeks, interned in France for months, and then allowed to return to Finland.

The destruction of *Killoran*, and a false rumour that Felix von Luckner was again commanding a raider, probably inspired Villiers' scheme 'for the confusion of merchant-raiders (with sail)'. He suggested on 5 January 1941, with all the desperation of a landlocked seaman, that the four-masted barque *Peking* be used as a decoy, with an experienced crew, guns and 'twenty keen boys'.

> Graf von Luckner was before the war a personal friend; I well know his almost fanatic enthusiasm for sailing vessels: I know the extent of his knowledge of them: and I know, too, that he could not resist the temptation, sighting one, to draw close to investigate. All I propose is that this weakness, which he shares in common with a good many other sail-trained German officers, should be exploited to bring destruction to his, and their, commands.[7]

Peking was a Laiesz nitrate barque that had been sold to the Shaftesbury Homes in 1932 as a stationary training vessel. When war began she had been requisitioned by the Navy, rigged down and laid up at Chatham Dockyard, where Villiers had seen her. His plan was almost plausible – cold deception in war was as useful a weapon as any other – but he revealed a little too much personal warmth in proposing it:

> The *PEKING* is a powerfully built steel ship, especially strengthened to beat to windward round Cape Horn and to carry heavy nitrate cargoes back that way: she is a magnificent vessel under sail, and could easily be given auxiliary power if that were considered necessary. … As for the crew, I could find them. For years we sailed her half-sister, *PARMA*, from Mariehamn in the Aaland Islands, with a crew of ten experienced men, and twelve boys.

Boys? Magnificent under sail? Auxiliary power *optional*? This was 1941, not 1914, harumphed their Lordships. They thanked Temporary Lieutenant Villiers for his most interesting suggestion and left him to serve his country in the store ship *Aberdonian* on a distant Scottish loch.

———

Aircraftwoman Wills started learning Morse and codes in West London. The desperate Battle of Britain began in August 1940, with massive German air raids on civilian targets night after terrible night. The school where Nancie was being taught was bombed, and the trainees had to go to live in an old workhouse.

On 24 December 1940, Nancie and Alan were quietly married at Fort William. Soon afterwards Nancie was selected to do a cipher course at Oxford. It was secret work and she was promoted: a lingering memory of her training as an officer was being taught the correct way to pass the port after dinner. Pilot Officer Nancie Villiers was assigned in May 1941 to Leighton Buzzard, north of London, and it must have been a relief to be out of the city. German air raids continued to cause heavy casualties, but at least the Royal Air Force was bombing Germany in return. It was at sea that the situation was far more unequal.

Over the year of 1940, German U-boat submarines sank 440 British merchant ships, more than eight a week. They communicated via cryptographic codes generated by a machine named Enigma. At Leighton Buzzard, Nancie was working on Type-X cipher machines, similar to Enigma devices, but said, 'I don't recall decoding any very interesting messages!'[8]

One U-boat incident would come to fascinate Villiers. In 1940, Erikson's barque *Penang* was the only square-rigger still taking grain to Europe. The previous year her cargo had earned about £3,900, but in 1940 the rate had soared to potentially £20,000: well worth the risk – to her owner at least. *Penang* loaded grain in South Australia and sailed on 3 July 1940 for Queenstown, Eire. She never arrived. In March 1941 she was posted missing by Lloyds, assumed to have been lost while rounding the Horn, but the truth was not uncovered until after the war.

In late November 1940, a pack of German submarines had taken up position off the Donegal coast. Among them was U-140, commanded by Hans-Peter Hinsch, and on 8 December he sighted *Penang*. Oddly, he first thought the barque was the four-master *Lawhill*, and Villiers believed that the mistake was because their identifying signal codes were similar. U-140 stalked the old sailing ship for two-and-a-half hours, before firing a single torpedo which exploded near *Penang*'s stern. She capsized and sank almost immediately. Every person on board drowned, including her female sailmaker Winifred Lloyd.[9]

The oddest aspect of *Penang*'s sinking was her location, off northeast Ireland at 55°25'N, 10°15'W – nowhere near any conceivable approach to her destination in the south of Eire. Even poor navigation or extreme weather could not account for such a discrepancy. One possibility is that British warships would often stop neutral vessels and send them for inspection at the 'contraband control' ports – Weymouth, Ramsgate or Kirkwall in the Orkney Islands. Perhaps *Penang* had been stopped and diverted north to Kirkwall, only to sail directly into the path of U-140.

A less fatal encounter took place in late 1944, when the four-master *Pamir*, then a New Zealand vessel, was stopped by the gigantic Japanese submarine I-12. *Pamir*'s crew rushed to abandon ship, but to their amazement the submarine's captain, Kaneo Kudo, allowed *Pamir* to go on her way untouched. Kudo had been a cadet on a Japanese sailing ship, and it seems that despite his orders to sink Allied vessels, he deliberately chose not to attack the square-rigger.[10]

U-140's commander Hans-Peter Hinsch had no such love of sail, and apparently never quite understood how people felt about his destruction of *Penang*. When Villiers attended the Cape Horn Congress in Mariehamn in 1976, he was told that Hinsch had also planned to attend, until someone made it clear to him that he'd probably be lynched if he turned up.

———

A worry for Villiers at this time was the fate of his brother Frank. In December 1941 he was quartermaster on a British refrigeration ship, *Duquesa*, carrying 14.5 million eggs and 3,000 tons of frozen beef from Argentina to Britain, via Freetown in Africa. *Duquesa* disappeared on the way to Freetown in late December 1940 in an area known for raider activity: Frank's family could only wait, hoping for a miracle.

Villiers lived aboard *Aberdonian* for the early part of 1941. He became interested in the recognition of aircraft for gun crews and started teaching himself and others the basics. Although this was something the Navy understood reasonably well, Coastal Forces was a body of mainly new volunteers. Every month or two, Alan managed to get to London to see Nancie, or she came up to Fort William. Travelling between the south and Scotland was tedious – trains from London to Edinburgh, then Glasgow, then Oban; and more trains, buses and a ferry to reach Fort William. Often the journey took two days from end to end.

The training base at Fort William was named HMS *St Christopher*, and was actually located in various buildings around the town. At the start of April 1941 Villiers was 'poached' to teach aircraft recognition at *St Christopher* by the Commanding Officer, Commander A.E.P. Welman DSO DSC RN (Retd): 'an alert and forceful man ... a fighter, and a not over-scrupulous one either'.

> This was depressing almost to the point of mutiny, for to change even a loch-bound wreck for a blasted hotel ashore was from the frying-pan into the fire with a vengeance. ... However, it soon became apparent that at any rate this was useful work.

It took some time for Villiers and Commander Welman to overcome conservative opinion in Coastal Forces that 'would <u>not</u> accept the view that Recognition should be taught, as part of gunnery, or that we could teach it'. But by the end of 1941 *St Christopher* had become an accredited Aircraft Recognition School, along with Devonport, 'good Chatham' – who had supported Villiers and Welman – and Portsmouth, who had not. (HMS *Excellent* was 'so ill-named', Villiers fumed.)

Welman's report on Villiers at the end of 1941 stated that his Intellectual Ability and Personal Qualities were 'exceptional':

> A first class seaman who has shown great keenness in any work entrusted to him. ... His influence with the Ship's Company has been most valuable to me as C.O. [Commanding Officer] and he has used his (well-known) talents as a lecturer to the advantage of all concerned, both on maritime subjects and aircraft recognition; the latter subject in particular he has tackled with great efficiency and unselfish application ... I can recommend him [for command at sea] with every confidence.[11]

Welman understood Villiers' frustration ashore. In July 1941 he managed to get him seconded to HMS *Furious* for a mission against a Nazi convoy, supposedly gathering in the ports of Kirkenes (Norway) and Petsamo (Finland) to attack Russian vessels. The Nazis and the Russians had recently become bitter enemies: relations between Hitler and Stalin, once so amicable as they'd gobbled up raw chunks of Europe together, had soured when the Germans suddenly turned on the Soviet Union on 22 June 1941.

After the experience of the Winter War, the Finns loathed the Soviets so much they threw in their lot with Germany in the

'Continuation War' against the USSR, allowing the Germans access to their ports. Gallant little Finland was no longer neutral, so in mid-1941 Erikson's ships became legitimate prizes to the Allies.

But by this time *Olivebank*, *Killoran* and *Penang* had been destroyed, *Moshulu* was in German hands, and *Winterhude*, *Viking*, *Passat* and *Pommern* were laid up at Mariehamn. Only three square-riggers were vulnerable to confiscation: and so *Archibald Russell* was taken over by the British Ministry of Food for a store ship, *Lawhill* was seized by the South Africans, and *Pamir* was arrested in New Zealand and put into trade by the Union Steamship Company.

But sailing ships were probably far from Villiers' mind when he joined HMS *Furious* at the Clyde on 17 July 1941 for Operation E.F., planned by Winston Churchill himself to show support for the USSR. The aircraft carriers *Furious* and *Victorious* were laden with Fleet Air Arm Hurricanes, Fulmars, Swordfish and Albacores.

They sailed for Iceland on 21 July. After five planes crash-landed on deck it became clear that many of the Fleet Air Arm pilots were 'woefully inexperienced'. A terrible accident also occurred: 'We arrived at SEYDISFJORD July 26,' wrote Villiers, 'having blown the bows off ACHATES in one of our own mine-fields on the way, and killed some two-score men.'

The flotilla left Iceland and was in position on 30 July, but a protective fog dispersed and a reconnaissance plane spotted them. The British knew the advantage of surprise was lost but the mission proceeded as planned. Twenty-four aircraft flew from *Furious* to Petsamo, but the pilots were surprised to find it almost empty of vessels. For want of better targets they attacked a couple of wooden jetties and a shipyard. They paid a harsh price, however, losing three aircraft and seven men.

Disastrous as Petsamo was, it was nothing compared to Kirkenes. HMS *Victorious* sent in twenty-nine aircraft, of which thirteen were shot down by the forewarned Luftwaffe. Villiers was appalled by the waste of lives on a mission that appeared to have been the essence of poor planning. He jotted down his impressions:

> ... the grim looks of the flight personnel as they went to their A/C for the raid in the bright Arctic sun ... the somewhat bumptious fighter boys, with the arrogance of youth and their cuff-sewn wings ... crashes on deck, crashes on the

fore-guns, crashes in the sea ... the heavy clump of landing A/C, sounding through the ship: the asbestos-clad fireman standing by for crashes: the hatred of the ship's company for all aeroplanes and most pilots.

He was scathing about relations between the pilots and the Royal Navy:

> [T]he Surgeon-Cdr, who asks me for ideas on the increase of neurosis in FAA pilots and ways to combat it, and says in the next breath that the ship's officers do not bother to get to know the air crews because of possible anguish at their frequent early deaths ... – no wonder there is neurosis! For they are mostly V.R. subbies [Volunteer Reserve Sub-Lieutenants], very new, very raw, and very scorned by their senior RN officers ... who have survived nothing but an over-dose of gin.

Villiers attended all the debriefings, and typed out four detailed pages on improving aircraft recognition with training routines, posters, silhouette charts, spotter's magazines and free recognition playing cards. He talked about motivating men and stimulating confidence in their own skills. His understanding of learning techniques was far ahead of his time, with the result that these sensible proposals were seen as both too radical and too hard to implement.

Villiers decided to go back to *St Christopher*. It was still preferable to battleships, with 'the drill, the routine, the crowded wardroom, the spirit (to me at any rate) of constant repression – these would get me down, and I don't think I could ever become a satisfactory "cog" officer no matter how hard I might try.'

———

Good news came from the Red Cross – Frank Villiers was alive, a prisoner-of-war. The pocket battleship *Admiral Scheer*, which had begun a ferocious career by sinking seven vessels in a single day, had captured Frank's ship *Duquesa* on her way to Freetown, on 18 December 1940. Her men were taken aboard *Admiral Scheer* as prisoners and *Duquesa* herself became notorious as 'The Floating Delicatessen', keeping the merchant raiders well supplied with delicacies for two months. The Germans did everything possible to keep her refrigeration plant working, including feeding *Duquesa*'s wooden bridge, masts and decks into the furnaces when her coal ran out.

Finally on 18 February 1941, after removing a final 360,000 precious eggs, they sank *Duquesa* with time bombs. By then, Frank and over 500 prisoners had been loaded on to another ship and taken to the prison camp Marlag und Milag Nord, near Bremen, where they stayed for the rest of the war. The camp was for Naval and Merchant Marine POWs only, and the men were treated reasonably well. Alan received postcards from Frank, and sent him numerous letters and parcels over the following three years.

In September 1941 Villiers received a painful shock. The head of Coastal Forces, Rear-Admiral Piers Kekewich, had watched him working earlier in the year, and wrote to Commander Welman, 'The very greatest credit is due to Lieutenant Villiers who is most certainly an incomparable lecturer.' Despite the honeyed words, Kekewich was against teaching aircraft recognition, and in September wrote again to Welman, warning him, Villiers reported furiously:

> that I was an 'adventurer', bent upon using Coastal Forces as a stepping stone to the position I thought I was entitled! ...
>
> This was dirty calumny, if ever there were any: and perhaps a reflection of the Admiral's own level of mind. God, all I wanted ever was to get back to Deodar, but being in the hated St Christopher I would do my best ...
>
> I never forgave Kekewich for that dirty letter, and when later he wrote congratulating me for some passing success at Whale Island [lecturing at Portsmouth], I did not answer him.

Diplomacy might have been the wiser course, rather than a snub to the Rear-Admiral Coastal Forces, who had handwritten 'My Dear Villiers' a rather pleasant letter. It would be a long time before he got away from *St Christopher*.

———

The rest of 1941 passed with travelling to various bases to lecture on aircraft recognition, and catching a few days here and there with Nancie, and occasionally Fritz and Kay. 'I requested a posting nearer Alan in Scotland,' said Nancie. 'The RAF's geography wasn't very good and I was sent up to Stranraer for a while – nowhere near Fort William! Eventually I got to Oban, although even from there it was a quite a trek.'

Villiers' exhausting teaching and travelling schedule continued. In June 1942 he requested a transfer to operational duties, pointing out that he had been teaching aircraft recognition thirty hours a week, day and night for a year, and was 'stale almost to the danger-point'. After letting him stew for another two months, Rear-Admiral Kekewich finally allowed Villiers to be posted for a short period to HMS *Forward II*, at Newhaven, near Brighton. He arrived on 19 August 1942, just missing out on the Dieppe Raid, which disappointed him.

Villiers was appointed temporary Commanding Officer of Rescue Motor Launch 513, whose captain, J. Francis Jones, was in hospital after being badly wounded at Dieppe: Jones and Villiers became friends. Villiers commanded RML 513 as it searched for downed aircraft and patrolled for E-boats. He enjoyed it very much, but on 9 October his posting was over and he had to return to *St Christopher*.

Nancie met him there with the news that she was pregnant. She was required to resign from the WAAF, but at least they could now enjoy life together in Fort William. To top the year off, on 31 November Villiers was promoted to the rank of Temporary Acting Lieutenant-Commander ('Temporary Acting' meant for the duration of the war only).

———

In January 1943 the news at Fort William was depressing: Villiers and Welman had been trying to set up a central school for aircraft recognition, but competing elements in Coastal Forces thought there should be two – one for themselves and one, a long way away, for Villiers; others preferred no school at all, believing that recognition was 'too hard' for most seamen.

In February 1943 Welman was posted to the Mediterranean; and in late March, after two years of heartfelt effort, Villiers was told by his new Commanding Officer that recognition would no longer be taught – at the same time as his latest class received a superb pass rate. He noted bitterly on April Fool's Day, 'Appointed to *St Christopher* 1941 – an appropriate date'.

It seems obvious now that someone like Villiers, with his unusual background, independent mind and progressive teaching skills would never fit easily into a traditional navy. But the war brought many innovations and one of them was Combined Operations, headed by Lord Louis Mountbatten. It carried out commando raids and was responsible for planning for the Allied invasion of Europe, which would need thousands of amphibious landing craft to carry men, weapons and supplies to the occupied countries.

Villiers was desperate to leave *St Christopher* and on 7 April 1943 he finally got his wish. He was posted to HMS *Dinosaur* at Troon, Ayrshire, the Combined Operations base for training officers and gunners for large landing craft.

On 15 April, Alan took Nancie to a nursing home in Glasgow, where she gave birth to a boy, the baby they had been jokingly calling 'Little Hank' for months. Villiers sent wires to Australia and London and a notice to *The Times*, and bought flowers for Nancie. 'This is HANK's week', he underlined in his diary. The baby was registered as Christopher Alan Villiers, and later known as Kit. Their good friends at Fort William, the Glassborows – Vernon taught aircraft recognition, and Gwen had a small girl – were of great help to Nancie over the coming months because Alan could not be with them: he had to leave for a new posting just days after the birth.

On 18 April, Villiers went to see Nancie and the baby, then left for Liverpool, where he boarded the RAF transport ship *Pasteur* for New York. From there he took a train to Washington, then a steamer to Norfolk, Virginia. On 1 May 1943 he first set eyes on the vessels that would dominate the next three years of his life: the Landing Craft Infantry (Large) – LCI(L)s – commonly known as Lice.

11

THE TERRIFIC
BUSINESS OF
MOVING ARMIES

Villiers' new job was to command a 'flight' of Lice across the Atlantic. The first LCI(L) had been launched in November 1942, and flotillas of ten to twenty craft had been sailing to Britain since January 1943: this would be the 10th Flight. The mass-produced Lice were angular and flat-bottomed, with a ramp on each side of the bow which was lowered in shallow water to let troops ashore, 'and there wasn't a curved line in them that couldn't be left straight', said Villiers.

> Their double bottoms and multitude of compartments made them mighty hard to sink, though they were hurriedly welded together by young women using metal so thin that to walk across the decks in places was to give one the willies, for the plates gave.[1]

They had four spaces for troops, a central conning tower and a wheelhouse with a tram-like steering handle which Villiers' gripman father Leon would have liked. They were powered by eight ordinary General Motors diesel truck engines, laid out in two banks of 'quads', driving two propellers. Their operational speed was 14 knots but at a pinch they could move slowly on just a single engine. Their above-water exhausts made 'a curious grunting' sound.

The war could not have been won without landing vessels. By 1945 there were well over a hundred different variations, from tiny boats to giant transports. Only the largest of them had the distinction of a name; the rest were known by acronyms and numbers. Some provided camouflage and defence with smoke, guns and rocket barrages, while others performed repairs, navigation, communication and command services. However, the task of the vast majority was simply to ferry people, trucks, tanks and cargo to beachheads.

Those more than 200 feet long were regarded as 'ships'; those less were 'craft'. The smallest landing craft, up to about 60 feet, could carry a few dozen troops or a single tank or 30-odd tons of cargo. The largest of the craft, about 190 feet, were the specialised Landing Craft Tanks (LCTs), which could carry three to ten tanks.

But Villiers' Landing Craft Infantry (Large) had a niche all to themselves. They were 160 feet long with a beam of 23 feet, transporting around 200 troops or 75 tons of cargo, and their versatility saw them adapted to many roles. Although their finish was austere by American standards, to the British they seemed almost luxurious, so they were often poached to become headquarters vessels too. (There was also a smaller version of the LCI, with space for about 100 troops and 18 bicycles.)

The British had designed the LCI(L)s but did not have enough free industrial capacity to build them, so the Americans fabricated 921 vessels on dockside assembly lines; Britain would get 214 of them under the Lend-Lease agreement. Their uncomplicated lines and ship-style bows made them fast, and they would be found to be magnificent sea boats, but their reliability under extreme conditions was not yet tested.

In his time Villiers had known the stately *Cecilie*, the noble *Parma*, the exquisite *Conrad*; it is hard to imagine him appreciating these welded 'orange-boxes'. Yet at heart he was always pragmatic about ships, even square-riggers: he was attracted by their beauty but he truly loved them for their honest, hard-working utility.

The Lice were hard-working too – like eccentric pack-mules – and Villiers came to be surprisingly fond of them. They did everything they were asked to, and in the end, more than anyone had ever dreamt possible.

———

The Battle of the Atlantic between the convoys and German U-boats had reached a climax in March 1943, with shocking Allied casualties. But the British had been gradually improving their U-boat defences and, at last, German submarine losses began to increase. Even so, in May 1943 there were still ninety-six U-boats skulking between Bermuda and Gibraltar – on the route Villiers would soon be sailing – and a loss rate of perhaps 40 per cent of his convoy was expected. In addition the LCIs were still on the 'Secret' list: because of their conning towers they looked like submarines from a distance, so they were at real risk of being attacked by ships from their own side as well as the enemy.

Each LCI(L) needed three officers and twenty-one crew. Villiers found that most had been taught 'a sort of get-there-quick method of navigating with air tables, … the only certainty was that they couldn't navigate at all'. He organised a course in a wharf shed, 'where every officer had to come and master just three things – the noon sight for latitude, the Marq St Hilaire position line, and the correction of his compass by azimuth'.

When it was time to leave, his Flight Sailing Orders to the young officers emphasised constant maintenance – 'If the ramps don't work God help the Pongoes [troops]. If God has to help the Pongoes HE'LL NEED OVERTIME FOR YOU.' His orders ended with a plea that clearly recalled some unhappy experience at Norfolk: 'AND FOR GOSH SAKES: Exercise the ELEMENTARY PRECAUTION of turning over your engines, working your helm and telegraph IN-VARIABLY, before slipping.'

The 10th Flight of nineteen LCIs left Norfolk for Bermuda on 25 May 1943. The weather was terrible, many crewmen were seasick, and some of the Lice had electric steering problems, leading to the random course changes that were always one of their least endearing features.

They arrived at Bermuda on 28 May, and after repairs set off again three days later for Gibraltar, sailing in five columns roughly 1,000 feet apart. Every day the lone Engineer Officer had to hurry from ship to ship in a small boat to fix breakdowns. Often by then half the convoy had drifted away, needing valuable time to round them up again.

Twice Villiers received coded Admiralty signals that U-boats were in the vicinity, but they were not attacked. He later heard through prisoners-of-war that German submarines had seen his convoy but kept their distance, fearing that the oddly shaped LCIs were a new type of sub-hunter.

They arrived in Gibraltar on 11 June after a passage of only eighteen days, one of the fastest crossings made by any of the LCI flights. At Gibraltar Villiers left the Lice and they carried on to Djidjelli, the headquarters of Combined Operations in northern Africa. 'I watch the Flight off with the Ocean C.O.'s, and feel lost without them', he wrote. He joined HMS *Melbreak* to return to Britain and immediately started the crew on aircraft recognition lectures twice a day. The ship had an easy run and Villiers was back in Fort William by 1 July.

He had several weeks of foreign service leave due. The baby was christened – Fritz and typographer Bruce Rogers were godparents – and Villiers spent much time with him: 'to the police station to get Hank a mask', 'we take a walk with the pram', 'a very happy day with Nanco and happy little Hank'.

A major turning point in the war occurred at this time – Operation Husky, the massive amphibious invasion of Sicily. The LCIs that Villiers had sailed from Bermuda took part, but to his frustration, he could not. Husky was a success, but many German troops got safely away to Calabria, the 'toe' of Italy. On 23 July 1943 Villiers finally received the news he was to be appointed to a squadron of LCI(L)s in the Mediterranean. Boarding a sleeper to Liverpool on 12 August he wrote, 'Little Hank is lovely at the station – poor mite! I resent having to leave him now!'

———

On 14 August Villiers sailed on HMS *Orontes* for Algiers. He immediately gave a talk on merchant vessels, and was soon teaching aircraft recognition classes twice daily. At Djidjelli he found he had been appointed to command LCI Squadron 'D', comprised of three flotillas of twelve LCI(L)s each, currently scattered around Sicily.

He took an LCI(L) to Malta to deliver troops and ammunition, then sailed for the east coast of Sicily, arriving on 3 September. That day the Operation Baytown attack on Calabria had begun, and there was no sign of Squadron 'D': 'Italy invaded this morning: damn! Late again … Sicilian children don't look like enemies', he noticed, with the eyes of a new parent.

They sailed to Messina, where Villiers finally took over 'D' Squadron. On 7 September he was sent to Tunisia with nine LCIs to load American troops for southern Sicily. The next day Italy surrendered to the Allies, and the day after Operation Avalanche began – the major invasion at Salerno, near Naples. To his frustration Villiers missed the action again.

At Messina he tried to reassemble the three scattered flotillas of his own Squadron 'D', but many ships had been taken over by other commands. He took fifteen LCIs to Sapri to load a brigade. Sapri had been badly damaged in the Salerno invasion and was a sobering experience. 'Horrible stench of the dead filling the harbour today, from a shelter near the Railway Station.'

That September he turned forty. He had a telegram from Nancie for his birthday and heard that all was well. He sent her nuts and lemons, delicacies now in wartime Britain. Messina was quieter now, the 'flaps dying off steadily'.

Villiers heard that LCI Squadron 'C' would soon become responsible for Sicily and southern Italy, but there was no news of what was to happen to his own 'D'. His Letter of Proceedings on 27 September 1943 estimated that in just a few weeks his versatile LCIs had carried at least 50,000 troops and performed the roles of salvage tugs, oil tankers, stores carriers, hospital ships, mine-field pilots and commando raiders.[2]

Then on 1 October, quite out of the blue, he discovered that a Royal Naval Reserve commander was being sent to take over his squadron. 'This is a damned unexpected smack in the face!' Next day it rained, a trawler came ashore, 9,000 troops had to be lifted to Taranto, and resignedly he wrote: 'I hear the Cdr RNR is at Augusta.' On 4 October, simply: 'Superseded.'

——

Villiers was retained as an administrative officer for the squadron, which was soon to start packing up to return to Britain. But there was still work to be done, and the LCIs sailed to the city of Catania at the base of Mount Etna, where they ferried thousands of soldiers to troop ships. It was getting colder now: Villiers could see snow on the peak of the volcano.

At last he had the time to look around at the local ketches and schooners – the sort of working craft he had always loved – noting their oddities and making lists of their evocative names. He watched convoys, merchant vessels and landing ships coming and going around the port. It was 'a lovely morning to say farewell to Sicily' when they left on 23 October for Algeria.

Since his demotion he had had difficulties with the officers of the squadron: 'I note quietly that I have been deposed in more ways than one …' he wrote unhappily. On 26 October he had 'a brush' with one F.O. [Flotilla Officer] about an unauthorised signal, and that night another F.O., 'with a smirk, wants to know from where I got the stories in my books. What a pair!' The situation hurt. Two days later, 'Not a very good day – the ignominy of supersession in command and retention as an underling gripes, where the standard of officer is so low.'

Then on Sunday 31 October he was suddenly reinstated as commander of 'D' Squadron – the head of another squadron was leaving, and the reshuffle left a post open for Villiers again. For a while it was an 'awkward 'twixt and between period', but he leapt gladly back into work, teaching courses and preparing the LCIs for their passage to Britain.

On 11 November the squadron sailed for Gibraltar, and finally Villiers and Flight 'U' of twenty LCI(L)s set off for Britain on 20 November. As the weather became steadily wilder, he was impressed by the LCIs' seaworthiness: 'vicious squalls from WNW: but all ships continue to behave beautifully – steering a little wildly now and then, of course, and leaping and rolling violently in the heavy sea. … I believe these ships could run before a full gale.'

By the eighth day out they were perhaps 100 miles from Land's End, when in the early hours of 27 November the destroyer HMS *Oribi* barged into the flight and collided heavily with LCI 178. When Villiers got to 178 he found she was badly damaged but, to everyone's amazement, was still floating on an even keel with working engines.

The damaged 178 and a group of other LCIs made slowly for Falmouth in deteriorating weather. Villiers finally got the rest into Plymouth on 28 November: 'At last – God, a difficult and worrying passage! Mist and sleet and WSW gale and no sign of Eddystone: minefields all around. … I am very tired.'

In London Villiers saw Kay Egerton at the American Embassy, who told him that Fritz had recently written a book on the Portuguese dictator Salazar, which was 'a great success'. At Combined Operations headquarters Villiers learned that Squadron 'D' was to be disbanded and handed over to the Canadians. He wrote angrily that it was typical of the 'iniquitous' bureaucracy which had such an 'unmitigated disregard of the value of experience <u>and</u> morale'. He took the train north, and at Troon had slightly better news: after a period of leave he was to be appointed commander of 'A' Squadron LCI(L) at Malta.

That evening Nancie was at the station in Fort William to meet him for three 'quiet, happy' weeks together – enjoying their third wedding anniversary, going for walks and sharing Christmas and New Year celebrations with friends. The baby was now eight months old: 'Kit is doing splendidly – what a grand little type he is!'

The new year found Villiers in a less gung-ho frame of mind than earlier in the war. 'Still on leave awaiting sailing orders for the Med. and wondering what is happening to the 21st and 22nd Flotilla: while I help Nancie with Little Kit, and saw wood. While I don't mind the life of a convoy commodore, this is scarcely the stage of the war to begin it.'[3] Four days later he regretfully left Fort William. At the station with Nancie and Kit in the afternoon, 'we pretend, with little success, that I am not going anywhere.'

He arrived at Algiers on 25 January. Villiers wrote bitterly in his diary, 'The new landing S. of Rome [Anzio] seems to be going well. Missed it again.' He had to get to Malta via Taranto, where he visited the full-rigged cadet ship *Cristoforo Colombo* three times while waiting for gales to pass.

He reached Malta on 14 February. The LCI refits were in a state of chaos and the previous commander had already left without formally handing over. Villiers found that 'ships don't work, floating dock doesn't work, no spares: even top overhaul of engines impossible'. There was now a sense of urgency to get the LCIs home to Britain for the invasion of France that everyone knew had to come. Yet even in the rush Villiers still managed to set up his beloved training courses for the LCI crews at Valetta.

He was weighed down with administration but still managed to get away to Anzio to see the situation for himself. Back in Malta he was shocked at the news of the fate of LCI 273, which had been bombed and sunk at Anzio after he left, with about twenty deaths among the troops.

Villiers received orders to command a flight of 21 LCIs back to Britain with nearly 1,000 men. It had no official designation so he called it Flight 'X'. They left Malta on 1 April. The voyage to Plymouth was the usual agony of breakdowns, straggling Lice, terrible weather and seasick passengers. Flight 'X' arrived at the mouth of the Thames on 24 April, and Villiers noted in his diary the frenzy of activity at the ports:

> All Plymouth and Devonport, and I hear Portland and Weymouth, and Cowes Roads and all these parts, jambed with ships and waterborn forts and queer constructions whose precise part in the invasion I cannot guess. But I expect we will soon see.

Villiers was given leave, 'and Nancie and Wee Kit are at the station – Kit with four teeth and a bonny smile!' For a sweet week they stayed at Oak Cottage, overlooking playing fields and the Great Glen. 'Raining and very cold, but it's pleasant and warm here and wonderfully happy.' All too soon it was over. On 8 May 1944, 'change into uniform again – blast it. Nancie and Wee Kit at the station: I can see Oak Cottage from the train.'

He returned to Tilbury, 'to cope with the madhouse'. The LCIs had been assigned to Force 'L', and Villiers got on very well with its head, Rear-Admiral William Parry. Parry had the disturbing news that Force 'L' was in effect only until D-Day, 'after which we are no-one's baby'.

The LCIs left for the Thames estuary on 16 May and began landing exercises on the local beaches. 'It is pretty difficult to retain any real secrecy about this great operation, except that people have heard of it for so long they don't really think it will happen', Villiers wrote. Five days later he went to Harwich for 'the conference in the old schoolhouse … We learn the plans for the 2nd Front which I think only Eisenhower ought to know.'

The LCIs loaded troops on 3 June and sailed to the Southend anchorage. The long-awaited invasion of France, Operation Overlord, was about to begin. Force 'L' was part of Operation Neptune, Overlord's naval arm, providing a second wave of reinforcements. The nineteen LCIs under Villiers' command were the 252nd and 253rd Flotillas of 'A' Squadron. On the morning of 5 June 1944 he wrote:

Sail. Delayed 40" for the green pennant. 242 [Villiers' LCI] is first through the boom of an Armada of ships bound towards France. Weather bad: we all fear postponement. Shelling in the Straits stops before we get there: go through by daylight.

The LCIs went on in the dark through the mineswept channel to France. In the early hours of 6 June, 'the gliders going over before 0300 show me the Day has come, but the weather is appalling on those open beaches.'

———

At 1415 on 6 June Villiers sighted the coast of France. His squadron split up, going to two of the five Normandy beachheads: Villiers took seven LCIs to Juno sector, nine went to Sword sector and three were used as rescue craft. At 1620 the landing began in bad weather. Focke-Wulfs dropped bombs but missed the ships. The sea was rising, and 'the cleared portions of the beach were so littered with wrecks and stranded LCT waiting to refloat on the tide that there was extremely little room. An explosion under the bow of LCI 268 soon indicated there were still mines ...'.

In a three-hour hour period of landing and disembarking under gunfire, one soldier drowned but they had no other casualties. The unfortunate 268 ran into another mine but still stayed afloat, 106, 110 and 243 were damaged, and 'most ships lost one or both ramps and at least one anchor'. As the troops were being helped ashore by LCI crew, some ships were damaged by attacking Junker 88s, others were holed by beach obstructions, and another by friendly flak.

'There were, however no casualties,' wrote Villiers, 'and as at all the other landings in which this Squadron has taken part, the LCI(L) seemed to have charmed lives.'[4] They sailed back to England on 7 June and next day took a company of Pioneer [engineer] troops to Nan beach. They could get no clear directions from any headquarters ship, except to follow another vessel, which promptly led them aground. They managed to get afloat again, landed the soldiers, then returned to Spithead to hear that LCI(L) 105, from Villiers' old 'A' Squadron, had been blown up by torpedo with seven crew members lost.

The next few days were spent in repairs and waiting impatiently. Then on 14 June they loaded Pioneer troops and a reconnaissance unit, and successfully disembarked them despite air raids. On the return to Britain they passed ten Mulberries (sections of floating harbour), twenty coasters, sixty Thames barges with ramps, a French chasseur, cruisers, destroyers, frigates, corvettes, minesweepers, motor gunships, motor launches, RAF Rescue launches and aircraft 'of all description too numerous to record' bound to and from Normandy.

There were no orders for them at Gilkicker, and now there would be none for two weeks – Force 'L' had been disbanded, and the chain of command was lost. The much larger infantry landing ships (LSIs) could now safely unload troops on Allied-held beaches, and no one seemed to need the Lice. Their crews repaired, painted, stored, cleaned and waited. Mail had been delayed but at last Villiers got a letter from Nancie, with 'her big news' – a second pregnancy. It was the only bright spot in the frustrating delay.

At last on 30 June they were given a job: to transport engineers rebuilding a French railroad. But on their return to Gilkicker, the Commodore of Landing Craft Bases informed Squadron Commander Villiers that his squadron was now regarded as part of the 'Shuttle Service'. 'Do I go on leave then?' Villiers asked himself in disbelief.

On 6 July twelve LCIs were sent to pick up 'coloured U.S. service troops' to take them to France. 'Since the poor fellows are sent by LCI(L) in obvious contempt, I am glad we have sunshine & calm and the best crossing yet.' When they returned to Gilkicker ('damn the place') Villiers won a small victory over bureaucracy: some of the LCIs were now allowed off the buoys in rotation, their crews given fresh food and leave ashore.

The war went on. 'From midnight until 0500, frequent air raids and rocket-bombs going over, some very low and one so close [it] lit the ship as with daylight.' Villiers also noted 'the pulsing of the horrible things beating the air violently as they pass over belching white flames'.

The LCIs were getting a few more operations now. They embarked an 'Army Field Hospital party 85 Nurses, 4 Masseuse [sic], 2 Women Doctors, 3 Welfare Officers. ... The Nurses settled down well, all possible being done for their comfort. [They] are in battle dress, complete to gaiters, and came carrying their packs.' After several more passages taking field hospital staff to France and bringing troops back to

Britain, Villiers moved to the shore base HMS *Vernon* at Portsmouth.

He calculated that from D–Day to the end of July 1944, the 252nd and 253rd flotillas – nineteen LCIs – had carried between 27,000 and 30,000 troops, engineers and medical personnel to France. They had lost one ship and seven men to a torpedo attack, and LCI 307 had had a confirmed shooting down of a Junker 88 aircraft. He sent Rear-Admiral Parry, who had headed Force 'L', a copy of the Operation Report. Parry replied with a friendly and gossipy letter, ending, 'Best of luck to your squadron – & I should like to add once more how impressed I was at the spirit you had put into them.'

———

In August 1944 Villiers took some leave at Fort William. 'Down-town in the morning and a little picnic along General Wade's road in the afternoon, with Wee Man paddling in the icy burn and dancing in the heather, chortling with joy.' At last there was something other than war to think about: Nancie and Alan had decided to move to Deddington in Oxfordshire, to lodgings in the 'Corner House'.

Villiers knew the cartoonist Brocksbank, and in late August discussed doing a children's picture book with him, *Tanky*, about a cheeky tank landing craft (LCT). Brocksbank drew some delightful preliminary sketches but the idea went no further.

Villiers visited the Old Croft at Elmsett, where the Egertons had moved after Bricett Hall had been taken over by the American Air Force. 'Both Fritz and Kay look better: but both have felt the war – especially Kay. Fritz … doesn't think the story of LCI(L) worth writing, not as a book, and not at this stage, anyway.' It was easy enough to assume then that no one would much care about the slogging, unruly LCIs, but it is a pity now that Villiers wrote so little about them.

He learned on 18 September that he was formally to disband 'A' Squadron, then take a reorganised 'A' Squadron to the Far East. The Americans had assisted the British with the invasion of Europe: it was now time for the British to help against the Japanese.

Lionel, Alan's youngest brother, contacted him at this time. He was seven years younger than Alan, who called him 'Leal'. He had joined the Australian Imperial Forces in 1941 and served in Palestine, the Western Desert and New Guinea. Now he was in Britain, a sergeant seconded to the Australian Prisoners' Rehabilitation scheme. In mid-September Lionel helped Alan move Nancie and Kit south to Deddington. Lionel had disliked Alan's first wife, Daphne, but was immediately won over by Nancie.

In mid-October Villiers was appointed Squadron Commander of the new 'A' LCI squadron. He also discovered two weeks later he had been promoted to Temporary Acting Commander at the same time, but no one had thought to tell him! He left for Oban and Squadron 'A' at the end of October. 'At Oban find half a staff, but no ships and no sign of any.' When the first of his new LCI(L)s straggled into port, it had a crew that had never beached, no engine-room tools, no spares and no stores.

On 15 November he read that he had been awarded the Distinguished Service Cross, granted to naval officers in recognition of 'gallantry during active operations against the enemy'.

> See in the Glasgow Herald Scots awards for Normandy which include 2 DSC's for old 'A' Squadron, 242 and 104. See in Times at 2200 we gained 8 DSC's that day, including one for me. And at least 9 DSM[edals] ... Telephoned Nancie and told her about DSC: very pleased.

Like his father Leon and brother Lionel, Alan would always be passionate about the benefit of education, and at Oban he sent flotilla officers to courses on current affairs and hired the local cinema to show films like *War in the Pacific*, *Facts About the Hon. Enemy* and *You Too Can Get Malaria* to his crews. The rest of 1944 passed in a rush, with the pressure of preparations mounting. 'A lot of the grief we have trying to prepare this Flight is due to culpable <u>criminal</u> blasted negligence! It is a soul-destroying business.'

Villiers spent Christmas Eve and Christmas Day with Nancie and Kit, then on 30 December 1944 commanded nine Lice down the west coast of Britain to Plymouth, where the landing craft flights for India, codenamed 'Appian', were assembling. On the tedious trip back north he had a disturbing meeting:

> In the Oban train, one Captain Bailey ex Cape-Horner (Colonial Empire, Oban Bay, Largs Bay etc) yarns of Capt de Cloux aboard the steamer BODIA at Leith and how he did not seem to like one Villiers. I'm afraid the failure of

the BODIA to collect much coin must have embittered Reuben: for I thought us friends. I gave him the PARMA shares at cost ... [sic]

The ease between de Cloux and Villiers is obvious from their writings, and Bailey's tale sounds more spiteful than plausible. Villiers did not seem to recognise that another ex-Cape Horner might be envious of him. He never quite understood that what came simply after decades of hard work and worldly experience – ease of expression in speech or writing (to deckhand or Admiral), uncynical devotion to duty and confidence at sea – did not come quite so naturally to other people.

On 13 January 1945 Villiers took Appian Flight 'P' of sixteen LCI(L)s from Plymouth to Gibraltar, arriving five days later after a quiet passage. The flight left for India under another officer, and Villiers returned to Britain by plane on 24 January. When he landed he learned, 'I have a daughter, born at Oxford, 19 January.' Nancie had given birth to Katherine Lisbeth while he was away, and a landgirl named Dorcas helped with the children.

A month later, on 24 February, Villiers left Britain in command of Flight 'Q', made up of twenty Lice bound for India. Villiers was in LCQ 491, a new Landing Craft Administration vessel, and despite its relative comforts he hoped he would be back as soon as possible. In fact he would not see his small family again for a long time.

When they were only eleven hours out of port they were shockingly reminded that, even as the Allied armies were closing in on Germany, the sea war was not yet over. The flight was being escorted by HMS *Ellesmere*, a 580-ton anti-submarine vessel converted from a Norwegian whaler, with a complement of thirty-five men. Villiers wrote in his passage Progress Report:

At 2340 a large upheaval in the water was seen on the port bow, where HMS ELLESMERE had been. A few seconds later, the thump of a violent explosion hit the sides of the L.C.Q. When the upheaval had subsided there was no sign of Ellesmere, and though I had my glasses on the place I saw nothing of the ship at all. ... A few calcium flares burned on the water where Ellesmere had been, and a widening smudge of fuel oil could be seen.[5]

Villiers sent a ship to investigate and rescue survivors, but there were 'no bodies at all, alive or dead'. 'They were a nice lot in Ellesmere', he wrote sadly in his diary. Some of the officers thought the explosion had been a mine but Villiers was convinced it was a torpedo, and was proved correct when it was later confirmed that *Ellesmere* had been sunk by U-boat 1203.

The convoy made its way to Malta, arriving on 5 March. Villiers wrote reassuringly to Nancie, carefully avoiding the topic of *Ellesmere*, 'Do you know, my lovely Family doesn't seem far away from me at all, and I'm so happy about them and proud of them and in love with them, all the time!'[6]

After the usual repairs the convoy left for Port Said four days later. It stayed only two days in each port for the rest of the trip, visiting Port Said, Kabret and Aden. At Aden he visited the port:

> The horde of dhows of all kinds jostling at the anchorage is as big and interesting as ever – ... Board a couple of Kuweit dhows at the anchorage and am well received, with coffee, halwa, and copious trays of sweet water-melon.

He joked to Nancie, 'my name seemed to be all right still. They can't have read the book!' He ended the letter: 'What a sweet pair of little babies the Lord has blessed us with! I am so grateful to you, Darling old Nance, and so happy to be your own loving old A.J.'

Flight 'Q' reached Bombay on 1 April 1945, after a very fast five-week passage. The date was significant to him: the fourth anniversary of his unhappy move to *St Christopher*, and, as he noted in his diary, '12 months ago I sailed for Malta with 21 LCI(L) of the old "A" Squadron, bound – though we did not know it then – for Normandy. Several of the same ships are here with me now.'

On 14 April the landing craft sailed south to Mandapam, near Ceylon. Next day was 'Little Kit's birthday: he is 2. I wonder what sort of world he will find at 22? And at 42?' He wrote, perceptively, to Nancie: '[T]he tragedy is that most people don't realise that this isn't a war that will <u>end</u>, but a sort of ghastly transition period brought upon ourselves from which we will have to fight our way back to sanity and sensible living.'

The LCI squadron left Mandapam on 18 April, sailed across the Bay of Bengal in lovely weather to Kyaukpyu, on the western coast of Burma. Suddenly the respite was over – Operation Dracula, the invasion of Japanese-held Rangoon, was about to begin. Villiers hurriedly readied the landing craft: 'Fuel, water, stores, fighting for everything.' '[Old Man] didn't quite expect to be in the thick of things so soon,' he wrote to Nancie. 'O.M. will be profoundly happy always in his love for you.'

By midnight on 1 May the LCIs had assembled off the vast mouth of the Irrawaddy River, while Rangoon was bombed from the air. On 3 May they sailed for the city among landing craft of all kinds, and began ferrying prisoners-of-war out to hospital ships. The invasion turned out to be an anti-climax as the Japanese had secretly abandoned Rangoon, but the city had been badly damaged by rioting and bombing. When Villiers had a chance to go ashore he noted:

Ruin – ruin – ruin – stench of rotting rice, busted go-downs, burned and wrecked small ships – and always the money to tread underfoot – 'Japanese Government one cent' … in the market, Jap yellow boots with crepe rubber soles, Jap one-toed jungle shoes, Jap equipment – the heap of refuse in the corner with the human thigh-bone –

The LCIs left Burma on 8 May and reached Mandapam, now their base, six days later. Alan received news there from Nancie: she had found them a small house known as The Cottage, in Leafield, about 18 miles north-west of Oxford, and had bought it for £800. She moved herself and the children to Leafield in June, helped by Alan's brothers Lionel and Frank. Frank had been released from his POW camp earlier in the year, and Lionel had plans to do a degree in education in Britain. For some, new possibilities were coming into focus.

For others, the war just dragged on. Villiers attended meetings in Bombay and brought back a small group of LCIs to join the others. He thought over lessons learned in Operation Dracula, organised fresh food and training courses to occupy the men, sent silk and shoes to Nancie and, as always, watched the local sailing craft with fascination:

Brigs, brigantines, schooners, large dhows daily. On beach 5 old ships, 1 building. Barque on beach. Brigantine SHAHULHAMEED, reg. no 3 of TUTI-

CORIN. Coppered, very few ratlines, carvel built, iron-fastened? above coppering. Men (7 men, 1 boy) climb aloft by toes. Dead-eyes and rope lanyards for rigging. Fores'l 24 cloths. Sails set well – very light cotton material (not canvas?). Crew pretty lean – no smoke from evening fire. All ties of chain. Rigging precisely as European Brigantine.

Slowly, agonisingly, the Japanese were being beaten back all over Asia. Plans to invade Malaya were short-circuited by stunning news: the annihilation of the cities of Hiroshima and Nagasaki with the world's first atomic bombs. Japan surrendered unconditionally on 15 August 1945.

Villiers prepared the LCIs for Operation Tiderace, the occupation of Singapore. He commanded a convoy of LCIs and frigates which sailed for Penang on 18 August, but they were ordered to halt two days later, 'returning to TRINCO on C-in-C's orders. GNASHING of teeth and groans.' A week later they left for Singapore: the Japanese had officially surrendered in Japan on 2 September, and in Singapore on 12 September Lord Mountbatten held another surrender ceremony and a fleet review. Villiers' LCIs transported 5,000 men ashore for the ceremonies.

The most essential job now was to rescue prisoners-of-war. Villiers left on 17 September to take LCIs and LSTs up the Siak River to Pakan Baroe (Pakanbaru) in central Sumatra. This was the site of a camp for a lesser-known 'Death Railway' – 137 miles of line through swamps and jungles, almost to Padang on the south-west coast. In stifling humidity and rain they evacuated about a thousand men to the LSTs waiting upriver, and loaded hundreds of sick POWs onto the LCIs. A Dutch doctor who helped with the evacuation told Villiers of terrible atrocities. Villiers' brief notes were sombre. 'On the way down, many large dark monkeys scampering in trees.'

———

On 23 September, Villiers' forty-second birthday, a Victory Service was held at Singapore Cathedral: he noted grimly that, as usual, the landing craft didn't rate a mention. The Pacific war was over and demobilisations began in October, but Villiers decided to stay in service for a few months longer as he knew he had no job to go to.

Some of the LCIs were to be handed over to the French in Indo-China, who were trying to reassert their rule despite the declaration of the Democratic Republic of Vietnam. In November 1945 Villiers took two LCIs to Saigon through still weather. He wrote, 'I can now understand why the tea clippers had such lovely hulls and so many "kites" – they had to, to ghost through these seas. These placid flying-fish haunts are the stuns'l waters, not the fresh winds of the artists' imaginings!'

In December Villiers was appalled to hear from one of his commanders in Saigon that he was taking French troops on patrols along canals to 'shoot up' junks, bomb trawlers and set fire to Annamite [Vietnamese] houses – with horribly predictable results: a British seaman was killed by a ricocheting bullet and two others were wounded. Villiers wrote to his superiors that 'Disquieting accounts of atrocities against Annamites committed by the French aboard H.M. LCI(L) have reached my ears ... It is submitted that the transfer of eight LCI(L) allocated to the French at Saigon may be treated as urgent.'

The days passed in endless administration – ship repairs, ship beachings, ship unbeachings, defaulter parades ('Hegarty again'), pump troubles, and still no news about the future of the LCI squadron. Villiers wrote bitterly: 'Situation at Singapore still a chaotic muddle, with no-one seemingly combining the wit to see with the power to act.' At a Christmas party for Force 'W' staff, Mountbatten confided cheerfully to Villiers that the reason Combined Ops used RNVR officers to bring the untried LCIs across the Atlantic was because they wouldn't know how much danger they'd be in.

In 1946 the LCIs were at last on the move: they were to be returned to the United States authorities in the Philippines. On 26 January Villiers took ten Lice from Singapore to Subic Bay. The British had told Villiers to deliver the ships 'as-is' but he found that the Americans wanted them back in good order, and it took four days' hard work to make them acceptable. He returned to Singapore to command the second flight of twenty-four craft, and despite breakdowns they arrived safely at Subic Bay on 11 March. The crews painted white lines at the ships' waterlines, so it would be obvious if they began sinking – a distinct possibility, as they all had leaks.

On 14 March 1946 it was finally done. Villiers signed the transfer papers and at 1300 the British colours were hauled down. He left LCQ

491, his headquarters for so long, and returned to Singapore, where he was granted leave to visit his mother in Australia. The Rear-Admiral Force 'W' noted on his application: 'Commander A.J. Villiers ... has worked hard and continuously to maintain his craft [and] has by his forethought and thoroughness looked after the welfare of some 130 Officers and 850 ratings in an exemplary manner and maintained a high morale throughout the squadron.'[7]

Villiers left Singapore on *Esperance Bay* on 22 March for leave in Melbourne, then six weeks later boarded *Athlone Castle* to return to Britain. He arrived home on 23 June and rejoined his family at Leafield after sixteen months apart.

12

SAIL'S TIME
IS UP

Villiers was officially discharged from the Royal Naval Reserve on 8 September 1946, with £162 and the thanks of their Lordships. He had served them for more than six years of his life and was now nearly forty-three. He spent the latter part of 1946 working on *The Coral Sea*, and settling contentedly into life at Leafield. Three-year-old Kit took some time to respond to the stranger, 'but Alan was very good with him', recalled Nancie.

At the start of 1947 Villiers, as usual, set out his plans for the coming year, which included finishing *The Coral Sea* and writing two new books: *The Way of a Ship* – 'a complete story of the development, history, trade, design, handling and demise of the big sailing-ship' – and *The Set of the Sails* – 'an autobiographical work more or less disguised? (Perhaps not at all)'. He had contracted to do *The Coral Sea* in the 1930s but now it would bring in very little money – and he was desperately worried about his prospects at a time of widespread unemployment. 'It is strange how one becomes almost <u>afraid</u> of writing, after so long a gap. I am finding this book hard going indeed.'[1]

He tried for a job in Sydney, editing the papers of Joseph Banks at the Mitchell Library, with little expectation of getting it. He also applied for work at the BBC and with the new United Nations, but had no luck. He and Nancie still thought about moving back to Australia but by now he had few friends there, he told Fritz: 'Naturally, when I spent so much time being a Finn, Norwegian, half-baked Yank and quarter-baked Arab, I haven't been seeing much of my own countrymen for the past 15 years.'[2]

The winter of early 1947 was bitterly cold and food was still rationed.

In an ironic reverse of their wartime relationship, Frank Villiers in Australia started sending Alan much-appreciated food parcels. Nancie was unwell and Villiers struggled with the housework, two small children, and his writing. In February Nancie realised she was pregnant again.

Fritz read the manuscript of *The Coral Sea*. Villiers wrote in his diary, 'Got the first six chapters back from Fritz with various rude remarks, but on the whole I must say I expected more.' During the worst snowfalls of the winter, Villiers submitted the book to publishers. They soon returned it, offering $500 for a major revision. 'They find mine a dull catalogue of voyages; and want more "drama". I'm afraid I'm not their man: but we will see. I might need that $500 yet.'

By April he was close to despair. He decided to begin *The Set of the Sails* and started reading through his old logbooks and diaries. 'I thought I had a good memory, but I am often surprised at what I find. Even 1929 is a long time ago now.'

In May Villiers received a letter from *National Geographic* magazine, written by Melville Bell Grosvenor, the son of the man who had invited Villiers to lecture in America in 1930. Mel was a passionate photographer, and was coming to Britain on a working vacation in July with his wife, Helen; Villiers invited them to stay at the cottage in Leafield. The outcome was a fifty-page spread in *National Geographic*, May 1948, describing Grosvenor's tour around the Cotswolds, north-west of Oxford, including a saccharine portrait of the life of the Villiers family in quaint little Leafield.

> There, in his garden, I saw my salty friend Alan, with his two youngsters laughing a greeting. 'Welcome aboard,' he beamed in his nautical way. 'And watch the overheads when you enter – Cotswold doors were designed for dwarfs!' Inside, Nancie, Alan's charming Australian wife, was waiting for me. ... 'You're just in time for some Australian meat pie and black currant pudding,' she greeted us. ...
>
> That night the rain pattered on the stone roof and the wind whistled. But in the morning the sun streamed in my dormer. ... 'What a fine day for color photography,' I commented to Alan at breakfast. 'Not a cloud in the sky.' A growl from the sea captain. 'It always rains in the Cotswolds after a sunny morning.' ... And how right he was!

The Grosvenors had only a vague idea of what food shortages might mean to the post-war British – let alone their unemployed 'salty friend' – and ate heartily. They went on their way with gifts of home-baked cakes and jams that Nancie had made from the raspberry patch. Mel confided to Villiers that his marriage was in difficulties and he was in love with his assistant, Anne. Villiers liked him but noted, 'The said M.B.G. goes through life like a man with two secretaries.'

All of Mel's letters after the visit mentioned Nancie's delicious jam, so they kept sending him jars. He invited Villiers to lecture to the National Geographic Society in early 1948, and it was the start of a brand-new direction in his post-war life.

———

Apart from the Finnish four-masters, only four others existed in 1939. During the war Sweden's training ship *Abraham Rydberg* was sold and reduced to barquentine rig. The Germans donated their cadet ship *Priwall* to Chile, but she was destroyed by fire. Two other German training vessels, *Kommodore Johnsen* (1921) and *Padua* (1926), were the youngest of the square-riggers: *Padua* was the final merchant four-master ever built. In 1946 they were awarded as German reparations to the USSR, which restored and renamed them – *Kommodore Johnsen* to *Sedov*, and *Padua* to *Kruzenshtern*.

The war had been painful for Gustaf Erikson. His younger son Gustaf-Adolf, second mate on the steamship *Argo*, died when it was torpedoed near the Åland Islands in 1942. His sailing fleet was gone too: *Winterhude* had been sold to the German Navy in 1944 then destroyed, *Moshulu* and *Archibald Russell* were laid up and neglected, confiscated *Lawhill* was sold to a South African business in 1946, and *Pamir* was still busily employed by the New Zealanders.

Erikson had only three square-riggers left: *Pommern*, *Viking* and *Passat*. In 1945 *Pommern* and *Viking* were used as grain barges, then *Pommern* returned to Mariehamn to stay, while *Viking* took timber to South Africa and brought wheat from Australia. Although Erikson was building up a fleet of small steamers, the four-masters were still profitable; so in 1946 *Passat* and *Viking* took cargo to South Africa, and in 1947 went out to South Australia to load grain.

Passat had a slow passage home and did not arrive at Falmouth for orders until October. By then there was no one to issue them: Gustaf Erikson had died on 15 August, aged seventy-four.

In mid-1947 Villiers attended the Annual General Meeting of the Society for Nautical Research: 'The proceedings are more than usually fatuous, except that I am appointed to Greenhill's committee for investigating means of collecting and preserving maritime negatives, both still and movie.' Later that year Villiers was elected Chairman of the Photographic Records Sub-Committee for the Society, a position he kept for many years. This was his second new post-war direction: the start of a long productive involvements with the Society for Nautical Research and the National Maritime Museum in Greenwich, which would one day become the home of the Society's – and Villiers' – collections of images.

Villiers rented the former Post Office in Leafield to have somewhere quiet to write. He began working furiously on *The Set of the Sails*. Fritz liked the idea of an autobiography, 'rounding it off with the end of the Grain Ship – make it my story, and theirs: the story of a passion for the sea.' Villiers wrote: 'At last I feel I am hitting my stride. The book is about something.'

He kept up a steady stream of letters seeking work and catching up with old friends, especially the Bay Ridge gang. Betty now had a daughter named Nancy, born in late 1945. Her husband, Ray Reed, had returned from the Army to his banking job but was restless. Tragically, her brother had died during the war and Captain Jacobsen died soon after from an operation. Elsie Jansen from *Joseph Conrad* had recently left the Coast Guard, and Marian and Eleanor Hansen were both married. Villiers was intensely relieved when Eleanor was able to send him the Arabian journals and films he had stored with her family before the war.

The summer of 1947 was as extreme as the winter had been: now they struggled with incessant heat and water restrictions. Nancie, eight months pregnant, bottled pounds of plums and tomatoes. In early September Villiers noted that since he had been demobilised the previous year he had spent £762 and earned £422. 'I have sold 15 articles, one book ... 9 lectures and 2 broadcasts. I suppose I could have done worse, but I shall have to do a great deal better! Getting back to wind'ard after seven years is hard.'

On 24 September, the day after Villiers' forty-fourth birthday, Peter John Villiers was born at Chipping Norton hospital. Villiers visited Nancie, sent telegrams, did the shopping, minded the two older children with the help of neighbours, and still managed to write about 4,000 words each day for *The Set of the Sails*. By late October he was up to the *Joseph Conrad* voyage, and wrote dryly in his diary, 'I think there is a lot in that story which is best left unpublished. It is in my log.'

During October Villiers toured and lectured in the west of England; in November he completed a draft of a children's book on whaling, and in December took a steamer to Copenhagen for a showing of his films. The BBC asked him to do an item on the four-master *Pamir*, then bringing a cargo of wool and tallow from Wellington. She arrived on 22 December after a fast eighty-one-day passage.

'As *Pamir* passed up the Thames, thousands marvelled at her beauty,' Villiers wrote in the May 1948 *National Geographic*. 'I have asked myself whether a nautical writer might take this occasion to draft the obituary of commercial sail. If we inspect the Orient ... the answer is "No". In Western waters, however, sail's time is up.'

———

Villiers left on 1 January 1948 for a lecture tour of America. He found he had more bookings than he had expected and rushed from city to city, meeting old friends and speaking to vast audiences, including 5,000 people at the *National Geographic* in Washington. The only rough bit was two days with Mel Grosvenor in February, 'ostensibly to go over the Cotswolds article ... but, as it soon became horribly obvious, in reality to pour out woe about his marital affairs. This is boring.' Villiers (of all people) should have understood, but he was probably kinder to Mel than this suggests: later Mel wrote, 'You were a patient friend and I appreciated it.'

He spent two days at Mystic Seaport, Connecticut, showing his films and seeing *Joseph Conrad* once more. Millionaire Huntington Hartford had soon lost interest in his new toy, and in 1938 had given her to the United States Maritime Commission. She was used as a training vessel during the war, then laid up in Florida. The Marine Historical Association of Mystic rescued the ship and made her the centrepiece of their museum. Villiers thought the staff had done a good job of the rigging, and he liked Mystic.[3]

At the start of 1948 Prime Minister Clement Attlee had asked Villiers to become a trustee of the National Maritime Museum, prompted by trustee Malcolm Glasier of the Blue Funnel Line. On the day Villiers attended his first quarterly meeting, 19 June, the twenty-six-year-old Duke of Edinburgh was also formally appointed. Other trustees included an earl (the long-standing Chairman, Lord Stanhope), a baronet, two knighted admirals, a knighted captain, a knighted Member of Parliament and a rear-admiral, but if the boy from Buncle Street felt intimidated he never admitted it.

After Fritz's comments and a revision, *The Set of the Sails* was accepted by publishers in Britain and America. In mid-1948 Villiers lectured at cities around England, and in August started a complete rewrite of the loathed *Coral Sea* manuscript. The summer was hot; their friends from Fort William days, the Glassborows, came to stay, and Villiers went blackberrying with the children. He sailed on Thames barges, and photographed the 'lovely ships, with their red-gold sails'. He arranged another lecture tour in America for early 1949, and this time Nancie would go too. The proofs of *The Set of the Sails* arrived, and Villiers gave a BBC broadcast on dhows that was well-received. The family finished the year in a happy flurry of Christmas.

———

In January 1949 Alan and Nancie left on the *Queen Mary* for New York: the speaking tour was as successful as the previous year. One highlight for Villiers was meeting the Portuguese Ambassador, Dr Pedro Teotónio Pereira, after a lecture in Washington – Pedro would become a lifelong friend. This was the beginning of Villiers' association with Portugal, the third new direction in his life. Pedro proposed that he sail with the Portuguese schooners which crossed the North Atlantic every year to fish for cod near Newfoundland and Greenland. Villiers was fascinated, but did not have enough time to prepare; instead he made plans to go in 1950.

He had earlier become involved with the Outward Bound Sea School, started in 1941 by educator Kurt Hahn and Lawrence Holt of the Blue Funnel Line, to teach young men the basics of seamanship in case of wartime emergency. Now it provided intense short sailing courses and mountain treks for teenagers from any background. Villiers thought highly of Outward Bound, and as the only sail-training venture in Britain he wanted in.

In May 1949, he was offered command of its new school-ship *Warspite*, a schooner only 80 feet long, with fore-and-aft sails. It was based at Aberdovey, North Wales. *Warspite* had berths for twelve lads and three permanent crew members – the master, mate and cook-engineer. She had been built as a yacht around 1911, had a straight stem, a long counter stern, a 12-foot draught and a 'rattletrap engine'.[4] In June 1949 Villiers sailed *Warspite* from Cowes to Aberdovey, loaded the first group of twelve boys and set off for five days in the Irish Sea. Most were seasick but all worked determinedly, and Villiers was pleased with them.

He wrote to Mel Grosvenor that he hoped to do a story for *National Geographic* about the programme: 'to take a photogenic boy through the whole Course, starting from his home some place in a big industrial city, and taking him mountaineering, sporting and sailing, and finally, away as a cadet in the Blue Funnel Line'.[5] Winter sailing on *Warspite* was much harder than summer, Villiers wrote. 'The light is lousy, the day short, the weather abominable ... Every week we get twelve raw boys and pound out into the Irish Sea, to do battle with the Atlantic gales. ... The function of the ship is to provide a <u>challenge</u> for Youth ... the strange thing is they thrive on it ...'.

In December Nancie took the three children on the steamship *Nestor* to visit Australia for six months. Her mother had recently died and she had not seen her father for over ten years. Alan was to continue with *Warspite* until March 1950 then go to Portugal until September to sail with the fishing fleet, so it was an ideal time to be away.

———

Edgar Erikson had taken over the company after his father's death. He kept the sailing ships working, and by early 1948 *Viking* and *Passat* were both loading grain again at Port Victoria. *Lawhill* was there too, working for her South African owners, but after this trip she was sold and laid up on a river in Mozambique, where she rusted until being scrapped a decade later. When *Viking* reached London in August 1948

Villiers went to see her at the docks before she went on to Antwerp. She was laid up there for two years, then sold to Sweden in 1950 to become a stationary school-ship.

Now the only seaworthy square-rigger the Erikson company owned was *Passat* – until in late 1948 the New Zealand government suddenly decided to return *Pamir*. It was trumpeted as a gesture of goodwill towards Finland, but *Pamir* had made losses on her most recent voyages and the New Zealand Navy didn't want her. Her Finnish master and mate from before the confiscation took charge, and *Pamir* sailed to Port Victoria in February 1949. *Passat* arrived from London soon afterwards.

They began loading grain to intense global press interest. Both four-masters were nearly the same size and registered tonnage. Both had been built in Hamburg for Laeisz – *Pamir* in 1905 and *Passat* six years later: they may not have been sister ships but the family resemblance was striking.

Pamir sailed for Falmouth on 28 May 1949 and *Passat* followed four days later. On 19 September, *Passat* won the Grain Race after a passage of 110 days. *Pamir* took 128 days to get to Falmouth but, welcomed by a flurry of small boats, sightseeing aircraft and nostalgic newspaper stories, *Pamir*'s was the final homecoming.

———

In early 1950 Grosvenor announced that his divorce had come through at last. Villiers replied, 'And what a wonderful difference it makes to all our living, to have the right mate, to be complete, to have a real solid foundation to the joys of each day, and against the trials … [sic] That's a grand start to 1950!'

The Set of the Sails, Villiers' autobiography, was doing extraordinarily well. It had been published in October 1949, and by January 1950 the first British edition was sold out, while in America it had already sold over 10,000 copies.

The National Maritime Museum was backing moves to save the famous tea-clipper *Cutty Sark*, and the newspapers talked of preserving one of the last steel vessels too. Villiers wrote in his diary: 'the PAMIR and PASSAT are now in Penarth Docks, laid up: VIKING ditto at Antwerp: POMMERN since before the war at Mariehamn. But I am not impressed. It is more sense to build a new ship. ... If the Ålanders cannot run them, nobody can.'[6]

He returned to *Warspite* in early January at Liverpool. 'Not for the first time I wish the Warspite was a real sailing-ship, going somewhere! ... She calls for a combination of Colonel Lawrence and St Paul.' He was offered the position of next director of the Outward Bound Sea School, but, 'I do not care for this at all though I well recognise the nobility of the work. ... How to make the place succeed when its finance pours away on two ships? The <u>idea</u> of the ships is magnificent; but the practice is ruinous.'

In late January Villiers contracted to do a book on the Indian Ocean. He wrote four articles, spent the second half of February on his last voyage on *Warspite*, then handed her over to another master. At Leafield he and Nancie had bought the cottage next door and a workman was opening up extra rooms for their tiny house through the common wall. In March Villiers worked on the house, prepared for the Portuguese trip, wrote three more articles and hosted a weekend meeting of the Photographic Sub-Committee at Leafield, which he enjoyed: 'They are live wires, especially Greenhill.'

———

On 10 March 1950 Villiers boarded the ship *Andes* for Lisbon. Portugal in 1950 was an unusual place. Since 1926 it had been ruled by the devoutly Catholic dictator António de Oliveira Salazar. This did not seem to bother most Portuguese, whose economy throughout the 1950s had a high growth rate. Portugal was unquestionably a frustrating and sometimes dangerous place to disagree with Salazar's views, but to many it offered prosperity and security in a tense post-war world.

It all came unstuck when Salazar refused to let the Portuguese colonies move towards independence in the 1960s, but that was yet to come. When Fritz published his biography of Salazar in 1943, and when Villiers visited in 1950, Portugal seemed the very model of a modern religious, nationalistic dictatorship. Disregarding the constitutional bans on press freedom, political opposition, collective action and universal suffrage, Fritz wrote optimistically of the Portuguese New State:

Above all, it places spiritual values above material values, and it considers the love of one's fellow men a far greater force in the attainment of social justice than an elaborate system of legislation based ostensibly on the will of a majority.[7]

When Villiers landed at Lisbon on 13 March 1950, he was especially looking forward to seeing Lisbon's great museums, as Portugal had been a maritime pioneer since the fifteenth century. Unfortunately, his hosts, the 'Gremio' – the Guild of the Codfish Shipowners – decided that the achievements of the New State were much more interesting. To Villiers' dismay, they kept dragging him off to look at rehousing projects instead of ships. Finally he got to see the Portuguese cod-fishing fleet, which still had more than twice as many sailing vessels as motor boats, including a barquentine and thirty-one enormous schooners.

Villiers was to sail on *Argus*, a four-masted schooner of about 700 gross tons and over 200 feet in length. She had an ice-strengthened steel hull, powerful engines and masts nearly 120 feet high. She had generators, refrigerators, electric lights, echo-sounder, radio telephone and steam-heating systems: *Argus* was a world away from any Cape Horner.

Argus set off on 1 April. She carried forty-four men, and after arriving at the Azores in mid-Atlantic, picked up another twenty-six. Apart from officers, deck boys and cooks, the vast majority aboard were dory fishermen, whose small wooden boats were piled up in neat stacks on the deck.

They arrived at St John's in Newfoundland in mid-April, and the fleet spent May on the Grand Banks. The tiny dories were launched over the side every day the weather allowed. Each carried one man who would lay out and haul in a heavy line with 600 hand-baited hooks for cod, three times over the exhausting day. The dorymen would gut, salt and store the fish away on the schooners at night, then start work again next morning at four.

After a disappointing catch, the *Argus* sailed north-east through broken ice towards Greenland. The dorymen fished day after arduous day, the ship moving slowly along the coast through June and July. Villiers wrote, without apparent irony:

Not that we endured a life of gloom. Far from it. Meals were always cheerful though cod was our staple. We ate cod fried and boiled (but always fried in olive oil); we ate cod fillets, whole cod, cod steaks, cods' heart, cods' tongues (fried in batter), cods' cheeks boiled and fried (and these were prime favourites); dried cod boiled, shredded, minced, made into fish cakes; we dried our own cod, and ate them in a dozen different ways; we ate some membraneous stuff scraped by the deckboys from cods' backbones, called samos, and served with a boiling of potatoes and tomato sauce. ... The food was good, the company excellent, the talk congenial though almost always of cod.[8]

In mid-July, possibly desperate for a change of diet, Villiers transferred to the fleet assistance-ship *Gil Eanes*, an old cargo vessel with a forty-bed hospital unit, which moved from schooner to schooner with stores, mail and the wireless link to the world. Villiers rejoined the *Argus* in mid-August, and in his heated cabin wrote a dozen articles and began *The Quest of the Schooner Argus*: he didn't have much else to do.

The fishermen were now having more success, but soon the fishing season was over. They sailed away on 10 September, dropped the Azorean dorymen at their island, and finally reached Lisbon. At the start of October Villiers returned to England, to rejoin his family after more than nine months apart.

———

At home Villiers worked on *The Quest of the Schooner Argus*, a valuable snapshot of an ancient livelihood now gone forever. A bland book too: no criticism, no irony, no vitality. Even the usually opinionated author has far less presence than usual. Villiers had gone with the cod-fishers not only to get a story for *National Geographic* but also to experience the last great sailing fleet for himself. In that he would be disappointed: he found that the schooners spread their canvas only as adjuncts to the engines.

In the book he broad-brushes the individual fishermen with a noble glow to the point of caricature: stoic, weather-beaten, uncomplaining, passionate about fish and grateful for life under the benevolent Guild of the Codfish Shipowners. However, it is possible he was being discreet: some of the men had told him hair-raising stories of life in Salazar's Portugal.

One said he been imprisoned by the Guild in the early days – 'we wanted liberty, he says – but he thinks the Gremio is a good idea now.' (Or perhaps a good idea when you're talking to someone with friends in the Gremio.) The outspoken Chief Engineer 'describes how he was a political prisoner for two years in Timor, and was beaten and strung up by the thumbs, and kicked ... the improvements in fishermen's lives are paid for by themselves many times over.'[9]

The men were paid on the basis of how much of the catch they brought in, and Villiers was perturbed at the way the captain appeared to underestimate the total. Part of him, like his father, loathed seeing injustice to workers, but another part had become increasingly conservative. His youthful reticence, his experiences as a journalist, a celebrity, a middle-ranking officer, all meant that he'd learnt to keep his real opinions to himself over the years. In any case, his dearest friend Fritz thought the world of Salazar's Portugal, and Villiers had four mouths to feed.

He may have been protecting the fishermen, he may not have wanted to embarrass his helpful hosts: whatever the reason, there would be no talk of political prisons in *The Quest of the Schooner Argus*.

———

Despite his absences and intense writing schedule, to his children he never seemed too busy for them. Kit remembers often stopping by his father's office after school – 'AJ would drop everything and draw a little picture of a ship so I could show it to Nance when I got home.' Kathy remembers Alan flying model planes with them in Leafield, and Peter that he was always ready to stop for a chat: 'a good listener and a spell-binding story-teller'.

Villiers completed the Portuguese article for *National Geographic*, and in January 1951 worked on *The Quest of the Schooner Argus*. It was finished a month later, then he began research for *The Indian Ocean*. From Leafield he made weekly trips to London to record a series of broadcasts for the Merchant Navy programme of the BBC General Overseas Service.

At Lisbon on 22 March 1951, Dr Salazar awarded him the decoration of Commendador of the Order of St James of the Sword, for outstanding services to science, literature or art. The honour meant a great deal to Villiers, since he would never be offered formal recognition from any other government for his many contributions to maritime heritage worldwide.

Early that year Villiers heard that *Viking* had been sold to Sweden, but *Pamir* and *Passat* were to be scrapped. In mid-year there was better news: *Pamir* and *Passat* would not be broken up after all. In June 1951 they were sold to Heinz Schliewen at Lübeck, to be worked as sail-training, cargo-carrying ships, and amid great public enthusiasm the German government agreed to subsidise the project. The four-masters were modified with ballast tanks, radios, extra lifeboats and 900-horsepower diesel engines. Transverse watertight bulkheads were installed as well as fittings for 'shifting board' dividers to hold cargo in place. Cadet applications were received from all over the world, and in the following year both ships made profitable voyages to Argentina.

August 1951 brought Villiers a devastating letter from Mel Grosvenor, who wanted the Portuguese article completely rewritten. He tried to soften the blow: 'In my estimation you are the Joseph Conrad of our day when you are at your best. But this article as it stands is not of that caliber. Also, like Conrad, you need now and then a bit of jacking from your editors!' Mel also wrote a separate, personal letter which ended, 'If you have a jar of jam to spare, would Nancy send us one because there's nothing like it anywhere!'

Villiers responded through gritted teeth: 'I will get cracking with it straightaway and you bet I will get something that we shall all like.' Grosvenor believed he had gone out laboriously cod-fishing himself when he had only briefly sailed in a dory, but he worked up a first-person adventure as required and it was finally published in May 1952.

On 18 September Villiers sailed (with a bottle of jam for Mel) on the *Mauretania* for New York. He started yet another lecture tour of America, and in nine weeks travelled to thirty cities. He was home by 24 December for the family Christmas festivities. His three months of non-stop lectures had brought them in good money. *The Set of the Sails* would continue to sell, *The Quest of the Schooner Argus* had received good reviews, and *The Indian Ocean* would soon be out. From these years onwards Villiers never again had to worry about lack of employment.

At the start of 1952 Villiers worked on a film script for MCA called 'Captain Silvio'. His script portrayed a feisty female pilot whose plane crashes at sea near the Portuguese fishing fleet. She is taken aboard a schooner but is disdained by the handsome, remote Captain Silvio. The inevitable storm brings them together for a future of matrimonial bliss – in Portuguese reality, her at home and him at sea six months of the year. The script was not apparently filmed.[10]

Alan and Nancie decided to move into Oxford so the children did not have to go to boarding schools. It meant leaving rural Leafield, but in January 1952 they put The Cottage up for sale. They chose a house in Davenant Road named 'Windrush', rather appropriate for Villiers. It was modern, spacious, on the city outskirts, and the children could easily get to school. They moved in on 1 April but their first month there didn't go terribly well: the children were seriously ill one after the other, and Villiers needed an adrenaline injection for severe hayfever.

In late May 1952 Villiers left once more for Portugal, to film the sail-training ship *Sagres* on a month's voyage to Madeira, Cape Verde Islands and the Azores. On this voyage *Sagres* carried twenty-eight cadets and 100 apprentice seamen, and Villiers was astounded: both at the number of hands, and how little work they seemed to do. The captain and officers did not have much square-rigger experience, and although Villiers liked them personally very much, he was concerned at their lax ship-handling.

This year he wrote three children's books, *And Not to Yield*, *Cutty Sark* and *Pilot Pete*. The first was a boys' adventure based on the Outward Bound Sea School, while *Pilot Pete* is about a porpoise from a remote New Zealand island which guides whaling ships into harbour, but also warns the whales to stay away from the hunters. The book is a delightful synthesis of Villiers' experiences, written by someone whose understanding of children had grown.

His approach to whaling was now very different too. In his 1934 *Whalers of the Midnight Sun*, it was a regrettable but necessary activity, but in *Pilot Pete* there is a sense of true horror when the animals realise why the beautiful ships are there. In the end, because of *Pilot Pete*, the island is declared a wildlife sanctuary: Villiers' thinking was ahead of his time again.

———

In February 1953 Villiers began probably his finest work on sail, illustrated by Harold Underhill and called *The Way of a Ship*. He had been planning it for years; a distillation of his understanding of the iron and steel vessels of the late nineteenth and early twentieth centuries. Through contacts since the late 1940s, Villiers had developed friendships among the German masters, especially Herman Piening, an ex-Laeisz captain; and *The Way of a Ship* focused on the great German sailing lines – Laeisz, Vinnen and Rickmers.

Villiers vividly portrays Laeisz 'Flying P' ships such as the spectacular five-masted *Preussen*, and in a section on 'Technicalities' provides readable and unique instruction on how to handle square-rigged sail, drawn from experience. Among the book's photographs is one of Betty Jacobsen in bad weather on *Parma*, looking appalled. It is captioned dryly, 'Girl cadets were a modern idea, found only in a few of the last Cape Horners. They did not stay at sea.'

Villiers also discussed school-ships and the fate of the ex-Laeisz barques *Pamir* and *Passat*: sadly, the grand scheme of working them as cargo cadet ships had recently run on to the shoals of bankruptcy. *The Way of a Ship* was a milestone; an affectionate leave-taking of the vessels that had dominated Villiers' early life. He would not revisit the topic again in depth for almost another two decades.

On 11 May 1953 he was awarded the Premio Camões – a prestigious Portuguese literary prize – for *The Quest of the Schooner Argus*, and in late May attended the launching of a new Grand Banks fishing motorship, named *Alan Villiers* in his honour: it was hardly surprising he felt appreciated by the Portuguese. In August he filmed the school-ship *Georg Stage* in Denmark for two weeks, and in early September sailed to America for another gruelling speaking tour, to last until mid-December.

On 28 October 1953, during the tour, his mother Annie died in Melbourne, aged eighty-two. The cause of her death was diabetes, which would eventually touch almost all of her children.

44. A lonely Atlantic convoy: Villiers commanded a 'flight' of LCI(L)s from America to Gibraltar in May 1943.

45. View from an LCI(L) of landing ships streaming towards France on D-Day, 6 June 1944.

46. Canadian Infantry landing from LCI(L) 299 on D-Day.

47. Villiers with some of his officers and crew, Far East, 1945.

48. Nancie in 1948, from her passport.

49. Alan in the early 1950s.

50. Traditional wooden Portuguese cod-fishing schooners in 1950.

51. Villiers broadcasting for the BBC, *circa* 1951.

52. *Mayflower II*, 1957.

53. Alan and Nancie Villiers after the arrival of the *Mayflower* in America, June 1957.

54. *Pamir*, lost with 80 crew and cadets in hurricane Carrie on 21 September 1957.

55. *Passat*, almost capsized in November 1957 like *Pamir*, but survived and today is a museum ship in Travemünde.

56. *Marcel B Surdo* as *HMS Serapis* in the film *John Paul Jones*, 1958.

57. Detail of movie ship *Angiolina H*.

58. Alan in costume for *HMS Defiant* or *Billy Budd*, *circa* 1961.

59. Captain Robert Miethe, aged 97, January 1975.

60. Restored iron barque *Polly Woodside* in Melbourne, 1989. Villiers' lifetime of work has inspired heritage vessel groups around the world.

61. Four-masted barque *Pommern*, built at Port Glasgow in 1903 as *Mneme* (the muse of memory), beautifully preserved at Mariehamn.

62. Alan in the garden at Lucerne Road, 1970s.

63. Villiers worked in 1920 on the 'lively, lovely' barque *James Craig*, built in 1874 in Glasgow, rebuilt by maritime heritage enthusiasts, and still sailing today in Australian waters.

Several square-riggers had recently been reprieved from the breaker's yard. *Moshulu* was bought by a Swedish company for a grain store in Stockholm, and *Pommern*, unused for years, was donated by the Erikson family to the City of Mariehamn. Once again, *Pamir* and *Passat* narrowly avoided destruction when they were auctioned off in April 1954 to the Landesbank [State Bank] of Schleswig-Holstein.

Also in April 1954 Villiers took his eleven-year-old son Kit with him to Denmark to show the *Georg Stage* committee the film *Schoolship* he had made from footage of their vessel. Kit remembers, 'He was a kind and considerate travelling companion, patient with a small boy's foibles.' Villiers then flew to Lisbon to meet up with Fritz and Kay, who had gone to live in Aviz in central Portugal, and to embark on three new sailing adventures.

His friend Pedro Teotónio Pereira had just been appointed Portuguese Ambassador to Britain, and he invited Villiers to help sail his beloved 40-ton yacht *Bellatrix* to London. It was a heady experience – the crew also included a rear-admiral and the pretender to the throne of Spain. A beaming Dr Salazar and the Minister for the Navy came to see them off at Lisbon. They had a rough but pleasant trip – 'The KING makes the scrambled eggs', joked Villiers.[11]

Next, he sailed from New York on the US Coast Guard barque *Eagle* on its annual training voyage to Europe. It was another job for the *National Geographic*, and over the seven-week period nothing much happened in 'Under Canvas in the Atomic Age'. He liked the master and enthusiastic crew but privately feared for their safety in other than easy conditions. He wrote glumly, 'I wish I sailed a sailing-ship and was not just busily making indifferent photographs of a cruise in one.'[12]

His wish was granted for his third venture of the year, as master of the literary creation *Pequod*. Director John Huston was filming *Moby Dick* at Fishguard in late 1954, with Gregory Peck as the obsessed Captain Ahab, and an elderly schooner standing in for his whaler *Pequod*. The schooner had been rejigged for glamour rather than sea-worthiness, but Villiers was fascinated by film-making on such a scale, and enjoyed it all. At one stage a rubber Moby Dick built around oil drums drifted away, and the BBC had to broadcast warnings that an artificial white whale had become a menace to shipping in the Irish Sea.

Pequod led Villiers to a new career with cinematic vessels, and also introduced him to Ike Marsh and Adrian Small, important future sailing companions. Ike was in his fifties, a rigger and ship model-maker, and young Adrian had joined *Passat* as a teenager in 1947, and was probably the last Briton ever to earn his mate's ticket in merchant sail.

———

In 1955 Villiers went on his usual full-throttle lecture tour of America between January and April, but his primary interest that year was research into vessels that had disappeared without trace. He attended inquiries at Lloyds and happily travelled around Britain, Norway and France gathering information: he appears to have greatly enjoyed the writing of *Posted Missing*. It covered all sorts of ships – coasters, trawlers, tankers, battleships, sailing vessels and liners – and was a unique study for its time, of enduring interest to salvage professionals as well as the general public.

Nancie was busy too. She had bought a real gypsy caravan, painted crimson and cream, with high wooden wheels. It was permanently parked near woods in a farmer's field near the River Evenlode, about 15 miles north-west of Oxford. She would take the children to camp out there for weekends; Villiers would sometimes go but he really preferred to be at home writing. Nancie then had another inspiration: she had always loved canoeing, and in 1955 bought a piece of land that ran down to the River Cherwell in north Oxford. They called it the River Garden, and would go swimming and boating there on the long summer evenings. It always amused his children that their adventurous father never wanted to learn to drive: instead, Nancie got her licence in June 1955 and became the family chauffeur.

In July Villiers completed *Pioneers of the Seven Seas*, an erudite, charming survey of innovation in seafaring, via primitive vessels, inquisitive mariners, engineering breakthroughs and bizarre ships. Villiers' views had now broadened, and here he expressed a new empathy for human complexity and ingenuity, rather than his usual sorrow for the 'passing' of sail.

At the same time, a group of German shipowners and the state of Schleswig-Holstein set up a non-profit foundation to operate *Passat* and *Pamir* – again – as cargo-carrying training ships. The four-masters were thoroughly overhauled, and in 1955 and 1956, with complements of about thirty-five crew and fifty cadets, they carried cement, coal and coke to the east coast of South America and brought wheat and barley back to Germany.

Although the 'end of sail' had been proclaimed often enough, sail itself clearly wasn't going without a struggle.

1 3

MAYFLOWER AND *MARCEL B*

In late 1955 *National Geographic* asked Villiers to check on the story potential of a replica ship project. He investigated, was impressed, and offered the promoters his services for free. They were ecstatic: you could not have asked for better publicity than the news that Commander Alan Villiers was going to sail the *Mayflower* replica from Britain to America.

As the *Mayflower II* was being built, Villiers carried on with the miscellany of other projects described in *Give Me a Ship to Sail*. As well as being involved with the film *Moby Dick* he travelled to the Maldive Islands, searched for two Italian brigantines for a (postponed) film project, and took part in a sailing-school ships race from Torbay to Lisbon in July 1956.

The race was particularly significant: it was the first of what would become world-famous events, continuing to the present day. It was organised by the Sail Training Association, whose patron was Villiers' friend, Portuguese Ambassador Teotónio Pereira. A dozen square-riggers and twenty smaller vessels took part, and Villiers crewed again on Pedro's yacht *Bellatrix*.

Sometime in 1956 Alan's older brother Noel died, aged only fifty-four. He had been a milkman, and was hit by a car on his rounds in Hobart.

Throughout the year Villiers worked on another of his Oceans books, which were crammed with readable history but gave him little pleasure. He had already 'done' the Coral Sea and the Indian Ocean, and this one was on the North Atlantic. It appeared in Britain as *The Western Ocean*, which made little sense in America, so it was released there as *Wild Ocean*.

Villiers also discovered a whole new audience when he started recording a television programme called *Sea and Ships* for the BBC in August. It became a regular series for some years, co-presented with a friend from Coastal Forces days, the naturalist Peter Scott.

Finally, Villiers was able to concentrate on the Mayflower Project. He had already lined up most of the crew, and on 22 September he watched the hull go into the dock at Brixham with great interest. It was the day before his fifty-third birthday: ten years since his discharge from the Royal Naval Volunteer Reserve, and twenty years since the end of the *Joseph Conrad* voyage.

———

At the beginning of 1957 Villiers took his family to Madeira for two weeks, for a holiday and to look over the Norwegian full-rigged training ship *Christian Radich*. He had signed a consulting contract with Louis de Rochemont, who was making a movie spectacular called *Windjammer*. De Rochemont, an American producer who had won two Academy Awards, was filming *Christian Radich* in 'Cinemiracle', using three cameras to create a single widescreen image.

Christian Radich left Madeira on 15 January and three days later her crew were amazed to see white sails on the horizon. Radio contact revealed it was the German four-master *Pamir*. So few square-riggers were still afloat that it was extraordinary for two to meet by accident, and a bonus for de Rochemont's cameras. They drew closer, and trim white *Christian Radich* circled great black-hulled *Pamir*, four times her gross tonnage. Cadets on both sides took photographs and called to each other, and the two beautiful vessels sailed southwards together for nearly a day.[1]

Pamir was carrying cargo from Antwerp to Uruguay: this time 2,500 tons of methyl alcohol in barrels. Just a few weeks before, the barque had had a nasty experience when she began to list sideways, and had to use her engine to rush into Falmouth harbour. An investigation found that her cargo had been poorly laden, and instead of water, methyl alcohol had been stored in her 750-ton ballast tanks.[2] Carrying cargo in ballast tanks on a well-loaded ship was not uncommon, but methyl alcohol was much less dense than water and the stability of the ship had been compromised. It should have been a salutary lesson.

Every maritime venture for Villiers was also a potential book, but oddly he did not devote many words to the 1957 *Mayflower* trip; it featured only in a children's picture book, a *National Geographic* article and a section of *Give Me a Ship to Sail*. Certainly the vessel's passage took less than eight weeks, and every reporting right had been flogged off before she even hit the water, but Villiers' main constraint was probably the law of libel, especially on the topic of Warwick Charlton.

Warwick Charlton was the promoter who first had the idea of the Mayflower Project – supposedly a goodwill gesture to honour Anglo-American bonds, prompted by the original 1620 journey of a Puritan sect on *Mayflower* from Plymouth (England) to Plymouth (Massachusetts), to found one of the early American colonies. Charlton was a newspaper and advertising man, a self-described 'expert in public relations'. He had been talking up the project for years and, probably to his own surprise, was suddenly offered seed funding in 1954 by real estate businessman Felix Fenston.

The idea of a re-enacted *Mayflower* voyage pleased everyone: Britain could take heart from its seminal role in world colonisation, and America could affirm its fantasies of benign Pilgrim Fathers. The Plimoth Plantation of Plymouth was happy to offer blueprints for a replica and to provide a future anchorage for the ship. Charlton could not believe his luck. Afterwards he would complain that he never made anything personally out of the project, but he lived very well off it. He had a persuasive smoke-and-mirrors approach to money that seemed to keep everything going, and the project gathered steam.

Villiers organised the *Mayflower* crew members, and helped with shipwrights, blacksmiths, riggers and chandlers. In March 1957 he flew to America to meet President Herbert Hoover on behalf of the project, and to lecture to the National Geographic Society. When he returned, a strike by shipbuilding unions had begun, but in an act of 'fraternal goodwill' *Mayflower* was exempted.

After intense efforts the completed ship was launched on 1 April 1957. She nearly capsized thanks to inadequate ballast, but that was quickly remedied; and Adrian Small, who shared lodgings with amiable Godfrey Wicksteed ('like a father to us'), today still recalls the extraordinary pleasure of being able to see *Mayflower* from their window every morning, floating like a vision in Brixham Harbour.[3]

———

Villiers' early friendliness towards Warwick Charlton became testier as deadlines were not met and vital documents did not appear. Like a mantra, he started telling himself (and everyone else) that he was only the master-designate of the ship, not the project organiser. Charlton tried raising money through donations, exhibitions and gimmicky schemes. The ship was carrying seventy large wooden 'Treasure Chests' filled with British export goods for sale, dozens of gold watches nailed around the vessel to promote their hardiness, and 130,000 envelopes the hapless crew had to stamp and frank en route, with 'Mayflower II – Maiden Voyage 1957'.

Charlton's perpetual-motion funding machine hit a snag, however, when the shipyard threatened a writ to prevent the ship from sailing unless at least £10,000 in costs were paid. The threat was lifted after guarantees were signed and cash dredged up (some contributed by Villiers and never recovered), and after the briefest of sailing trials the ship slipped out of Brixham on 17 April 1957.

At Plymouth the Lord Mayor held a departure ceremony attended by 10,000 people, with Villiers, Charlton and the crew dressed in seventeenth-century costume. Finally *Mayflower* sailed for America at 5.00 p.m. on 20 April. Before they had even left the harbour they found a stowaway. Villiers was convinced he had been planted by Charlton for publicity, and bundled him off into a press launch, doused with a bucket of galley-slops.

Mayflower was a handy barque, Villiers said, of 220 net registered tons and about 90 feet long. Her masts did not appear very strong, which confirmed his decision to take a southerly trade wind passage across the Atlantic rather than the stormy northern route of the original ship. She sailed well, however, and Villiers soon came to know her capabilities and limitations; although he wrote grimly in the Journal, 'I would feel a lot happier about this ship had she been built under Lloyd's survey – indeed, under any survey.'

But at last Villiers had the kind of shipmates he'd always hoped for. Mate was Godfrey Wicksteed, friend since 1921 and master in sail and steam. From *Pequod* came Adrian Small as second mate, Ike Marsh as bosun, and the cheerful seamen Joe Meaney and Joe Powell. From *Joseph Conrad* came Jan Junker (a master too, now) as third mate, and Andy Lindsay and Harry Sowerby as crew. A good friend from Oxford, Jack Scarr, was there; and a real doctor too – 'surgeon-sea-man' John Stevens had even brought along leeches. And this time, definitely, absolutely – no women.

By this stage, however, Villiers strongly mistrusted Charlton, referring to him only as 'the "ideas" man' in *Give Me a Ship to Sail*. Charlton said in an interview some time after the voyage:

> It has been rumoured that Villiers and I were always at loggerheads. Certainly there was a good deal of friction between us. I don't think he ever got used to the idea of a mere landlubber like myself building the *Mayflower*. But although Villiers was frankly critical of the way I sometimes publicised *Mayflower*, he was determined to hold onto his job of captain. He was usually able to smother his resentment until we were at sea. But then he could contain it no longer and we hardly spoke a civil word to each other during the fifty-four-day voyage.[4]

In the same interview he also confided breathlessly: 'I was the only one aboard who knew that the *Mayflower II* could perish and take her crew to the bottom of the Atlantic.' He claimed that the ship's surveyor had told him, 'She is unstable … liable to capsize in heavy seas …'.

Apparently unaware that a surveyor would be guilty of criminal neglect if he knowingly let such a vessel sail, Charlton bravely kept the terrible news to himself. During a storm he agonised over whether he 'had been right in concealing from the crew the real dangers of the voyage'. Given that all of the officers were veterans of Cape Horn, this statement probably exasperated Villiers beyond endurance.

———

The voyage proceeded pleasantly through the weeks of May 1957. *Mayflower* made slow, steady progress. In early June she entered the shipping lanes near America, to be greeted by liners, tankers and British naval vessels, including the massive carrier *Ark Royal*. On 8 June they had their only decent storm for the passage, which everyone rather seemed to enjoy. On 11 June the liner *Queen Elizabeth* glided past, and later in the day the US Coast Guard barque *Eagle* sailed up.

Captain Zittel, a friend of Villiers, called, 'What ship?' Villiers replied, '*Mayflower*, three hundred and fifty years out from England!'

They arrived at Provincetown on 12 June. 'Our welcome was terrific, colossal, magnificent!' wrote Villiers. Boats, yachts, cutters, aircraft, the full-rigged ship *Christian Radich* and even two Navy dirigibles came out to greet them; and Nancie had flown across the Atlantic to be there as well.

The following day they sailed across Cape Cod Bay to Plymouth. Dressed in period costume, Villiers, Charlton and the crew landed near famous Plymouth Rock, to the acclaim of tens of thousands of people. Charlton wrote, 'As we were rowed towards the shore I glanced at the Captain with whom I had been so proud to sail, sitting beside me with his black pilgrim hat in his hand, and thought how like the younger Churchill he looked, with his air of imperious determination.'[5]

But fine words would butter no parsnips with 'the younger Churchill'. Charlton had to leave immediately, which landed Villiers with the loathed task of handling publicity. Parties, press and politicians were coming at them from every side – even Vice-President Richard Nixon and young Senator John F. Kennedy turned up. Villiers wrote in *Give Me a Ship to Sail*:

> There were parades, receptions, dinners, lunches, engagements ... There were television programmes, radio programmes, sports fixtures, visits to ceremonies and functions at Boston and all sorts of places with never a quiet moment ... it was all sincere and wonderful. It was also extremely tiring ...

Mayflower was towed to New York for another riotous welcome. On 1 July there was a ticker-tape parade up Broadway, Alan and Nancie in a limousine and the crew marching behind in their seventeenth-century costume, with Felix, the ship's kitten. *Mayflower* was berthed in midtown Manhattan and thousands of people visited her over the next few months.

Charlton and his associate John Lowe were the remaining directors of the Mayflower Project. Once the voyage was over, the ship's ownership was to be transferred to an education trust, with a board made up of a duke, a knight and Felix Fenston Esq., who had supported the project with large sums of his own money. Fenston had been waiting for Charlton when the ship landed. He dragged him back to England on the next plane to transfer *Mayflower* from the project to the trust so its finances could be untangled: Charlton's smoke and mirrors had triggered a public relations disaster.

Dozens of tradesmen and an 'elderly widow' were seeking payment of thousands of pounds of outstanding *Mayflower* debts. A tugboat owner had instructed New York lawyers to arrest the ship unless the promoters paid his accounts, and accusations flew back and forth in the international press. Charlton insisted they'd all be paid by 'next week'. In the meantime, he told reporters, he was issuing writs of libel and slander.

He was also refusing to resign from the Project to allow the trust to be set up. His Mayflower Project still owned the ship, he told Villiers smugly.[6] Fenston then cut the money – or Charlton – off at the knees, and within a fortnight the assets of the Project were transferred to the trust. Charlton disappeared to America for a lucrative lecture tour about how he had built and sailed the *Mayflower II*.

The official receiver began winding up Mayflower Project Ltd in mid-1958. He said he could not locate Charlton, so had no access to the company books. Charlton complained to a reporter, 'I know where the books are. They are in my London home ... I have nothing to be ashamed of. I didn't make one penny from the entire venture.'

In 1959 the receiver gave his opinion that 'a disproportionate amount of the moneys raised was spent on organisational expenses'. He stated that the income from exhibitions and other sources had been about £56,000, while the ship had cost roughly £85,000 and expenses added up to another £43,000. Those expenses included £4,000 for public relations, £4,000 for advertising and publicity and £8,000 for travelling and entertainment – at a time when the price of the average house in Britain was about £2,500.

———

Money was on Villiers' mind too. One of his *Mayflower* publicity tasks in July 1957 was to go on the television quiz show *The $64,000 Question*, where he won $16,000. Not only did it create a potential tax problem, but he was particularly sensitive to any hint that he had sailed the ship for personal gain. He decided to donate $3,200 (the maximum permitted) to Plimoth Plantation, but first had to get permission from the Bank of England. The Bank approved, and Plimoth Plantation gratefully awarded him lifetime membership.

Villiers left for England at the end of August 1957. He took two weeks of summer holidays with Nancie and the children at Cwm-yr-Eglwys in Wales, where they had been going for years, and where they had first met their lifelong family friends, the Scarrs. (Jack Scarr had sailed on *Mayflower*, and one of his children, Tessa, would nurse Villiers in his final days.)

The *Mayflower* crew had been required to sign an agreement not to publish anything about the voyage for twelve months, to give priority to Charlton's 'quickie' on the project. Villiers had refused to sign, and actually did a *National Geographic* article on the technical aspect of sailing the ship. In September 1957 one of the on-board reporters, Maitland Edey, wrote to tell him that Charlton's book contained chunks lifted directly from his own writings and those of Villiers, passed off as 'conversations' on the ship. Villiers sent a sharp reprimand to Charlton's publishers. At the same time he was horrified to see newspaper articles calling him Charlton's partner, and consulted a lawyer about potential libel writs:

> Owing to the fact that the associates of Mayflower Project may be exposed at any time for the fraud which they have perpetrated on the American people, it is very necessary that my name should not be associated with theirs. At the same time, everyone honourable connected with the enterprise, on both sides of the Atlantic, is working to keep the matter from public exposure, for the sake of Anglo-American relations.

The lawyer pointed out that any action would bring the matter into exactly the sort of public scrutiny Villiers did not want, so he let it drop. He settled back into normal life, and returned to America in September 1957 for a three-week lecture tour. At San Diego, where the dilapidated iron ship *Star of India* was laid up, Villiers drew attention to her fate in the local press and inspired a volunteer group to begin the ship's long restoration. It helped him feel more philosophical about the events surrounding *Mayflower*, and he wrote to Mel Grosvenor:

Charlton and Lowe, the London promoters, were really a pretty terrible pair of fellows – their trouble, I suppose, was (at any rate in part) that it took crazy people to make such an idea work, anyway. At least they produced the ship, and we sailed her, and Plimoth Plantation are very glad to have her. Those are the important things.

Adrian Small had written happily to Villiers at the start of the project, 'What an opportunity to see how those ships sailed', and it was true: Villiers and his crew had been given the chance to experience something no other mariners had known for centuries. For all of its complications, the task had been a blessing.

On 21 September 1957, two days before his fifty-fourth birthday, Villiers heard on the radio that the four-masted barque *Pamir* was 'in trouble'. After *Pamir* had parted from *Christian Radich* and Louis de Rochemont's cameras earlier that year, she had delivered her barrels of methyl alcohol to Montevideo and returned to Hamburg in May with a cargo of barley. She left in June for Argentina with thirty-five crew and fifty-one teenaged cadets.

Pamir took on another load of barley at Buenos Aires and set off again for Hamburg on 10 August. As she was approaching the mid-Atlantic in early September, a tropical storm heading towards the Americas grew into hurricane Carrie. It reached Bermuda, then changed direction, looping back the way it had come. By 20 September Carrie was only 350 miles from *Pamir* but its path was safely southwards of the ship. Then suddenly it changed course towards *Pamir*, speeding up as if it were trying to catch her.

It did so on the morning of 21 September 1957. At about 8.00 a.m. on *Pamir* the wind rose to a shriek. Sails blew out and had to be cut away. At 10.36 a.m. the radio operator sent the distress message in Morse code, 'Pamir afloat in heavy hurricane without sails'. She had been on the starboard tack, heading to safety away from the eye of the hurricane – the standard procedure – but as she heeled over in the wind the cargo began to shift, and she could no longer right herself. At about 11 a.m. she transmitted, 'All sails lost, list 35 degrees, still increasing'.

The captain ordered everyone to the Hochdeck (the raised middle deck). Cigarettes and brandy were issued and the cadets were calm, but there was flooding below that the pumps could not handle. At 11.27 a.m. a general SOS went out, 'German four-mast barque Pamir in danger of sinking', and again a few minutes later: 'Hurry now. Ship makes water. Danger of sinking.'

The final message from *Pamir* was sent just after noon, but was lost in static. In the howling storm she listed so far her masts touched the water. Men were flung into the waves and choking spray. *Pamir* lay on her port side, then rolled over, her long keel and red hull in the air for about twenty minutes, then sank by the bow. Those who were tangled in rigging or too close to the ship were dragged under.

A massive search and rescue effort by the ships and aircraft of fifteen countries took place over a week of dreadful weather. Two days after *Pamir*'s sinking, five men – two sailors, two cadets and an assistant cook – were found in one lifeboat, and the following day a single sailor was discovered half-submerged in another: only six out of eighty-six men had survived.[7]

Forty-five days later it was *Passat*'s turn. She had left Buenos Aires with 4,200 tons of barley for Hamburg on 18 September. Four days into the voyage Captain Grubbe passed on the news of *Pamir*'s loss to his shocked crew and cadets. It was clear that their own cargo might shift too – by the time they had passed the Equator it had already settled by 6 feet. Over the following days they re-stowed most of the contents of Hatch No. 1 into the other three hatches to top them up.

It was not a moment too soon. In the North Atlantic, on 4 November, *Passat* was struck by a terrible storm, and the captain ordered her hove-to. Men were up to their hips in tons of water swirling over the deck, and the ship was rolling heavily. Seventeen-year-old able seaman Lothar Friis, who had been on *Passat*'s previous three voyages, could see her red underwater hull emerging as she wallowed. Next night conditions worsened. *Passat* heeled horribly to port by 60 degrees before recovering, and was left with a 16-degree permanent list.

The captain gave orders to flood the starboard ballast tank immediately, even though it was full of grain. *Passat* gradually righted herself by about 10 degrees. Lothar Friis wrote soberly in his diary, 'Last night we escaped by a thumb's width from sinking, the cargo slowly but surely shifted.'[8] The storm abated; they raised the sails and proceeded towards Portugal, working desperately to bring the ship back into trim. Reaching Lisbon on 9 November, they removed the wet grain, then sailed to Portsmouth to pick up a stability testing expert. *Passat* returned to Hamburg on 8 December 1957 and never went to sea again.

———

In early November 1957 Villiers went to Germany to see his good friend Captain Hermann Piening, now Marine Superintendent at Hamburg, and one of the assessors in the official inquiry on *Pamir*'s loss. *Passat*'s experience provided useful clues. Both vessels had been in sudden violent storms, both began listing after their cargoes shifted, and both had barley in their ballast tanks. But *Passat*'s tank had been flooded so she recovered her stability, while *Pamir*'s had not. She remained listing and water had poured in, probably through a smashed hatch.[9]

But why had both cargoes shifted in the first place? It was now standard for grain to be carried in bulk, not sacks, and although feeder boxes and 'shifting board' bulkheads minimised any flow, it could still move in extreme conditions: and tall sailing ships were far more likely than squat steamers to reach the large, sustained angles of heel that might trigger such a shift. Although the inquiry concluded that inexperience with sail had been a major factor in *Pamir*'s loss, Villiers always felt it was the decision to carry grain in bulk on square-riggers that had been horribly wrong from the start.

Even after *Pamir* was lost and *Passat* laid up, there was still a single four-master at sea. An 1887 iron ship named *Drumhill* had become the German-owned barque *Omega*, which Villiers himself had almost joined in 1921. In 1926 she was bought by a Peruvian company, then plodded her way around South America for decades until 26 July 1958, when she sank beneath 3,000 ton of guano off Lima. Christened with uncanny foresight, *Omega* had the distinction of being the final four-master ever to engage in merchant trade.

———

After his experiences with *Pequod* and *Mayflower*, Villiers became the first port of call for anyone in Hollywood needing a photogenic ship; and the work became a source of great pleasure to him. The two Italian wooden barquentines he had located for a project in 1956 – *Marcel B Surdo* and *Angiolina H* – were not used until March 1958. Then Villiers was contracted to supervise their makeover into movie frigates, and to sail each of them 900 miles from Fiumicino near Rome to Denia on the Spanish coast near Valencia.

When he took *Marcel B* to Denia in June 1958, Nancie, Kathy and Peter came along for the sunny five-day passage, signed on as steward, second steward and boy. Villiers also found a few ex-*Mayflower* seamen for crew – Adrian Small (who captained *Angiolina H*), Ike Marsh, Joe Lacey and ship's boy Graham Nunn. Villiers sailed *Marcel B* for two months during shooting.

The film *John Paul Jones* was loosely based on the life of the American Revolution naval commander. In an important battle, *Angiolina H* (173 tons) played Jones' famous ship *Bon Homme Richard*; while *Marcel B* (278 tons) played his opponent HMS *Serapis* and, after cosmetic work, also had a role as USS *Ranger*. Shooting took place from late June to early August 1958.

The movie's writer and director was John Villiers Farrow, father of actress Mia Farrow – Villiers called him his 'cousin from Sydney' and believed (incorrectly) that he was actually Leon's step-brother[10] – and starred Elliot Ness as a somewhat sanitised Jones, with Bette Davis in a cameo as man-hungry Catherine the Great. *John Paul Jones* got generally good reviews, although one reporter clearly couldn't tell real ships from fakes: 'Apart from a few unavoidable model shots in the sea fights, the production is big and handsome.'

———

Villiers endured another lecturing tour in America and Canada, from October to December 1958. The winter weather was appalling but he seemed to have developed an extraordinary ability to keep going week after week, working with good and bad projectors, large and small audiences, accepting whatever (and whoever) he was landed with, and generally making the best of it. If the projector broke down he'd yarn; if the plane was late he'd re-book; if a city was snowed in he'd go to

another. He had no fear of speaking to women's clubs now; he'd found
they could be delightful audiences, though sadly more interested in
Felix the kitten than the rigging of the spritsails. He didn't take it personally.

Things were going well and would continue to do so. A children's
book *The New Mayflower* was selling nicely; he was finishing off *Give
Me a Ship to Sail* 'with a new and more hopeful ending', he had started
collecting maritime tales for *A Seaman's Selection of Great Sea Stories*
(1959), and was planning a major work with *National Geographic –
Men, Ships and the Sea* – still three or four years away from completion.

Mel Grosvenor approved expenses for three sailing trips – Scotland,
southern England, and something Villiers had wanted to do for some
time: East Pakistan and the Brahmaputra river. (His children, as
adults, agreed that it seemed perfectly normal for him to come and go
in this way – it was some time before they realised not every father did
likewise.)

In early 1959 Villiers began looking for a boat for the Scotland voyage, and found the wooden Dutch botter *Cristoden* in Wales, 60 feet
long. She had a diesel engine, cabins and a bathroom. Villiers, Ike
Marsh and Graham Nunn spent five weeks preparing her, then they
sailed on 9 May for the starting point, the Firth of Clyde. Godfrey
Wicksteed, Nancie and the children came and went at different times
in the voyage.

Over twenty weeks they took the boat through the Inner Hebrides,
the Outer Hebrides, up through Loch Linnhe – revisiting Fort
William and wartime memories – the Great Glen, Loch Ness, Moray
Firth, Edinburgh, and the Forth and Clyde canal to Glasgow. A professional photographer was used for the story so only a few of Villiers'
own shots appear, but they are beautiful, especially a spectacular
panorama of islands and sea:

> It rained, of course, but it was often the soft and gentle rain, so common in
> those Scottish lochs, that touches the water with swift, soft circles and is so
> light the brief perfection of these circles is its only evidence, for it cannot be
> felt on face or hair.

National Geographic was one of the few institutions that provided an alternative to America's parochial view of the world. Over a period of forty-five years Villiers researched, travelled, took photographs and wrote thirty-one articles for the magazine; and despite the biases of the period the *Geographic* offers us today an extraordinary record of cultures on the verge of irrevocable change.

In February and March 1960 Villiers made his long-anticipated trip to East Pakistan, where his friend Basil Greenhill was Deputy High Commissioner. Greenhill helped him with arrangements in East Pakistan and also visited Villiers during the Scotland voyage. Sadly, soon afterwards his wife, Gillian, died unexpectedly, and letters between Villiers and Greenhill were warm and supportive.

In June 1960 an auxiliary gaff-rigged ketch, *Tectona*, was chartered for the 'UK interest piece' on southern England. Between June and September *Tectona* was sailed from the Isle of Wight to the tip of Cornwall, then back along the Cornish and Devon coasts to the starting point at Cowes. They stopped frequently at little villages, and passengers came and went, including Mel and Anne Grosvenor and their son Eddie. This single voyage gave Villiers enough material for two long *National Geographic* articles and two smaller pieces.

He briefly visited Portugal in early August for a naval review in honour of Prince Henry the Navigator. He sailed on Pedro Teotónio Pereira's yacht *Bellatrix* again: Pedro now had the exalted position of Deputy Prime Minister of Portugal, and 'looks a lot older, and worried – as well he might.'

Villiers left at the end of September for his annual speaking tour of America and Canada. He still attracted enormous audiences – at one venue there were 10,000 people at two shows. He visited *Mayflower* at Plymouth and *Joseph Conrad* at Mystic. In Washington he saw Mel Grosvenor, who gave him the go-ahead for a major new project in eighteen months' time: Australia.

———

The year of 1961 began for Villiers with a speaking tour in England and Scotland, then with Nancie and sixteen-year-old Kathy he flew to New York, where they dined with old friend Betty Jacobsen Reed and her fifteen-year-old daughter Nancy.[11] At *National Geographic* he was perturbed that Mel Grosvenor was favouring his own shots for the first *Tectona* article: 'it was only with difficulty that we avoided photographs of the excellent and indisciplined Eddie at the cross-trees, holding a bucket of mackerel, etc., etc.' (Eddie and his mackerel were slipped into the second *Tectona* piece.)

Undoubtedly Villiers' most pleasurable venture for the year involved sailing *Marcel B* for two sea movies, *Billy Budd* and *HMS Defiant*, released as *Damn the Defiant!* in America. *Billy Budd* was filmed from May to July, and starred Peter Ustinov and young Terence Stamp as the gentle-natured Billy, in a powerful tale from Herman Melville about good and evil, mercy and justice.

At the beginning of May, Villiers, Adrian Small, Ike Marsh and local seamen took *Marcel B* and *Angiolina H* from Valencia to Alicante for *Billy Budd*. Loaded with film crew, cameras, lights, generators, actors and extras, the ships worked for three months. Villiers greatly liked Ustinov, who also directed the film, and in Ustinov's autobiography *Dear Me* he describes Villiers on the ship as 'howling archaic commands to the winds, interspersed with expletives in no recognizable language.'

In early August, with his sons Kit and Peter aboard, Villiers and Adrian Small took the two vessels to Denia for a month of work for *HMS Defiant*. The producer was John Brabourne, son-in-law of Lord Louis Mountbatten, who came sailing on *Marcel B*. Mountbatten wrote to Villiers on 22 September:

> It is many years since I have had the pleasure of doing a cruise in a reasonably big ship under sail, and it brought back all the thrills of those days. ... I thought you handled your ship magnificently and all the film people most tactfully. Thank you so much for three enjoyable trips.[12]

HMS Defiant starred Alec Guinness and Dirk Bogarde. Like *Billy Budd* it was set in the tumultuous year of 1797, with its press-gangs, hell ships and famous mutinies at Nore and Spithead. The film is less of a psychological drama than *Billy Budd*, but the fine performances and striking sailing sequences have made them both classics, and they are still available today.

In September Villiers went to Portugal to lecture and to see Fritz and Kay. In late October he flew to America for two weeks for another intense speaking tour and meetings with *National Geographic* editors. He was still working on *Men, Ships and the Sea*, and noted to himself: 'Personalise, dramatise, humanise! Reduce: use ship to get there, follow a definite highlight routine, a discernible route, not hop – skip – jump.'

'Personalise, dramatise, humanise': the 'what' of ships rather than the 'why' of people had been the focus of his work for so long, but age had brought him some interest in human complexity. Under the heading of 'Ideas' he jotted notes for a new manuscript: a biography of Captain James Cook.

———

In interviews Villiers would sometimes mention his dream of one day sailing a replica of Cook's ship *Endeavour* to Australia. He started seriously considering it after an old friend, Colin Chapman, told him that the New South Wales government might buy the movie-ship *Bounty* to preserve in Sydney, and that 'some persons were considering, as a nucleus of an Australian Maritime Museum, the refurbishing of a coal-hulk named the POLLY WOODSIDE. I simply thought that here was the interest ...'[13]

In early 1961, the idea developed after maritime artist Oswald Brett suggested to him that the *Bounty* replica could be used in 1970 to mark the two centuries since Cook first landed in Australia.[14] A few weeks later, when Villiers was in America, he made a special trip to California to check over the *Bounty* but decided she was a 'second-rate facsimile'. What was needed was an authentically built replica, and he wrote enthusiastically to Brett:

> But I would really like to launch the idea properly myself, in Sydney, and not have it go off at half-cock. With whom do I launch it? Not a newspaper, certainly. Is the R.A. Hist. Soc. [Royal Australian Historical Society] live enough? And what do you think of Calwell?[15] [Arthur Calwell, then leader of the Australian Labour Party, was an old friend of Villiers' father.]

He was, as always, intensely busy with other work. In January 1962 Villiers went to Denmark and Norway to scout out ships for a new Hollywood extravaganza, *Hawaii*. He recommended that a Danish ketch named *Grethe* be converted to the movie brigantine *Thetis*, and sailed – by him of course – to Hawaii for shooting in 1963 or so: it was something to look forward to.

The hard-working *Marcel B* and *Angiolina H* appeared in an Italian film, *Son of Captain Blood*. It was not a raging success but it kept Adrian Small and Graham Nunn employed, and there was the promise of more movie work to come. In the meantime Villiers got them work rigging HMS *Victory* for the Society for Nautical Research.

In March 1962 he visited Washington for yet another bout with the *National Geographic* editors. He had, he hoped, finished *Men, Ships and the Sea* at last, but when he arrived, 'long session over SHIPS which to me is all profoundly depressing because these so-called "editors" do not edit. They rewrite, murder, add mistakes.'

On 22 March he joined the first nuclear-powered merchant ship, NS *Savannah*, for three days of sailing trials, mostly spent trying to understand nuclear power 'until my head reels'. *Savannah* was a combination of elegant cruise ship and cargo carrier, an 'Atoms for Peace' initiative to showcase the safety and cleanliness of the friendly isotope. Villiers' story appeared in the August 1962 *National Geographic*, and today seems more charmingly outdated than anything he ever wrote about sailing vessels.

Savannah was undoubtedly beautiful but her working life was short – the need for large numbers of highly trained technicians and extra space for the nuclear plant made her uneconomical from the start, and she was decommissioned within a decade. Forty-six years after Villiers first saw *Savannah* she is still waiting to be decontaminated.

14

RETURN TO
CAPE HORN

When Villiers set sail for England on *Grace Harwar* in 1929 he did not realise he was leaving his birthplace forever, but he probably would not have cared if he had. He always enjoyed his identity as a prominent 'Australian writer' but preferred to keep the narrow-minded world of his youth at a distance. However, when Alan, Nancie and Kathy arrived in Australia on the liner *Oriana* on 9 June 1962, he discovered that it was now an utterly different country – a powerhouse of optimism built on post-war prosperity, European migration and great engineering schemes.

The Villiers visited Tasmania, Victoria, South Australia, the Snowy Mountains and Sydney. In late July Peter joined them and they went north to Queensland. In mid-August Villiers flew on alone to Darwin. As an Australian he had grown up with all of the usual lazy biases against 'Abos', but at this stage of his life he had met, liked and lived with 'natives' from all over the world. He regarded the Aborigines thoughtfully:

> [T]hey seemed, at first, a wild lot ... Close up I noticed that their eyes were gentle, their features mild, their aspect cheerful. They chanted in low voices while they performed weird dances ... their choreography was really astonishing ...
>
> Outside the cathedral a bearded black man in long trousers and neat shirt leaned against the fence with a little chap, aged three, seated on his shoulder. In the cathedral is a striking painting of the Madonna and Child as natives. The little chap looked just like the Child.[1]

From Darwin he flew to Broome, which charmed him with its blue-jade water, red soil, sailing luggers and handsome, mixed-race locals.

Broome's days as the pearl shell capital of the world were long since over, yet there was new hope in for a future in cattle, fisheries, tourism and cultured pearls. Villiers was shown a lugger under construction – a pearling ketch about 55 feet long – and thought she had 'wonderful lines and was fit to sail around the world'.

He went on to Port Hedland, Kalgoorlie, Woomera, Adelaide and Alice Springs in the centre of Australia (he rearranged the travel sequence for his articles). His family flew home and he went on to Canberra, Alice Springs again, Sydney and Melbourne, before boarding *Helenus* on 12 November for the passage back to England.

The time on the ship was spent dashing off another Oceans volume – *Oceans of the World: Man's Conquest of the Sea*, a cheerful gallop through maritime history via Villiers' own experiences. He arrived home in mid-December then left after Christmas for Washington, where Mel Grosvenor greeted him with news of the excellent sales of *Men, Ships and the Sea* – already more than 125,000 copies.

—

Villiers spent much of 1963 consolidating interest in the *Endeavour* project. He had made useful contacts during the Australian visit, especially Norman Wallis and R.A. Dickson of the Royal Sydney Yacht Squadron, who set up a committee in March 1963 to organise an *Endeavour* Trust for Australia. In May that year an unidentified newspaper clipping enthused:

> The command will go out: 'Cast off on the starboard tack, me hearties!' ... A gallant 98 ft sailing ship of 370 tons will forge her way into open seas for the Southern Cross – 20,000 miles over the horizon. ... Commander Villiers, 60, a vast, rumbustious character who looks and curses like a sea dog, has his crew ready to sail with the tide.

Villiers' crusty captain persona was now so well established it didn't seem to matter that 'damn' was usually the extreme of his cursing! At this time too he received a reminder of how not to do a replica ship, when the *Daily Express* reported on 11 May 1963:

> Author and journalist Warwick Charlton left London Bankruptcy Court yesterday and admitted: 'I am bust because I became obsessed.' ... His creditors

were told yesterday he had debts of about £6,600 ... Assets were put at £38. ... 'It's ironical, but here I am broke, while the *Mayflower* has grossed over a million dollars since it reached America.' But he had no regrets.

In July 1963 Villiers signed a contract to write a biography of Captain Cook, and set to work with pleasure. In October he left for another two-month lecture tour of America but this time Nancie joined him. Rather than his usual one article per year for *National Geographic*, during 1963 Villiers published four major pieces: ship history, cruising off Devon and two on Australia. They were all popular, and it would be the peak of his fame at the magazine.

———

In February 1964 Villiers lectured in England, and in March went back to Australia to drum up support for the *Endeavour* project. In May he got to go on a square-rigger again for the first time in almost three years. *Sagres* was taking part in Operation Sail, the Sail Training Association's race from Lisbon to Bermuda; Louis de Rochemont was filming the race for a *National Geographic* movie, and Villiers was helping him. The race began magnificently on 5 June, with eight large training ships and barques, plus a four-masted schooner.

Sagres was not the vessel Villiers had sailed on in 1952, now a museum ship in Hamburg under her original name of *Rickmer Rickmers*. She had been replaced by the 1937 German-built steel barque *Albert Leo Schlageter*. The vessel might have changed, but the lack of experience that had so perturbed Villiers before was still evident: 'I have been critical of the way the ship is run (I don't want to be here in any hurricane!) but whatever I may think of some aspects of running the ship – and they are <u>terrible</u> – these are very nice fellows and there is a happy spirit aboard.'²

At Bermuda, Villiers realised he was being snubbed by the Sail Training Organisation:

> For my part, to my chagrin and surprise, I am not counted in at a single one of the official and semi-official affairs, and am invited to nothing, although the S.T.A. know very well I am here ... I'm afraid that the absence of <u>all</u> invitations ... was deliberate. I do not assume that I ought to be invited anywhere

by these arrogant and snobbish Britishers: but I am trying to write their story for a rather well-known international magazine …

Villiers believed there was sometimes prejudice against him, perhaps because of his popular success, his Australian origins, his intolerance of officialdom and his support of non-British maritime heritage. He was probably correct on all counts.

Operation Sail was to end with a triumphant 'sail-by' in New York harbour. During the procession Villiers broadcasted an enthusiastic live commentary, but was privately appalled that the ships motored rather than sailed past, despite the good conditions.

> Of the eight captains who sailed on the S.T.A.'s Lisbon–Bermuda race, two only were really competent square-rigged shipmasters … The governments which trust ships to such officers don't appreciate what they are doing … The Lord preserve them if they ever try anything other than power-assisted summer sailing.[3]

In early October Villiers was contacted by the Mirisch Corporation, which was going ahead with the film *Hawaii*. He went to Copenhagen with the director George Roy Hill, to start turning the ketch *Grethe* into the movie brigantine *Thetis*. He then spent time in New York with Louis de Rochemont, editing the *Operation Sail* movie. Unfortunately, the *National Geographic*'s Television Service wanted de Rochemont's footage for itself. Mel Grosvenor preferred it as a movie but his increasingly influential son Gilbert prevailed: in early 1965 the film was cut down for television.

It was a pity, but Villiers had other things to look forward to: in 1965 he would be sailing for the film *Hawaii*, and there was action at last on the *Endeavour* project. The HMS *Endeavour* Trust was established in Sydney in November 1964, with Vice-Admiral Sir John Collins as President, and the Australian government had donated an encouraging £10,000.

———

Villiers sailed the brigantine *Grethe* from Denmark to Panama City in early 1965 as calmly as other people drive to work: by now there was perhaps not another man alive with his breadth of personal experience in square-riggers. *Grethe* left Copenhagen on 24 January, with Adrian Small and a temporary crew. Nancie joined them at Lisbon, to make a trans-Atlantic passage on a sailing ship for the first time in her life. They reached Barbados on 5 March and Nancie greatly enjoyed the experience.

Mirisch had located a second vessel for the film, so Adrian Small took over *Grethe*. Villiers and Nancie were flown to California, where the three-masted schooner *Wandia* was being converted by the Art Department into a barque, the whaler *Carthaginian*. He found crew for *Wandia* from friends he had made during his American tours – Kenneth Reynard, master of the *Star of India*, and Karl Kortum, who had preserved *Balclutha* and founded the San Francisco Maritime Museum.

Nancie flew back to Britain and Villiers took *Wandia* to sea on 20 April. The voyage was mostly spent undoing the excesses of the Art Department, and they arrived at Honolulu on 7 May after an easy passage of 2,500 miles. The next few months for Villiers passed in travelling between Oxford, California and Honolulu, and sailing ships for the filming of *Hawaii*. It starred Julie Andrews and Max von Sydow, and was probably the most famous movie Villiers worked on, but it was not a major success; and unlike with earlier films, no one seemed to even notice the lovingly rebuilt ships.

He was back at home in July: 'I work a 7-day week, which is ridiculous. I take on some difficult things … I get older too – 62 now, and sometimes feeling it … And I have a book or two to write which I hope may be of a little more worth than useless *National Geographic* articles.'

Villiers was away again to lecture in America in October and early November, then spent a few days at Mystic Seaport. He was very fond of 'the gentle, competent, visionary founder – later ruthlessly discarded – Carl Cutler', but less fond of the new management, although he still thought 'the achievement is tremendous'.[4]

———

The *Endeavour* project gathered steam over 1965. The three members of the technical group, Villiers, Norman Wallis and building supervisor Marcus Fletcher, got on very well together. In Sydney, the HMS

Endeavour Trust set up a company, Captain Cook's *Endeavour* Ltd, to handle a funding appeal and expenses. The first quote they received for timber was ludicrously high – about £130,000. Villiers quickly found them another merchant quoting two-thirds less, but the Australians began to wonder what they'd let themselves in for.

Some progress seemed to occur when the British Committee for the Endeavour Trust was formed, with Viscount Boyd of Merton in the Chair and Admiral Sir Charles Madden as Executive Secretary; Madden and Villiers became close friends. But, sadly, Norman Wallis died suddenly in November 1965, and a driving force for the project was lost. An unpleasant note was also struck when R.A. Dickson – whom Villiers had brought into the project in the first place – offered Villiers a contract to sail the replica which seemed to him a 'slap in the face', designed to 'pin down a confidence man' rather than trust in his integrity as master.

The timing was becoming urgent too – if the ship was to go around the Horn, the keel had to be laid as soon as possible, but the Australian appeal for funding had raised only £42,000 by mid-1966. Then the shipyard asked for a guarantee up front for the full cost – £220,000 – rather than the more usual incremental payments. The Australian government and banks declined to underwrite it. In June 1966 newspapers reported that the project had been postponed for six months, 'because the public appeal for funds in Australia had started a little late'.

Now *Endeavour* no longer had time to sail around Cape Horn and arrive in Botany Bay by 1970. The project decided on an alternative route of Cook's, via the Cape of Good Hope instead. But Australia was in the middle of a drought, a half-built Opera House and the deepening quagmire in Vietnam: few people cared about sailing ships. Yet even towards the end of 1966 there was still hope, until the project received a second blow: the 'irreplaceable' Marcus Fletcher died after a short illness in November 1966.

On 13 January 1967 the HMS *Endeavour* Trust announced: 'in view of the unavailability of the necessary funds at this date the building of the replica of HMS *Endeavour* in sufficient time to arrive in Australia to coincide with the Bi-Centenary of Captain Cook's landing is not practicable and the project has been abandoned.'

Villiers thought the trustees were 'asses'. He did not live to see the launch of the Australian-built *Endeavour* replica, twenty-six years after the end of the project he had so hopefully initiated.[5]

———

Throughout 1966 Villiers had kept working on his biography of Captain Cook. It went more slowly than usual, which frustrated him but probably made it a more thoughtful work. His other major project for the year was a study of Holland for *National Geographic*, but even after three visits that did not proceed easily either.

A little house on Lucerne Road abutting their River Garden land on the Cherwell came up for sale, and Nancie, ever the optimist, wondered about the small house next to that too. In August 1966 they bought both properties: the 'Villiers Estate', they joked. Windrush, the family home for fourteen years, was put up for sale.

Alan attended meetings of the National Maritime Museum trustees and the Society for Nautical Research as often as he could. In November, Frank Carr, the Director of the Museum, retired with great reluctance and noisy controversy; Villiers had little respect for Carr. Together with fellow trustee Malcolm Glasier, Villiers strongly supported Basil Greenhill's successful application for the post. Greenhill had married Ann Giffard after the death of his first wife, Gillian, and they would often visit Alan and Nancie: Villiers was god-father to Basil and Gillian's son Richard.

In March 1966 Villiers went to Alaska for two weeks to lecture on James Cook at Anchorage, Juneau, and the University of Alaska at Fairbanks, and in November also lectured for a week at the University of Lisbon: the boy who never finished high school had come a long way. His children were doing well too. Kit had taken a degree in politics, philosophy and economics at Oxford, Kathy was about to graduate in geography and anthropology from Durham University, and Peter was just starting Latin American studies at the University of Essex.

———

Since the days of his Arabian voyages, Villiers had never lost touch with the Abdul-Latif family or Ali al-Nejdi, the captain of *Bayan*. In

January 1967, Nancie and Alan flew to Kuwait for a holiday. They found that al-Nejdi had come far from his days as a humble nakhoda and was now a very rich man; and the Abdul-Latif family had similarly prospered, especially politically. The Villiers enjoyed a busy a week of visits and gifts and feasts with old friends and met a bewildering number of their descendants.

In early February 1967 Villiers began another six-week lecture tour in America. After his return the family completed the move from Windrush to the new house in Lucerne Road. In May the BBC asked him to broadcast the arrival of Francis Chichester at Plymouth, after a single-handed sail around the world, including Cape Horn. Villiers thought the voyage had been foolhardy, but he had known Chichester for some years and enjoyed marking his safe return.

In June, Villiers' book *Captain Cook: The Seaman's Seaman,* beautifully illustrated by Adrian Small, was released to excellent sales. At the same time Alan was busy setting up a major trip for *National Geographic*, following the path of Charles Darwin in the *Beagle*. Villiers and his son Peter flew to New York in July 1967, then left for South America with photographer James Stanfield.

They arrived in Chile, and travelled to the notorious West Coast. In the days of the nitrate barques no one had to ask 'West Coast of where?' There was only one West Coast, and without it four-masters might never have survived long enough for Villiers to enjoy. But Valparaiso was 'a bit of a disappointment, for the great old windjammer port retains nothing of that atmosphere'.

They went on to the Galapagos, Brazil, Uruguay, Argentina, chilly Punta Arenas and even further south to Puerto Williams, where they were marooned by a blizzard for five days. Back at Punta Arenas they took a bus up the coast to Santiago, where the ninety-year-old Laeisz master Captain Robert Miethe now lived:

> What a wonderful old man he is! This blue-eyed, strong-featured, grand old sea-dog, in full possession of all his faculties (he still is a marine surveyor, one of the only two in the whole district) and perfect health. We get along splendidly: it is obvious the old man doesn't get many chances now to talk of the Cape Horn days to an interested listener. He is fascinating.[6]

A few days later it was Villiers' sixty-fourth birthday. He was only halfway through a trip that would have left most people reeling: dozens of aircraft, bus, boat, truck and even mule rides, tedious Customs, difficult hotels, and all under severe time pressure. It was not surprising he could not sleep: 'For this past week I have been bothered at night by considerable irritation, sometimes in spasms, of the skin of the feet. What is this – getting old?'

In late September Peter left for home and Nancie arrived. They flew to Tahiti for two weeks, then Tonga and New Zealand, where Alan met the likeable Cook scholar Professor John Beaglehole, who became a good friend. They landed in Brisbane in early November then travelled south to Melbourne: Alan's brother Frank had now retired from the merchant service, and Lionel was a highly respected headmaster. After Australia they visited Mauritius and South Africa, where they spent time with Villiers' friends from 1928, Alan and Betty Deverall.

Back in Britain by late November, there was no time to rest. Villiers had to go to Amsterdam then almost immediately to freezing Washington to give lectures. He was home at last in mid-December. He went to the doctor for a check-up, and found that the odd symptoms he had noticed in his feet had a rather grim cause: like his mother, he had developed diabetes mellitus (Type II). Just after Christmas 1967 he was admitted to a nursing home for a week of medical tests.

———

The year 1968 brought fundamental changes in the lives of the Villiers family. In January Alan started on the diabetes drug chlorpropamide and responded well. He and Nancie learnt how to modify his diet and he started on regular exercise. The illness gave him the chance to withdraw from the arduous lecture circuit, and he was content to stay at home and work on his writing and frequently grumbled-about correspondence.

The Villiers offspring came and went, staying for weekends and holidays, bringing friends to go punting on the Cherwell, or for picnics or parties or dances. Kit, twenty-five, was restless in a job with a London newspaper, and left for Japan to work for a shipping firm in August 1968. Kathy, twenty-three, completed a postgraduate diploma in town planning at the University of Manchester, and Peter, twenty-one, was still studying at Essex University. Alan and Nancie were supportive and at ease with their children's lives.

But Villiers at sixty-four was perhaps a little less supportive of his fifty-two-year-old wife's interests at this time. For several years Nancie had attended Workers' Educational Association courses and was passionate about the North Oxford Residents' Association. 'Nance to a Wives meeting in Christ Church hall, on education for women, or some such nonsense. How seriously they all take themselves!' 'Nance off to the [M40 motorway] inquiry (after some remonstrances from me: she is home to fix lunch).'

The harmony of their household flowed directly from Nancie's prodigious efforts. The many visitors to their home were always greeted with her food and hospitality. She assisted elderly friends, maintained two rental properties they owned in Oxford, and drove Villiers wherever he wanted. During lectures he would show compilations of his films, and it was Nancie who had often done the work of editing them with a splicing machine.

She was sometimes 'poorly' or had a bad back – 'Nancie not feeling very well, which is sadly often the case and has been for some years' – but medical examination never found a reason. Her ill health may have been linked to the heavy load of responsibility she carried, especially during Villiers' frequent absences, because her family noticed that after Alan's death such episodes almost disappeared. Still, times of irritation between them were rare, and their long marriage appears to have been a happy one.

Villiers wrote his first draft of the South American 'Darwin' article, and delivered it to the faithful Mrs Templeton, who typed and retyped copies of his work over many years. He also worked on a book that *National Geographic* had commissioned, which he called *The Ship and I*; an update on his autobiography *The Set of the Sails*. 'In the evening reading through my early diaries from the *Bellands*, the *Herzogin Cecilie*, and the *Parma*, and am appalled at their crudity and inadequacy. I was obviously a very late developer.'[7] It is not clear whether he meant emotionally or as a writer.

He kept up his attendance at his various maritime committees, although he was more cynical now. In April he wrote: 'Society for

Nautical Research more than usually useless: little concerned with things nautical (except HMS *VICTORY*) or research, it is more and more a private hobby, almost, for a few cronies.' Still, the fruits of involvement could be sweet: in October 1968, when the *Victory* Advisory Technical Committee [VATC] met on the ship, 'the lunch in the great cabin with Nelson's silver at Nelson's table is a fine occasion ... the first time the VATC has been so honoured. There are four admirals present and several captains.'

Villiers had also been asked to join an advisory committee for the Hudson's Bay Company, which was building a replica of the seventeenth-century ketch *Nonsuch* to celebrate its three-hundredth anniversary. Adrian Small was appointed master, and Villiers went several times to Devon when she was being built and sailed on her during sea trials.[8]

But what he most enjoyed during 1968 was working on a new book which re-awakened his passion for the great square-riggers. He went to Hamburg in June to interview retired Laeisz masters, and they visited maritime museums, bookshops and galleries, yarning happily for hours. In August he began checking early ship documents at the Public Records Office in Hayes, near Heathrow. He was fascinated by what the logbooks revealed about life aboard the Cape Horners, 'more social history than seafaring'.

———

Villiers' diabetes seemed to have stabilised. In early 1969 he took up a guest lectureship on the liner *Kungsholm* for a Pacific tour. When Nancie and Alan joined the ship they were told by a crew member that the prospect of him lecturing on Captain Cook 'had filled' the cruise. They visited New York, Florida, the Galapagos, Tahiti, the Cook Islands, Samoa, Fiji, New Zealand, Hobart and Melbourne; and by then Villiers had given seven lectures, three broadcasts, and written two articles.

They went to cocktail parties every night, and almost despite himself Villiers started to enjoy the life. At Melbourne they were met by Lionel and sister Enid, who seemed well, but Frank was 'looking old, ashen, tired' – he was affected by diabetes too, and had recently spent time in a tuberculosis sanatorium.

Kungsholm went on to Sydney, Thursday Island, Bali, Singapore, Bangkok, Hong Kong and Yokohama, while Alan gave five more lectures and Nancie took Japanese lessons. On the passage to Panama Villiers did another four talks while Nancie learned Spanish and got a nice tan. They finally reached New York in mid-April, where Villiers lectured to raise funds for the South Street Museum and its barque *Wavertree*: at the New York Yacht Club he received a standing ovation.

Over the next six months Villiers made dozens more visits to the Public Records Office repository at Hayes, working his way through the logbooks of British sailing ships from 1905 to 1908. Nancie or Peter would sometimes drive him there and help with summarising, but he usually went on trains and buses, taking two-and-a-half hours each way. He chided himself for putting in so much effort but clearly enjoyed it – 'they carry the human story' – and eventually read the logs of 470 vessels, mostly Cape Horners. He was particularly touched to come across the records of seaman Korzeniowski: Joseph Conrad himself.

His friend Admiral Sir Charles Madden asked Villiers to write something on the work of the Royal National Mission to Deep Sea Fishermen, so he spent three weeks in the Arctic from late August on the trawler *Arctic Vandal*. He found the experience dispiriting as he did not seem to connect with these sailors as he had with the Portuguese, but did his best with the book *The Deep Sea Fishermen*. He really preferred to concentrate on his 'Cape Horn magnum opus', and decided he must visit Captain Robert Miethe again in Chile.

The year ended well: the old sailing ship crew lists at Hayes had been under threat of being culled by 90 per cent because of lack of storage space, but Basil Greenhill agreed they should be preserved by the National Maritime Museum. And Basil and his wife, Ann Giffard, had written a book on the experiences of women on sailing ships which, to her great pleasure, they dedicated to Nancie Villiers.[9]

———

Villiers went to stay with Robert Miethe in the small town of Quilpué, Chile, in January 1970. Miethe met him at the railway station: 'I move in and we are soon yarning away – we are still at it towards midnight. A wonderful old boy, in excellent form and quite unimpaired memory.' They talked for three days.

Villiers then flew from Chile direct to Portugal. He saw his old friend Pedro Teotónio Pereira, whose encroaching Parkinson's disease had now ruled him out of political life, although he had once been Salazar's chosen successor. Alan also visited Fritz and Kay in Aviz, who were finding life there increasingly difficult, but they had neither the energy nor funds to move back to England. Fritz, now eighty-six, was confined to a wheelchair.

In mid-February Kit came home from Japan. The three children would visit at weekends, and Villiers delighted in their busy lives: the clapped-out cars, the career ambitions, the conversations, the meals, the movies, the unusual friends. An acquaintance of his late brother Noel came to talk about the old days in Melbourne, prompting Villiers to write in his diary, 'Thank the Lord I had the big sailing ships to take me forever out of Collett St and give me something to stick to – yet I'd have found that, even without them'. It was perfectly true that his curiosity, perception and self-discipline would have taken him far in just about any field.

In March 1970 Villiers began writing one of his major works, *The War with Cape Horn*. Nancie hated the title but Villiers insisted he couldn't think of a better one – which was perhaps unimaginative of him as it was confusingly similar to *By Way of Cape Horn*. He found the writing difficult. The official logs of British ships around 1905 depressed him, with their depictions of gruesome conditions and inadequate masters. He turned to the well-run German ships with relief, but then worried about the 'image of British Sail' that suffered in the inevitable comparison.

In 1970 the Duke of Edinburgh convened the Maritime Trust with the Duke of Westminster and other titled luminaries, and Villiers was asked to join the Ships Committee. He was already a trustee of the National Maritime Museum, chairman of the Photographic Records Sub-Committee of the Society for Nautical Research, a member of the *Victory* Advisory Technical Committee, the *Cutty Sark* Preservation Society and the *Nonsuch* Committee, and in mid-1970 he was elected President of the Society for Nautical Research.

The bi-centenary of Cook's landing in Australia arrived in April 1970. A reporter asked Villiers if he were bitter about the failure of the *Endeavour* scheme: 'of course not (not publically, anyway)', he joked in his diary. He was saddened that when he was invited to Australia House to mark the event, it was to represent the Society for Nautical Research: they had no idea he had written a major work on Cook, or even that he was Australian himself.

Villiers would sometimes grumble about Nancie's extension classes and memberships of associations, but he gave as freely of his own time himself. He did the preface for a popular Brooke Bond tea-card series on ships, supplied historic photos for museums and exhibitions world-wide, and researched queries from historians, movie-makers, mod-ellers, artists, an Oxford barge group and (apparently) anyone who'd ever had a relative go to sea.

In September 1970 there was a break from the constant round of meetings, letters and books: lecturing on another cruise on *Kungsholm*. Nancie did not come this time, but visited when they berthed at Plymouth, England. After she left, Villiers wrote, 'much missing my wife … it was lovely to have her even for a little while.' They had been married for twenty-nine years. Later 'a number of old ladies, remark-ing on her beauty (so obviously uncocted: "grown from inside", one says) express regret that she is not here.'

The voyage and lectures went well, but back at home Villiers found Peter thinking of joining the Army, while Kit had a new job in Japan and was busily preparing to leave. One evening they watched family films, 'of early days with the children … very pleasant to see. But I feel old.'

In January 1971 Villiers was told that the official logs at the Hayes repository were being dispersed after all. He managed to save the early twentieth-century documents for the National Maritime Museum, and curators across Britain pounced on those for their own ports, but – he heard with incredulity – the remainder were to be sent to the uni-versity at St John's in Newfoundland. He contacted the National Library of Australia to see if they wanted logs with Pacific or Australian links. They certainly did, so he filled several boxes and had them shipped to Canberra. He also helped staff from the State Library of New South Wales select logs for their archives.

Disillusioned with the British approach to Pacific maritime history, he spent weeks at Hayes in the first three months of 1971, finding out as much as possible about nineteenth-century ships before it was too late. He began planning a book based on Joseph Conrad's life at sea.

Villiers' committees continued: the Society for Nautical Research was his favourite – 'this lively organisation'. He also enjoyed the recently formed Maritime Trust (Prince Philip would turn up in his red helicopter and call him 'Alan') and was pleased that the *Cutty Sark* Preservation Society had decided to put that ship into the care of the Maritime Trust.

He had been a trustee of the National Maritime Museum now for twenty-three years. He began to notice that the director, Basil Greenhill, seemed to be getting rid of people: 'I wonder – one after another, all the pioneers, out they go ... Basil can be abrupt not to say curt.' He was surprised at Greenhill's growing 'obsession with status' but they still worked well together.[10]

In March 1971 Phillip Donellan from the BBC planned a film on sailing ships, and Villiers helped him with documents, artefacts and introductions to elderly seamen in Germany and Britain. The film, *Before the Mast*, was shown later that year and Villiers was pleasantly surprised at its quality.

On 1 April he flew to Australia to continue with research for the book on Conrad: 'it might "knock" the Xmas card image of the "clipper" somewhat. It will not be good for the "nostalgia" market: well, I'm not writing for that, nor ever have.' He enjoyed two peaceful weeks burrowing through records at State Libraries and made a quick visit to Melbourne. On 3 May he was 'warmly received' by the National Library of Australia in Canberra, who tape-recorded his comments on the official logs he had sent them. Best of all, on the way home he stopped in Tokyo and had nearly a week in Japan with Kit.

In mid-1971 Villiers took the train to Nantes to study Conrad's early life on French ships. Commandant Marc Paillé gave him a manuscript by ex-sailor Henri Picard listing the French Cape Horn ships, and asked him to write an introduction and help get it published. It was a diversion from Conrad, but Villiers had found much on French ships in the Hayes logs and was happy to write several chapters for the book.

It appeared in 1972 as *The Bounty Ships of France*, by Villiers and Picard.

He quietly helped other struggling writers too: he edited large sections of *Four Captains* by George V. Clark, and submitted it several times until it found a publisher. He also did a great deal of work on *Windjammer 'Prentice* by Captain V. Large and D. Jackson – even collating the index – and again pushed it until successful. He took no credit for such efforts, content that these histories were preserved.

In June the commander for the *Apollo 15* Moon mission, David R. Scott, wrote to Villiers to say that he had been inspired by a draft of his article on Cook, so had named their Command Module 'Endeavour'. The article that Scott saw appeared in *National Geographic* that September. It was enormously popular, but Villiers found it depressing that so many people who congratulated him on it had never read 'even one' of his books.

Mel Grosvenor's son Gilbert was now in charge at *National Geographic*, and Villiers noticed with resignation that they did not want his work as in the past – they were not even interested in a manuscript they had already paid for. Still, *War with Cape Horn* was doing well, and Villiers was asked to select a third anthology which would appear as *My Favourite Sea Stories*. It did not demand much work, which was a relief, as 'one can so easily keep putting off any difficult writing – and it is <u>all</u> difficult now'.

In November, twenty-four-year-old Peter left to join his regiment in Northern Ireland. His parents kept their fears for his safety to themselves: Pete was doing 'a man's job', Alan said. Kit was still in Japan and the place was lonely. But one bright spot was Kathy's frequent presence. She always seemed cheerful, attending parties, redecorating her flat, enjoying her job and going to planning enquiries with Nancie.

In December, 'Nancie was off by the 1525 for London to attend some meeting of surveyors, planners, road engineers and the like: I trust they are not too greatly taken aback when she and Kath walk in.' Probably not – the Vice-Chancellor had recently written to Nancie approving of her idea for a public environmental study with Oxford University.

Part of one of their two small properties at Lucerne Road was rented out, but at the rear Villiers had his study, with a glassed-in veranda looking on to the Cherwell River. As if he were still at sea, his diary entries usually began with notes on the wind, weather and barometer reading; and he watched the ever changing River Garden with loving interest:

> The backwater and our 'dock' full of thick ice, the trees of hoar frost, the lawns of frozen snow.
>
> Colder … but a full moon rises splendidly over the river and the night is beautifully clear.
>
> Willow seed lies fluffily on the water and everywhere, with more in the air.
>
> The hail hits the earth and the roofs savagely and quickly heaps high on the lawn … and the rain drops hit with such force that each one bursts.
>
> Still very grey and misty across the fields … though the sun is visible as a white disc.

The river rose and fell with the weather, sometimes flooding the lawn or retreating so far in summer that the backwater behind the island, 'Cromwell's Ditch', was just mud. Despite the efforts of gardeners, grass-cutters and Nancie, work in the River Garden was never-ending. Villiers still suffered agonies of hayfever every year. His energetic family would call him out to the garden in the milder weather for picnics and punting and sitting in the sun, but all he really wanted to do was write.

Nancie also kept up her busy 'errands of goodwill and mercy, of which she and Kath do the family's share and more'. And Villiers wondered about one of her friends: 'The old lady – 88 I think – has lost her memory. What is left?'

15

VOYAGE INTO
THE UNKNOWN

In January 1972 Villiers, aged sixty-eight, agreed to a request by the Prime Minister to continue as a trustee of the National Maritime Museum for another two years, although he was becoming increasingly concerned at the director's approach:

> There is an almighty long screed from the excellent Basil telling the Trustees what to do – really an alarming lot of it. ... It is noteworthy how his appointment to Greenwich as Director has gone to Basil's head – this was something I did not foresee. Who could? ... And yet, dammit, no-one more than I – with Malcolm [Glasier] – put him where he is. There were those of the board who found him stuffy, sticky, dull: he has become arrogant, hostile (to inferiors), a manipulator.[1]

Villiers had always had a willingness to temper his judgements with recognition of multiple facets of any situation, but now his likes and dislikes seemed to swing to extremes, and some of his attitudes had hardened into prejudice. He was convinced that *The Times* and the BBC were 'grievously' biased towards Jews and against Arabs, and towards the 'treacherous' Irish and against the British Army.

Yet he was the kindest of men at a personal level, patient and thoughtful with the stream of visitors and letters demanding his attention, although he grumbled in his diary, 'There is also an undue proportion of silly, unwanted mail from persons quite unknown to me asking fool questions ...'. Still he answered them all – a dozen typewritten replies in a day was not unusual – and despite two months of postal strikes in 1971 he had every sympathy with the coalminers when they began striking in 1972 – at least until rolling power cuts reduced him to writing by candlelight.

Pleased by the interest the National Library of Australia had shown towards the Hayes records, Villiers decided at this time he wanted his own papers to go to Canberra one day too. Unfortunately the Conrad manuscript was not going well. Something seemed 'wrong' with his health, and he felt weighed down by work.

In August 1972 Alan and Nancie flew to Travemünde and Kiel for a 'splendid' gathering of sailing ships, but the highlight of the year was an unexpected commission from *National Geographic* for an article following Sir Francis Drake's voyage around the world. Villiers wondered if he'd have the stamina, but the doctor reassured him he was 'as fit as a man ten years younger'.

The Times noted his sixty-ninth birthday on 23 September, 'which I regard as pretty good recognition for a lad from Buncle St, N. Melbourne, with not much in the way of obvious advantages except that greatest advantage of all – parents of ability and character'.

Nancie and Alan left for the Drake trip in late September. In Portugal there were sombre meetings with old friends. They visited Fritz and Kay in Aviz: frail Fritz predicted (correctly) it was the last time they would meet. Then they saw Pedro in Lisbon, still working despite his Parkinson's disease: 'A long, trying day with poor Pedro yesterday', Villiers wrote.

They flew to the tip of South America, then a few days later Villiers got to Quilpué to see Captain Robert Miethe, now ninety-three. They followed Drake to Panama, the Caribbean and San Francisco. Then Nancie stayed with Kit in Japan while Alan visited Drake sites in Indonesia. They were home by mid-December, intensely relieved it was over – 'I don't have to go anywhere today or tomorrow, or the next day!'

Then it was back to work: 'I still try to cope with the masses of papers, mail, etc ... but this time I don't feel up to it at all. I don't remember things as clearly as I did for one thing.' And among the letters was one with bad news: 'our wonderful old friend Pedro has died in Portugal. We shall have no other friend like that.'

———

Villiers wrote in 1973, 'Looking back in some of these older diaries, I am appalled at the amount of almost wild rushing about the earth that I have done in the process of making a living.'[2] That didn't stop him going on a debilitating speaking tour in America from late March to late April that year, but it was the final one: the promoter was 'trying to get me to sign on for next season. Tell him I'd rather live.'

Pan Books released paperback editions of *The Set of the Sails* and *Cruise of the Conrad* in March 1973, 'both with the most atrocious and unsuitable ships under alleged sail on their covers', fumed Villiers. He wished they had used the excellent young maritime artist Mark Myers, who had painted the covers of *War with Cape Horn* and *The Bounty Ships of France*.

In 1973 the price of oil soared, and ideas for new forms of wind-assisted shipping became popular. Since the late 1950s Villiers had exchanged letters with German engineer Wilhelm Prölss, who had come up with the idea of the Dynaship: a modern six-masted cargo vessel with semi-rigid sails and auxiliary engines. In the early 1970s, the newly formed Friends of the Earth had written to find out more about the Dynaship, and a bemused Villiers put them in touch with Prölss.[3]

Villiers had always feared that sail-handling skills might eventually be lost completely, but took heart from the growing popularity of yachting. But he was dubious that sail could ever become commercially viable again, and when cheap oil returned he was not surprised when modern wind-ship ideas were discarded.

The National Maritime Museum asked him in 1973 to write a booklet 'on the handling and voyage-making in square-rigged ships'. When he re-read his *The Way of a Ship* for background, he was pleasantly 'surprised to see what a useful book that is. I think that is probably the best and most useful book I have written'.

Intrigue still bubbled at the National Maritime Museum. Villiers received an 'appalling whallop of verbiage from the industrious Basil', who was trying to eject George Naish, the Museum's ships and ship model expert for many years. Naish was also Secretary of the Society for Nautical Research, and Villiers held great affection for him: 'George is George – unique, scholarly, hopelessly inefficient. We admire and support him for his scholarship, clarity of memory; and forget the rest.' Staff at the Museum whispered of mutiny against the 'grimly ambitious Basil'. But they had been friends once and Villiers saw his vulnerability too: 'it is a pity he is so ruthless, inhuman, and so unsure of himself. Why?'

In June 1973 Villiers spent a week in Sweden with his son Peter. They took a brief trip to the Åland Islands and Mariehamn's 'most excellent small museum'. Moored alongside was the handsome four-master *Pommern*, maintained as she had been before the Second World War. Villiers enjoyed their holiday together enormously, but in retrospect Peter recalls that this was when he first noticed that his father's memory 'was beginning to decline … he seemed his normal cheerful self, but was unable to form short-term memories, so that he would forget where our hotel was. It seemed quite funny at the time, and I don't remember attaching any real importance to it.'[4]

Villiers' health was worrying him. Although his diabetes had cleared up almost completely, he often had high temperatures for no reason, and it was hard for him to concentrate. In mid-July 1973 his doctor sent him for X-rays and blood tests. A month later he was admitted to a nursing home, with a temperature of 103 degrees and 'a marked loss of weight – to 10st 6lb', which was low for a man of nearly 6 feet in height.

Tests continued for two weeks, 'some of them beastly personal', he wrote glumly. X-rays also showed 'one rather astonishing thing … evidence of the damage done by my fall in the four-masted barque LAWHILL off Port Lincoln. There is evidence of serious injury looking as if the pelvis may have been broken … I am astonished that the X-rays here today should show up damage I have lived with for so long.'

He would need his youthful stoicism again. On 27 August a deep abscess in his lower bowel was operated on. The partly external wound had to be kept open for months, packed with sterile gauze so it would heal from the inside as it drained. Villiers learned to change the dressing himself, painfully, twice a day in a hot bath. He called it wryly his 'stern wound'. But the operation had left him exhausted; he sometimes wrote or attended events, but more often, 'do nothing, think nothing, write nothing'. He watched the river, the swans, the garden and the night:

> I chanced to look out from our bedroom window and saw all the trees so beautifully picked out in frost and all lighted from the new lamps in Water Eaton

Road that it looked like fairyland, and I called Nance to see it. Soon after dawn every trace was gone as if it had never been there: but Nance and I had seen it.[5]

Kathy's presence was always a comfort. Compared to some of her friends, Villiers wrote tenderly, 'it is our small Kath who always knew where she was going.' He started to feel stronger, and attended the British branch of the International Association of Cape Horners as guest of the president, the 'always human' Malcolm Glasier. (Villiers was a member of the Finnish and German branches.)

In December the Museum still seethed, the miners went out on strike again, and the country faced petrol rationing and a three-day week. Villiers was well enough by then to write diatribes about Basil, publisher Robert Maxwell, Opposition Leader Harold Wilson, the 'stupid Minister' for the Museum ('a <u>Mrs</u> Thatcher, I believe') and Edward Heath ('should have taken a job playing an organ and not become the biggest fool Prime Minister of the century').

———

In January 1974 Villiers learned that his 'stern wound' was not healing because of tuberculosis mycobacteria, which had probably caused the original abscess. Like many people he may have carried the latent infection for years, given the prevalence of TB in some of the places he had sailed. He was started on a course of five large injections ('prangs') a week and six tablets daily.

For the first fortnight of prangs he was too sick to get out of bed. His health returned towards the end of February, but perhaps not his equitable mood: election day brought 'contempt for the unscrupulous Wilson, the conceited woffling ass Heath, the vile opportunist Powell and the frightful Wedgwood Benn'. He yearned to see that honest old man Captain Robert Miethe again, and made plans to visit South America. In May 1974 he flew to Chile with his son Peter and they spent three days making tape-recordings of Miethe's memories.

After much effort Villiers submitted his little book on sailing square-riggers to the National Maritime Museum. He still hoped that his papers would be archived in his home country rather than Britain, and had begun negotiations with the National Library of Australia.

'The English are unforgiving with one who hasn't conformed and yet succeeded,' he believed.

He wanted to retire from the presidency of the Society for Nautical Research as he no longer had the energy, and did so in June that year. In August he returned to working on his Joseph Conrad manuscript, but although his health was officially 'all clear', his concentration was not. 'It is so hard to hold all the threads – indeed to get them into a pattern at all', 'Repetition creeps in very readily when one is past 70': but he did not seem to notice how much was creeping into his own diaries.

The Marine Academy of France awarded Henri Picard and Villiers medals for *The Bounty Ships of France*. He could not attend the ceremony but in October received the 'simple silver medal engraved with a very fine, well done early 19th century sailing ship … and my name on the reverse … if any book of mine deserved any award whatsoever, it is NOT that odd collaboration which I scarcely believed would be published.'[6]

In October Villiers enjoyed a dinner in honour of the three trustees retiring from the board of the National Maritime Museum, which included himself and his friend Malcolm Glasier. He also heard at that time from Lionel that their brother Frank had gone into hospital with a gangrenous foot from diabetes.

In late 1974 *National Geographic* asked Villiers to write an article on Ferdinand Magellan. He took on the job but no longer had the energy for the tedious rushing around after tickets and visas for South America, and it was Nancie who now had to deal with the arrangements.

———

Alan and Nancie left for Portugal in mid-January 1975 to start work on Magellan. They flew to Rio and rested for a few days – Villiers was already tired – then went on to Santiago. There they took the now-familiar route to Quilpué to visit Robert Miethe. Villiers realised that the ninety-seven-year-old was wearing his best suit because he thought they would not meet again. 'Good, great Miethe. He is ready to ship his last moorings.'

Alan and Nancie joined the liner *Gripsholm* at Valparaiso for a ten-day passage through the Straits of Magellan to Buenos Aires. It was pleasant and easy, especially compared to the next few weeks, flying on to Tahiti, Honolulu and Guam. In March they visited Manila, Cebu, Brunei and Singapore. By mid-March they were home again, where two sad letters were waiting. Villiers' brother Lionel wrote that Frank had died in Melbourne on 22 January, and Robert Miethe's son told him that the old captain had died of a heart attack on 7 April 1975.

The Magellan article was 'curiously heavy going', Villiers found, as was his tax return, and the proofs of *Voyaging with the Wind*. At last he submitted the Joseph Conrad manuscript to his British and American publishers. But, disappointingly, both returned it in October 1975. As well as Conrad's life at sea 'they wanted more about the <u>writer</u>. This has been dealt with by far more competent minds', he puzzled, with good reason: there was much in print on Conrad the author but nothing about him as a seaman.

But good news arrived too: a reprint of *Posted Missing* was a selection of the American Book of the Month Club, and selling very well, apparently because of the success of the sensationalistic *The Bermuda Triangle*.[7] The Kuwaiti government wanted to do a translation of *Sons of Sinbad*, and the National Maritime Museum was holding a party to launch *Voyaging with the Wind*.

Trivial misunderstandings had left Villiers annoyed with the production of their 'piffling little booklet', but he later admitted to himself 'it reads well in spite of them'. The delightful *Voyaging with the Wind* does indeed read well. It skillfully distills a lifetime of love and understanding of sail into fewer than sixty pages. It was to be Villiers' final book.

———

A tourist agency asked Villiers to be a guest lecturer on yet another South American cruise, so he and Nancie joined the Greek vessel *Apollo* in mid-January 1976 at Rio de Janeiro. They sailed down to the tip of the continent, where 'gaping at Cape Horn seemed almost obscene':

> There are times when I have become quite confused aboard this vessel – where is she, why?, what the devil Nance and I are supposed to be doing here ... I give some sort of talk which is listened to in respectful silence with perhaps also some bewilderment, for I am not at all sure what it is supposed to be about.[8]

They were back in Oxford by the start of March. Kit came home on leave and 'suggests that it is the diabetes which has affected my capacity for drive and work, this past year or so. It could well be so: I know that I am different.' In April the National Library of Australia sent him a 'long, fat envelope' on his papers being archived at Canberra – 'all very intimidating indeed, so much so that the only sensible course would be to give the idea up'. He put the envelope aside.

He realised with surprise it was the first time for many years that he did not have some plan 'cooking' for an article or trip. He spent weeks trying to get his office into order, but his desk never seemed to clear. He felt almost overwhelmed by the task of dealing with his correspondence and wished he had a secretary-typist to help, as in 'the old Bay Ridge days in N.Y./Brooklyn. They were good … [sic]'.

He edited and re-submitted the Conrad manuscript to his publishers, but in May 1976 one of them returned it with proposed editing. They 'have taken a lot of the tang out of it, the seamanlike side-lights'. On further reading he was horrified at what they had done. 'There may well have been some repetition but they seem to have taken out at least 40/50000 words'.

In late May he and Nancie flew to the Åland Islands for a meeting of the Cape Horners Association, AICH. Mariehamn was now 'greatly changed', and he met only two people he knew – Harald Lindfors and Werner Öjst, though there seemed to be nearly a thousand attending. He felt out of place and was glad to get back to Oxford.

———

Britain suffered a major drought in 1976. Day followed day of dusty heat, and the Cherwell was scum-covered and stagnant. Villiers felt unwell, with painful hips and legs, and 'my memory becomes worse and worse, which is trying for it was one of my few assets'. The doctor reassured him that his diabetes was well under control and there was nothing wrong.

In late June he received his Conrad manuscript back from the other publishers, 'with a letter that is not all that cordial – not at all!' He was downcast, and his memory was worse than ever – after a friend's party, 'I don't seem, for one point, to remember a single person we met.'

And Nancie seemed always to be busy: 'I should have been warned by the example of her mother, in Melbourne – another gad-about, meeting attender, champion of women etc etc.' Still, he admitted, 'I suppose the understandable truth is she doesn't want her whole life to be in my shadow.'

In July they attended the Royal Garden Party at Buckingham Palace: 'It was a long hot afternoon for a couple of cups of the Royal tea … dear Nance looked very attractive.' He liked to watch her at work in the garden, and noted the beautiful blue Morning Glories that she grew over 'Nance's arch' every year. He helped her sort out some slides for a talk she was giving on the Straits of Magellan for a local group and was surprised to hear her name mentioned on the radio.

Villiers was furious that Basil Greenhill had finally moved George Naish out of the main section of the National Maritime Museum: 'the damned, bad-tempered, arrogant and scheming fool, for Naish is one of the very few there worth consulting on <u>anything</u>'. Every few weeks he would write about it, outraged, as if the situation was new: 'that fool had managed to throw George Naish out now … I am very sorry I did the Museum so much lasting harm in so warmly (and mistakenly) backing Greenhill for Director after the futile, quarrelsome ass Carr …'.

He did not have the heart to revise the Joseph Conrad manuscript but worried terribly about family finances if he could not work. Although they owned several properties and had substantial savings, he feared inflation would take it all. His income tax return was over-due: it normally took him little time as he had always been excellent with numbers. Now he simply could not do it, although he tried almost every day from August to November 1976. 'I find that after a solid morning of it, when I come again in the afternoon I am soon sunk – can't stay afloat on all these figures long at all and the only thing is to wait until the morrow.'

He increasingly reported the same incidents in detail over and over. Time seemed to disappear; 'The day goes by very quietly but very quickly too: I don't know what happened to it.' 'Once or twice of late I have felt my age here at home, at least once with slight alarm with what seemed horribly like a threat of losing consciousness …'.

He was, he thought, to give a talk to the Royal Institute of Naval Architects on 15 December 1976, on 'Use of the Wind at Sea':

The affair from my point of view at any rate was something of a disaster of which the less said the better. I don't think I knew that such collections of snoots existed ... I met no one, knew no one, was neither introduced nor thanked – not that there was anything much to thank me for! It was appalling.

He was still a fluent speaker on maritime subjects, so perhaps the 'disaster' was that he had mistaken the date, the topic or the audience. Still, Christmas was good: Nancie invited all of their neighbours to their house for a highly successful 'Lucerne Road Residents' Party'. Peter was home from Northern Ireland, Kathy arrived from her new job in Manchester, and Kit rang them from Taiwan.

Villiers wrote on 31 December: 'I have a new diary ready but I find it rather hard to keep the days apart at the moment.' The new diary was never used: the wisps of confusion grew into the fog of Alzheimer's disease.

———

In 1977 Villiers' sister Enid died of complications from diabetes. She had been the youngest of the family, born nine years after Alan. His other sister Hazel was also diabetic and died in 1978, but his brother Lionel remained healthy, dying at ninety.

In his younger days in Tasmania Villiers had known Dr William Crowther, now Sir William, who wished to mount an exhibition in honour of Villiers at the State Library of Tasmania. Villiers was not well enough to attend the event in March 1977, so Crowther wrote: 'I attempted to describe the depth and variety of your writings which made you the historian of the last phases of the square-rigged traders of commerce in sail ... Your artistry and mastership of photography was an eye opener to those present.'9

In May a representative of the National Library of Australia visited the Villiers. The 'long, fat envelope' he had discarded the year before had contained a draft agreement, approved by Villiers' solicitor, for his papers to be bequested to them. Now Alan's failing memory and his concerns about taxes made this unlikely, so the library decided not to push the matter, but simply stay in touch.

Villiers had commissioned maritime artist Mark Myers to illustrate his Joseph Conrad book, but had to tell him he could not use the paintings as the manuscript had been rejected: 'The plain facts are that I have been somewhat not myself for maybe a year now … I have to rewrite the work just about, and that takes time and some courage too: but I am glad to do it.'[10] In fact he did little more on the manuscript, although it remained a major preoccupation.

In early June a week of reunion at Plymouth, Massachusetts, took place to celebrate the twentieth anniversary of the *Mayflower* voyage. Alan and Nancie attended but it left him tired. In late 1977 and early 1978 he resigned from the Society for Nautical Research, the *Victory* Advisory Technical Committee and the Maritime Trust Ships Committee: 'the time has now come when it is too much for me'.

In early 1978 Villiers' closest friend Fritz Egerton died, aged ninety-four. After thirty years his wife, Kay, left Portugal and came to Oxford. She stayed in the Villiers' flat next door – 'she was an angel, a delightful person', said Nancie, who would cook her lunch. Sadly, after just a few months, Kay had a stroke and died in hospital. Towards the end of his life Fritz had not been able to write, but a few years before he had recalled the beginning of their long friendship at what was a momentous time for Villiers:

> My mind often goes back forty years to the days when … I first knew you. To one day in particular when I went to the Times office, when you were doing some job connected with the Australian Press: then to Wardour Street or somewhere, where you were cutting film, and finally to a little boarding house somewhere near Golders Green Station.[11]

Fritz had been Alan's father-figure for forty-five years. He wrote in 1973: 'Do take care of yourself, lad. It may be wrong, but I must confess that you mean more to me than most of my own children.'

———

The National Library of Australia came up with a proposal in April 1979 to purchase Villiers' papers. The Liaison Librarian found that Villiers was still healthy and active but had forgotten about the previous negotiations. 'He is certainly quite lucid and can make decisions about what he wants to do with his papers; the only trouble is that he cannot remember, literally from one minute to the next, what he has decided.'

The NLA suggested an exhibition of his work; Villiers insisted he was still using some papers for the Joseph Conrad manuscript which would have to be retained. By September 1979 Nancie had done a magnificent job of sorting the collection into some order, and the NLA had organised a professional valuation. The Liaison Librarian noted that Villiers' health appeared to be deteriorating rapidly, and that Nancie was under strain. She simply wanted the material packed and shipped as soon as possible, as it was presently occupying most of one of their two houses in Lucerne Road.

The valuation of the collection came as a surprise to everyone. Villiers had accumulated thousands of maritime books: only a selection had been examined but some appeared to be extremely valuable. The manuscripts and letters (since there were few from 'distinguished correspondents') were rated of less value, while specialists were required to check over the films. It was clear that the books needed a more thorough valuation and the National Maritime Museum agreed to examine the films, so in January 1980 the NLA proposed a separate purchase of the correspondence, manuscripts, notebooks, journals, charts and miscellaneous items. Nancie was only too happy to agree, and by April 1980 twenty-eight cartons of material were on a ship to Australia.

The Director-General of the National Library, Dr George Chandler, wrote to Villiers then to say that in his retirement he hoped to research some of the major sea voyages between England and Australia, so it was 'a matter of great personal pleasure that ... the papers of one of the twentieth century's most outstanding sailors and chroniclers of the sea, should come into our custody'.[12]

———

In October 1978 Stephen Murray-Smith, Reader in Education at the University of Melbourne, contacted Villiers. They had met in 1962 when Villiers had travelled around Australia, and Murray-Smith wrote:

> As you are in my opinion the most distinguished living writer who has emerged from Melbourne, and an equally distinguished educator, it is a particular wish of mine to see you honoured with the award of an honorary degree from the University of Melbourne. While I was in England recently I wrote to the Duke

of Edinburgh on the subject, and he was kind enough to support my interest strongly. As I am a member of the Faculty of Education I am proposing the award to you of a Doctorate of Education.'[13]

It took some time to arrange. In October 1980 Villiers' daughter Kathy married Roger Chetwynd, a fellow town-planner, but by then Alan was not able to make a speech; their old family friend Jack Scarr spoke at the wedding instead.

It was in December that Villiers became a Doctor of Letters of the University of Melbourne. In Britain and Australia, Litt.D. is a doctorate above even that of Doctor of Philosophy, awarded to those 'whose record of published work and research shows conspicuous ability and originality, and constitutes a distinguished and sustained achievement'.

By then Villiers was too weak to travel, but he was pleased to be honoured by the University of Melbourne. Annie and Leon would have been so proud of him.

———

Peter wrote about his father's final years:

> His memory did decline from the age of about 70 onwards and in retrospect, it was the onset of Alzheimer's, which was irreversible, and made him incapable of continuing the life he had led. Alan had always relied on an excellent memory, and was not a great filer or systems man, although he was meticulous about accounts. As his memory declined he became unable to work, as his work depended on his memory; and when he could no longer work he was no longer happy, until the very end, when some sort of peace set in.
>
> Alan never became bedridden, and was cared for at home by Nancie and a very cheerful family friend called Tessa Scarr, who had trained as a nurse and was invaluable. Like many whose memories fail, he could be both anxious and brusque, as he no longer knew who people were; and they handled him extremely well. In the end I believe he suffered a stroke, but it was no surprise that he died: he was a shadow of the man he had once been, but still an impressive figure with an abiding force of personality.[14]

Kathy added:

> I agree with Peter that Dad's personality remained strongly there. Also it was striking that he always thought he was working – the motivation to work and

support his family was very strong. We have a number of copies of his books in which he has written comments and alterations – Mum gave him copies to remind him of his achievements.

Mum bore by far the greatest burden of Dad's decline, and it was a great burden. I was working at the time, from late 1976 to late 1979 in Manchester; the rest of the time in London. Tessa Scarr was absolutely marvellous; she came two to three days a week, and I don't think Mum could have managed without her. I personally feel a great debt of gratitude to her.

There was no question of Dad going out for the day to a day centre – he wasn't the clubbable sort! – or of a home. Towards the very end – the last three to six months or so – I think Mum advertised for help, and this was the way to discover the local saints – those prepared to sit with the dying. I was very impressed with them.

Dad was very strong, and did not depart quickly. He finally succumbed to what was thought were some mini-strokes. I only recall him being bedridden at the very end. Mum says he walked to Summertown a fortnight before he died.[15]

Alan Villiers died on 3 March 1982 at the age of seventy-nine. It was a 'Cape Horn' night, Kathy vividly remembers – appropriately wild and windy. Six weeks later she gave birth to her first child, Georgina, who became a great comfort to Nancie.

A service of thanksgiving for Alan's life was held in Oxford at the University Church of St Mary the Virgin in May. The Address was given by Viscount Runciman of Doxford, who had worked with Villiers for decades on maritime committees, and the Lesson was read by his old shipmate Captain Godfrey Wicksteed, who in his seventies was still rigging the *Cutty Sark*.

During the war Villiers had taken temporary command of Rescue Motor Launch 513 from his wounded friend J. Francis Jones. In 1985, Jones wrote:

Alan Villiers was one of those astonishing people that seem somehow to combine the qualities of several people in the one persona. To a natural authority he added great charm. His intellectual equipment was formidable; but he shewed [sic] it mostly through his great gift of communication ... Alan Villiers to my mind so towered over his fellows in personality and accomplishment that even now I'm not reconciled to his death.[16]

Peter Villiers, who has published books on ethics, policing and human rights, had always been fascinated by his father's final incomplete manuscript, although it was more incomplete than Alan ever quite understood. After significant additional research Peter incorporated it into *Joseph Conrad, Master Mariner* (2006), in which Mark Myers' superb paintings at last received the showing they deserved, thirty years later.

After Alan's death, Kit Villiers qualified as a solicitor and worked in shipping law in Asia. After retiring he returned to Oxford and now lives in the house where Alan had his office overlooking the Cherwell and the River Garden. Kathy Villiers and Roger Chetwynd had a second child in March 1985, named Alan after his grandfather. They are also now retired, but like her mother, Kathy has retained her intense interest in community issues all of her life.

For a long time Nancie Villiers continued her environmental work with the Oxford Preservation Trust and the North Oxford Association; she also set up the Friends of the Cherwell Valley. Kathy said, 'as an Australian she is a tremendous Anglophile, and values Oxford and the English countryside greatly – almost more than the English'. Alan, the seaman, never understood the hold that the land had on his wife, or appreciated her significant contribution to local conservation.

In recent years Nancie has been slowed down by a stroke, but still loves to visit country gardens and the Oxford theatre. Now in her nineties she looks decades younger, her beauty 'grown from inside', as Alan said. In 1980 George Pierrot, an old friend, wrote to Nancie, 'Tell Alan ... I often think of him with a great deal of admiration. I think you were the greatest thing that ever happened to him.'

———

It was a wild 'Cape Horn' night when Villiers died, which sits in pleasing symmetry with the first sentence of *The Set of the Sails*: 'The equinoctial gales howled about the little weather-board house and roared through the riggings of the square-rigged ships at the bottom of our street, on the night when I was born.'

While Villiers was never one to let an awkward fact spoil a nice image (Buncle Street is well over a mile from the nearest dock), this was how it was in his mind's eye, and it was essentially true: there were windjammers enough in 1903 Melbourne to play the gales like an orchestra. That was far from the case when he died. Had all the four-masted barques left on earth been crammed into Victoria Dock that night they would not have raised more than a mournful hum: only seven remain.

Four were once Erikson grain carriers: *Moshulu* today is a restaurant in Philadelphia and *Viking* a hotel in Gothenburg, both much altered. *Passat* is a handsome museum vessel at Travemünde; while honest, unchanged *Pommern* floats at her home in Mariehamn. The other three were German nitrate carriers: *Peking* is a museum vessel in New York, while *Kruzenshtern* (ex-*Padua*) and *Sedov* (ex-*Magdalene Vinnen*) are Russian sail-training vessels. *Kruzenshtern* recently circumnavigated the globe, while *Sedov* has sailed more than 300,000 nautical miles in the last forty years. They are the acknowledged monarchs of the square-rigger kingdom.

A greater number of three-masters have survived, iron and steel, ships and barques – many linked in some way with Villiers. Among them are *Star of India*, *Balclutha*, *Wavertree*, *Christian Radich*, *Gorch Fock*, *Rickmer Rickmers*, *Sagres II*, *Eagle*, *Georg Stage*, *Polly Woodside* and *James Craig*. His odd little *Mayflower II* at Plymouth, Massachusetts, and much-loved *Joseph Conrad* at Mystic Seaport, Connecticut, are visited by thousands of people every year.

At around the time Villiers died, the second of the great oil price shocks struck the world, and again people looked at schemes for wind-assisted shipping. The Japanese built two prototype rigid-sail cargo vessels, and in the late 1980s the cruise industry launched a handful of luxury liners with automated sails, but again they lost their relevance once oil prices fell.

Now, in the first decades of the new century, it is becoming clear that cheap, bountiful, easily extracted oil is a thing of the past. Perhaps the expense of developing sail for modern ships will soon have to be set against the growing cost of fuel. God's wind needs no bunkers, after all.

———

Alan Villiers' life has had enduring influence. In 1982 his library was acquired by the University of Melbourne. 'It is a collection that could never be assembled again,' Stephen Murray-Smith stated in an undated press release. 'More of a scholar's working library than a collection of desirabilia, this Villiers collection ... must serve as a considerable incentive to maritime historical studies in Australia.'

For decades Villiers gave generously of his expertise to maritime organisations – the National Maritime Museum, the *Victory* Advisory Technical Committee, the *Cutty Sark* Preservation Society and the Society for Nautical Research all owe some part of their success to his efforts. He was the first person to bring the concepts of ship preservation and sail-training into broad public consciousness. Basil Greenhill declared that 'Modern youth training in sailing vessels can trace its origins largely to the inspiration of Alan Villiers' long voyage in the *Joseph Conrad*.'[17] Certainly there had been naval cadet ships before Villiers, but he was the first to promote sail-training as a means of developing self-reliance in just about anyone.

Although Villiers would often joke that all he ever did was point the camera and click, in fact he had a marvellous eye for detail and composition, and developed a professional's knowledge of film technology. His own work promoted public interest in the photography of merchant vessels, and he helped facilitate the growth of the Historic Photographs archive of the National Maritime Museum, which today holds over a quarter of a million images. Nearly 10 per cent of those were taken by Villiers himself, and the Museum recently published a beautiful large-format book drawn from his collection – *Sons of Sindbad: The Photographs*.

Villiers' books still appeal to modern readers and some have been reprinted recently, for example, *Captain Cook*, *Joey Goes to Sea* and *Cruise of the Conrad*. Every sailing-ship enthusiast met during the course of this work had been inspired in some way by Villiers: 'I loved his books when I was young!' was a common exclamation. Among them was a schoolchild who began a correspondence with Villiers that lasted for years, a fisherman visiting Oxford who shyly rang him and was invited around for a warm chat, a teenager who decided to go to sea for a lifetime (and did) and many others who dedicated themselves to the preservation of historic vessels.

But every positive has a negative. Because of its appeal and uniqueness, Villiers' work has come to almost define the sailing-ship era of the 1920s and 1930s, yet his portrayal was decidedly biased. In Villiers' square-rigger world there could be no *genuine* sailors who were women or Jews or blacks, but in the real square-rigger world they existed. Unfortunately, we don't know much about them today because Villiers himself wrote them out of the picture.

If there is ever a rational cause for misogyny or racism, there was none apparent in his life, apart from the usual terrors of a young, inse-cure male. We are left with the feeble justification that 'everyone else was like that then' – which is only partly true. The period between the wars may have been conservative but it also bubbled with social change and new views of women and other cultures. In loving the old ways of ships Villiers chose to take on the old ways of thinking: his travels may have brought him empathy for foreigners he knew personally ('decent chaps'), but he rarely questioned the stereotypes of his parents' era.

His myth-making was also unfortunate. As a journalist he was used to bending the truth to 'improve' a yarn, but it became a bad habit. While he was careful about details of ships themselves, people aboard were less honestly rendered, and his own persona – the reader's trusted eye-witness – was the least reliable of all. His autobiography *The Set of the Sails* was essentially true, but it was also selective, embroidered and emotionally false. Even respectable *National Geographic* was compro-mised – Villiers' imaginary cod-fishing adventure (May 1952) led mod-ern researchers to believe that he spent 'days alone paying out and hauling in long-lines in a flimsy dory on a treacherous sea'.[18]

A sense of exclusion – a classic Australian 'chip on the shoulder' – always stayed with him, although that at least was excusable. Villiers was not a naturally lucky man – his success was based on single-minded vision and endless hard work. It is shameful, then, that he was never offered formal recognition by the countries whose square-rigger heritage he laboured to commemorate – Finland, Britain, America and Australia – and if he felt bitter about it he had every right to.

The difficulty for many was that the talented Villiers did not fit into any simple category. He was a high-school dropout who wrote mar-itime history, an unqualified master who circumnavigated the world, a foc's'l hand who made movies and a junior officer with more sea skills than many admirals. He could be pedantic, stubborn and irritable; and witty, thoughtful and charming. His obsessive focus brought him a satisfying career but left him sometimes oblivious to feelings and experiences outside the maritime world.

Villiers wrote over forty books but feared that none were 'worthwhile'. He was wrong: his work will always be remembered for its passionate commitment to an extraordinary era. But despite its historic value, some of his writing lacks human depth. He never understood that emotional evasion and knee-jerk prejudice must, in the end, diminish the reach of any art.

——

Out of the intricate tangle of steel and spirit that drove the wind ships, Villiers found an expression for his own pain that resonated with the world. 'Some were lost,' he would growl. 'That's the way life is. Something's always lost.' And in showing us the enormity of that loss, he taught us to love what remains.

In January 2006 the restored barque *James Craig* came to Melbourne. She passed through The Rip and into Port Phillip for the first time since 1920. It had been eighty-six years since her final trading voyage; eighty-six years since Villiers himself last stood on her deck.

She blossomed on the skyline like a half-remembered dream or a promise of the future – a vision so new and true and hopeful that words cannot convey it. Perhaps Villiers came as close as anyone could:

> She rolls lightly and runs with the shadow of her sails on her foam-creamed bow wave as it streams past the clean hull: the three trucks circle slowly and with grace against the vast immensity of the blue sky ...[19]

That much-lamented 'end of sail' seems to be taking its time to get here. With any luck it never will.

ACKNOWLEDGEMENTS

This book really began when I was writing the life of *Redbill* the pearling lugger, whose dashing owner Captain Gregory had worked in his youth on square-riggers. Research on his vessels revealed striking photographs of ships in Melbourne and books by Alan Villiers. In November 2004, curiosity led me to the National Library of Australia and Villiers' intriguing journals.

His family in Britain supported the idea of a biography, and Nancie, Kit, Kathy and Peter have given me great support. They responded to questions, copied photographs, read through drafts of the manuscript and discussed their own perspectives on Alan as a husband and father: I much appreciate their many contributions. In Melbourne, Elizabeth Sullivan, daughter of Villiers' sister Hazel, also provided fundamental assistance: Elizabeth trusted me with family letters, haunting photographs and valuable insights into Villiers' early life.

Historic vessel enthusiast Miles Allen put me in touch with Hanna Hagmark-Cooper, Director of the Ålands Sjöfartsmuseum, who kindly allowed me to stay in the museum's guestroom during an unforgettable visit to Mariehamn in June 2006 (*Pommern* was moored just outside). In Mariehamn I also had the pleasure of meeting Australian Jocelyn Palmer, who helped enormously by translating Swedish documents that shed light on the lives of the female sailors of the 1930s.

My late husband Captain David Hancox offered encouragement, documents and background information; and introduced me to Captain Lothar Friis, who shared his chilling memories of *Passat*'s near-loss in 1957, and Tim and Dinks Boden, who provided hospitality in London in June 2006.

Maritime heritage stalwart Lindsay Rex shared his images of restored vessels, and introduced me to artist Oswald Brett, who knew Villiers from the days of *Joseph Conrad*, and Geoff Andrewartha, who sent me a photocopy of Daphne Villiers' diary from the Tasmanian Maritime Museum. Sailing historian Garry Kerr provided photographs of Daphne Villiers and the Bass Strait ketch *Hawk*. Gunela Astbrink and her parents translated letters from Ruben de Cloux to Villiers, Phil Helmore and Neil Cormack supplied papers on the loss of *Admiral Karpfanger*, and Adrian Kelly transcribed Villiers' idiosyncratic shorthand notes.

The excellent Internet maritime archives created by Lars Bruzelius, Mori Flapan, Gary P. Priolo and Philippe Bellamit were fundamental to research for this book. I also much appreciate the support of my colleagues from the Maritime Heritage Association of Victoria, World Ship Society (Victoria), Williamstown Maritime Association and the Internet Society of Australia.

As always, I am grateful for the resources of libraries, archives and museums, and their amiable and professional staff. I would especially like to thank the National Library of Australia for its careful stewardship of Villiers' papers, and for providing such a magnificent environment in which to study them. I have also benefited from the fine collections of the Melbourne Maritime Museum, State Library of Queensland, State Library of Victoria, Maritime Museum of Tasmania, National Archives of Australia, Mystic Seaport and the Ålands Sjöfartsmuseum.

I greatly appreciate the efforts of the staff of the National Maritime Museum in Greenwich who midwifed my manuscript into a book: my thanks to Rachel Giles, Eliza Marciniak, Pieter van der Merwe, Abbie Ratcliffe, Beth Huseman, Sara Ayad and Bob Todd.

Others who have assisted in various ways include Adrian Small, Glen Stuart, Steven Cooke, Janet Boglio, Joan Wills, Mark Sullivan, Michael Chapman, Stan Bowen, Norman Quinn, Chris Roche, Jonothan Davis, Maurie Hutchinson, Tony Larard, Yetta Krinsky, Daisy Searls, Tony Hill, Jane Keany, and Dorothy and Victor Prescott.

My gratitude goes to my family in particular, for their support during the last few complicated years.

Kate Lance
Melbourne
August 2008

APPENDIX A

PRODUCTION OF FOUR-MASTED IRON AND STEEL MERCHANT VESSELS

This data was drawn from the *Catalogue of Four-Masted Ships and Barques* by Lars Bruzelius, which lists 442 four-masted vessels built from 1801 to 1989. I have excluded 28 vessels: 12 made of wood, 10 converted from steamers, 5 Japanese ships and 1 yacht, so these are *only the iron or steel four-masted merchant barques and ships*, a total of 414 vessels built between 1875 and 1926.

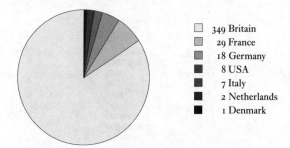

	349 Britain
	29 France
	18 Germany
	8 USA
	7 Italy
	2 Netherlands
	1 Denmark

Figure 1: Origin of the total 414 four-masted iron and steel merchant vessels built in Britain, Europe and America.

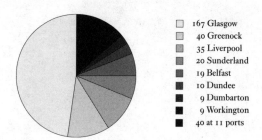

	167 Glasgow
	40 Greenock
	35 Liverpool
	20 Sunderland
	19 Belfast
	10 Dundee
	9 Dumbarton
	9 Workington
	40 at 11 ports

Figure 2: Locations of shipyards that built the 349 British four-masted iron and steel merchant vessels; 62 per cent came from Glasgow, Greenock and Dumbarton on the River Clyde.

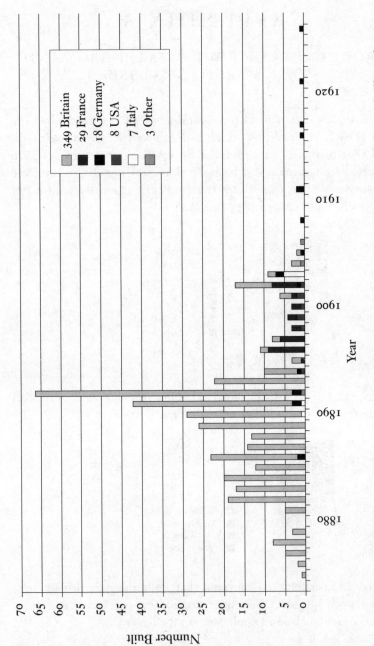

Figure 3: Country of origin of the 414 four-masted iron and steel ships and barques built each year between 1875 and 1926.

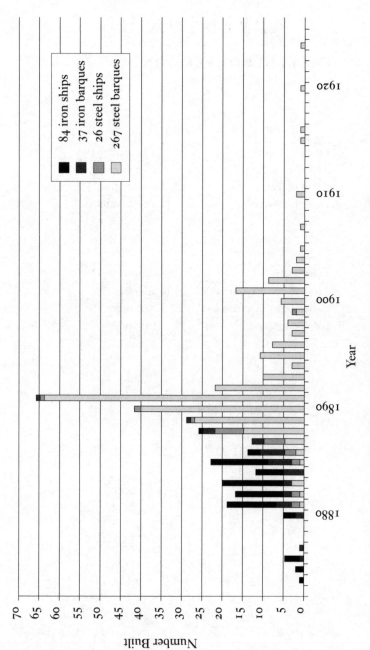

Figure 4: Type of metal used and rigging style of the 414 four-masters built each year between 1875 and 1926.

APPENDIX B

METRIC CONVERSION TABLE

1 inch	2.54 centimetres
1 foot (12 inches)	0.30 metres
1 yard (3 feet)	0.91 metres
1 mile (5280 feet)	1.61 kilometres
100 miles	161 kilometres

1 centimetre	0.39 inches
1 metre (100 centimetres)	3.28 feet
1 kilometre (1,000 metres)	0.62 miles
100 kilometres	620 miles

NOTES

CHAPTER 1: HELL AND MELBOURNE

1. Villiers, A., *The Set of the Sails*, Hodder and Stoughton (1949), p. 123.
2. Villiers, A., *The Set of the Sails*, p. 16.
3. National Library of Australia, Alan Villiers Collection (NLA), MS6388, Series 3, Box 75, Folder 662.
4. Villiers, A., *Whalers of the Midnight Sun*, C. Scribner's Sons (1934), p. 21.
5. NLA, MS6388, Series 2, Box 64, Folder 570.
6. NLA, MS6388, Series 2, Box 64, Folder 570.
7. NLA, MS6388, Series 3, Box 75, Folder 662.
8. Private communication, Peter Villiers, June 2006.
9. NLA, MS6388, Series 2, Box 64, Folder 570.
10. NLA, MS6388, Series 2, Box 64, Folder 562.
11. NLA, MS6388, Series 2, Box 64, Folder 565.
12. National Archives of Australia, C102/0 Tape SCE08.
13. Villiers, A., *The Set of the Sails*, p. 33.
14. A ship's gross registered tonnage, GRT, is not a physical weight at all but a measure of its volume in units of 100 cubic feet. Net registered tonnage, NRT, was the cargo-carrying volume left over after excluding living, storage and engine spaces. In square-riggers, unlike steamships, the difference between GRT and NRT is small.
15. The list of over 1,700 German sailing ships larger than 140 gross tons is from the Introduction to Middendorf, F.L., *Bemastung und Takelung der Schiffe* (1903) reprinted Kassel (1977), trans. Flapan, M.: http://home.iprimus.com.au/mflapan/MiddendorfWebpage1.htm.
16. Excludes the 1931 barque *Hussar*, built as a yacht for an American millionaire, and the Japanese sail-training ships *Taisei Maru*, *Nippon Maru* and *Kaiwo Maru*. Data from the Maritime History Virtual Archives; see http://www.bruzelius.info/Nautica/Ships/Ships.html.
17. NLA, MS6388, Series 4, Box 80, Notebook 1.
18. NLA, MS6388, Series 3, Box 70, Folder 616.
19. NLA, MS6388, Series 3, Box 70, Folder 616.
20. NLA, MS6388, Series 4, Box 80, Notebook 1.
21. Villiers, A., *The Set of the Sails*, p. 105.
22. Greenhill, B., 'The Alan Villiers Collection', National Maritime Museum, 1998.
23. NLA, MS6388, Series 4, Box 80, Notebook 2.
24. In an undated reply to a friend who had mentioned meeting Lusitania in Antwerp in 1930, Villiers wrote, 'What a coincidence that you also know "Lusitania" – he must have had some dynamic or memorable quality that we seem both to remember him so well.'

CHAPTER 2: *THIS* WAS SAILING!

1. Less than 2 per cent of the tonnage lost was under sail. Calculated by author from data in *British Merchant Ships Lost at Sea Due to Enemy Action, 1914–1918*, His Majesty's Stationery Office (1919), digital version, http://www.naval-history.net. Almost 2,500 British Merchant ships were destroyed in the First World War. Yet it is hardly surprising that the sailing ships among them received little attention – they comprised only 10 per cent of the casualties, and they were much smaller ships too.
2. Karlsson, E., *Mother Sea*, Oxford University Press (1964), p. 11.
3. NLA, MS6388, Series 4, Box 80, Notebook 15.
4. Kemp, P., *The Oxford Companion to Ships and the Sea*, Oxford University Press (1988), p. 942.
5. Kendall, N., 'Wind-some Words', *The Christian Science Monitor*, 6 May 2004. See http://www.christiansciencemonitor.org/2004/0506/p18s03-hfgn.html.
6. Allen, O., *The Windjammers*, Time Life (1979), p. 6.
7. NLA, MS6388, Series 1, Box 36, Folder 310.
8. Villiers, A., *Falmouth for Orders*, Geoffrey Bles (1930), p. 63.
9. Karlsson, E., *Mother Sea*, p. 72.
10. NLA, MS6388, Series 4, Box 80, Notebook 1.
11. Villiers, A., *The Set of the Sails*, p. 117. Quotes without attribution in Chapter Two are from this book.
12. Cato, J., *I Can Take It*, Georgian House (1947), p. 160.
13. Villiers, A., *The Set of the Sails*, p. 157.
14. State Library of Victoria Pictures Catalogue, Jack Cato Collection, Accession Number H98.150/62.
15. NLA, Hazel de Berg Collection, ORAL DeB 470, Conversation with Alan Villiers, 1970.
16. NLA, MS6388, Series 8, Box 98, Item 2.
17. Greenhill, B., and Hackman, J., *Herzogin Cecilie*, Conway Maritime Press (1991), p. 37.
18. Karlsson, E., *Mother Sea*, p. 75.
19. NLA, MS6388, Series 4, Box 80. Notebooks 8 and 9a.

CHAPTER 3: WHAT COULD A GIRL LIKE ME DO?

1. NLA, MS6388, Series 4, Box 80, Notebook 7.
2. Greenhill, B., and Hackman, J., *Herzogin Cecilie*, p. 115.
3. NLA, MS6388, Series 4, Box 80, Notebooks 7, 8 9 and 9a. Quotes without attribution for 1928 are from these diaries.
4. NLA, Hazel de Berg Collection, ORAL DeB 470.
5. Greenhill, B., and Hackman, J., *Herzogin Cecilie*, p. 114.
6. Greenhill, B., and Hackman, J., *Herzogin Cecilie*, p. 115.

7. NLA, MS6388, Series 4, Box 80, Notebook 7.

8. NLA, MS6388, Series 4, Box 80, Notebook 7.

9. One verse from 'R. Alcona to J. Brenzaida' and two from 'No Coward Soul Is Mine'.

CHAPTER 4: HE IS DEAD

1. *Grace Harwar* diary: NLA, MS6388, Series 4, Box 87, Item 170. Quotes without attribution for 1929 are from this diary.

2. Sequence of events from *Grace Harwar* diary, not as depicted in *By Way of Cape Horn*.

3. The encounters with *Orangeleaf* and *Conte Biancamano* are reversed in chronological order in *By Way of Cape Horn*.

4. *Orangeleaf* was then a ship of the Royal Fleet Auxiliary, supplying British naval bases in the West Indies with fuel and stores. Her crew were being most generous with His Majesty's provisions; they might have been less so had *Orangeleaf* been just an ordinary tramp steamer. Private communication, Captain David Hancox, 2006.

5. NLA, MS6388, Series 1, Box 13, Folder 120.

6. NLA, MS6388, Series 3, Box 71, Folder 619.

7. NLA, MS6388, Series 1, Box 59, Folder 524.

8. NLA, MS6388, Series 3, Box 71, Folder 620.

9. NLA, MS6388, Series 3, Box 76, Folder 665.

10. Publicity brochure, Shearwood-Smith, Inc, 1932.

11. Newspaper clipping, courtesy of Villiers' niece Elizabeth Sullivan, does not show the name of the newspaper.

CHAPTER 5: DAPHNE AT SEA

1. NLA, MS6388, Series 23, Box 132, Scrapbook 4.

2. Diary for 1931, NLA, MS6388, Series 4, Box 80, Notebook 10a. Quotes without attribution for 1931 are from this diary.

3. From the exhibition programme for Skeppet och Flickan, Ålands Maritime Museum, 1985, translated by Jocelyn Palmer.

4. Diary for 1932, NLA, MS6388, Series 4, Box 80, Notebook 13. Quotes without attribution for 1932 are from this diary.

5. NLA, MS6388, Series 4, Box 80, Notebook 13a.

6. NLA, MS6388, Series 4, Box 80, Notebook 4.

7. Jacobsen, B., *A Girl Before the Mast*, Charles Scribner's (1934), p. 1.

8. NLA, MS6388, Series 1, Box 13, Folder 120.

9. Newspaper clipping, courtesy of Villiers' niece Elizabeth Sullivan, does not show the name of the newspaper.

10. Daphne Villiers' Diary, Maritime Museum of Tasmania, D1993-134, Box 5.

11. Villiers, A., *Voyage of the Parma*, Geoffrey Bles (1933), p. 165.

12. NLA, MS6388, Series 1, Box 61, Folder 537.
13. All of the shorthand quoted was translated by Mr Adrian Kelly, an official Court and Hansard Reporter for Australian government departments and State and Federal Parliaments. See http://www.transcriptsplus.com.au.

CHAPTER 6: APPRENTICE GIRL

1. Chapman, S.P., *Whistled Like a Bird*, Warner Books (1997), p. 146.
2. NLA, MS6388, Series 4, Box 88, Folder 697.
3. NLA, MS6388, Series 1, Box 61, Folder 537.
4. NLA, MS6388, Series 4, Box 80, Notebook 15. Quotes without attribution for 1933 are from this diary.
5. Betty's letter refers to Villiers' letters stopping 'last spring'. In the spring of 1934 they were together on *Parma*; in 1935 and 1936 Villiers was away on *Joseph Conrad*, but there is no reference to that ship. However, in the spring of 1937 Betty married Ray Reed – significantly, the letter is monogrammed 'R' – and at the same time Alan became involved with another woman.
6. NLA, MS6388, Series 2, Box 65, Folder 573.
7. NLA, MS6388, Series 4, Box 80, Notebook 15.
8. NLA, MS6388, Series 1, Box 13, Folder 120.
9. Lovell, M.S., *The Sound of Wings*, Hutchinson (1989).
10. Ruben de Cloux letters, translated by Gunela Astbrink, NLA, MS6388, Series 1, Box 24, Folder 212.

CHAPTER 7: AN EXQUISITE MOMENT

1. Quotes without attribution in Chapter Seven are from the diary of the *Joseph Conrad* voyage, NLA, MS6388, Series 8, Box 98, Item 2.
2. He wrote four articles: Conley, G., *The Yachting World*, 13, 20 and 27 December 1935 and 3 January 1936.
3. *The Marine Magazine*, 15 August 1936, p. 39.
4. The reliability of articles that Conley wrote later are questionable, as he claims in one that he was actually on board for the passage from Nassau to New York.

CHAPTER 8: THERE CANNOT BE TWO VOYAGES SUCH AS THIS

1. Quotes without attribution in Chapter Eight are from the diary of the *Joseph Conrad* voyage, NLA, MS6388, Series 8, Box 98, Item 2.
2. Private communication, Oswald Brett, 2006.
3. NLA, MS6388, Series 8, Box 101, Folder 740.

CHAPTER 9: ADRIFT IN ARABIA

1. Greenhill, B., and Hackman, J., *Herzogin Cecilie*, p. 162.

2. Sometimes known as Sewer Mill Cove.
3. Karlsson, E., *Mother Sea*, p. 239. The fittings from *Herzogin Cecilie*'s saloon and some cabins were taken back to Mariehamn, where they were later rebuilt as part of the Ålands Maritime Museum.
4. NLA, MS6388, Series 1, Box 61, Folder 541.
5. Newspaper clipping from folder on women in sail, Ålands Maritime Museum.
6. NLA, MS6388, Series 2, Box 65, Folder 572.
7. Private communication, Peter Villiers, February 2007.
8. NLA, MS6388, Series 2, Box 65, Folder 572.
9. *Van Nuys Tribune*, 3 June 1937. Rita played 'Conchita' in *Ladies Love Danger* and an uncredited role in the Fred Astaire movie *Top Hat* in 1935.
10. Ghys, R., and Cormack, N.W., 'An Investigation into the Loss of the Steel Bark Admiral Karpfanger ex L'Avenir', *Marine Technology*, Vol. 41, No. 4, October 2004, pp. 141–60.
11. Private Journal, October 1938–May 1939, NLA, MS6388, Series 13, Box 119.
12. Private Journal, October 1938–May 1939, NLA, MS6388, Series 13, Box 119.
13. Villiers, A., *Sons of Sinbad*, Hodder & Stoughton (1940), p. xvi. Quotes without attribution on the Arab voyages are from this book.
14. Diaries of Hilgard Pannes, Collection 209, Vol. 6. G.W. Blunt White Library, Mystic Seaport.
15. Private Journal, October 1938–May 1939, NLA, MS6388, Series 13, Box 119.
16. Facey, W., Al-Hijji, Y., and Pundyk, G., *Sons of Sindbad: The Photographs*, National Maritime Museum (2006), p. 32.
17. Journal, 'Voyage of the *Bayan*', 7 December 1938–14 May 1939, NLA, MS6388, Series 13, Box 119.
18. Villiers kept the certificate in his papers all his life. NLA, MS6388, Series 2, Box 64, Folder 562.
19. Journal, 15 May 1939–7 June 1939, NLA, MS6388, Series 13, Box 119.
20. Facey, W., Al-Hijji, Y., and Pundyk, G., *Sons of Sindbad: The Photographs*, p. 17.
21. NLA, MS6388, Series 13, Box 121, Folder 878.

CHAPTER 10: AIRCRAFTWOMAN WILLS

1. Lance, K., *Redbill: From Pearls to Peace*, Fremantle Arts Centre Press (2004), p. 21.
2. Eric Newby's irreverent *The Last Grain Race* was written in 1956, and his stoic sailors are eccentrics, his noble officers are nuts, and he cheerfully highlights all of the ghastly stenches that Villiers carefully never mentioned.

3. Hurst, A., *The Medley of Mast and Sail: A Camera Record 2*, Teredo Books (1981), p. 322.
4. Private communication, Nancie Villiers, June 2006.
5. Downe, P., *Wind on the Heath*, Georgian House (1946), p. 74.
6. Diary 5, NLA, MS6388, Series 7, Box 90. Quotes without attribution for 1941 and 1942 are from this summary by Villiers of those years.
7. NLA, MS6388, Series 7, Box 91, Folder 681.
8. Private communication, Nancie Villiers, January 2007.
9. See http://www.uboot.net.
10. Parrott, D., *Tall Ships Down*, McGraw Hill (2004), p. 28. Japanese submarine I-12 sank the Liberty ship *John A. Johnson* on 31 October 1944 (shortly after this meeting), killing ten men, and two weeks later was destroyed by American vessels.
11. Welman's report on Villiers at the end of 1941: NLA, MS6388, Series 7, Box 91, Folder 681.

CHAPTER 11: THE TERRIFIC BUSINESS OF MOVING ARMIES

1. NLA, MS6388, Series 1, Box 53, Folder 461.
2. Letter of Proceedings, NLA, MS6388, Series 7, Box 91, Folder 687.
3. Diary 13, NLA, MS6388, Series 7, Box 90. Quotes without attribution for 1944 are from this diary.
4. Official Report of 'A' Squadron LCI(L) in Operation Neptune and during Build-up. NLA, MS6388, Series 7, Box 94, Folder 706.
5. Passage Progress Report, NLA, MS6388, Series 7, Box 91, Folder 689.
6. NLA, MS6388, Series 7, Box 90, Folder 680.
7. NLA, MS6388, Series 7, Box 95, Folder 714.

CHAPTER 12: SAIL'S TIME IS UP

1. NLA, MS6388, Series 4, Box 81, Diary 18. Quotes without attribution for 1947 are from this diary.
2. NLA, MS6388, Series 2, Box 64, Folder 568.
3. Diary 20, NLA, MS6388, Series 4, Box 81.
4. NLA, MS6388, Series 1, Box 39, Folder 338.
5. NLA, MS6388, Series 15, Box 124, Folder 900.
6. NLA, MS6388, Series 4, Box 81, Diary 22.
7. Egerton, F.C.C., *Salazar: Rebuilder of Portugal*, Hodder & Stoughton (1943), p. 329.
8. Villiers, A., *The Quest of the Schooner Argus*, Hodder & Stoughton (1951), p. 97.
9. Diary 22, NLA, MS6388, Series 4, Box 81.
10. NLA, MS6388, Series 1, Box 14, Folder 129.

11. Diary 44a, NLA, MS6388, Series 4, Box 82.
12. Diary 45, NLA, MS6388, Series 4, Box 82.

CHAPTER 13: *MAYFLOWER* AND *MARCEL B*
1. NLA, MS6388, Series 1, Box 40, Folder 344.
2. Parrott, D.S., *Tall Ships Down*, p. 32.
3. Private communication, Adrian Small, February 2008.
4. Undated *Today* interview with Warwick Charlton, *c.*1958.
5. Charlton, W., *The Voyage of Mayflower II*, Cassell (1957), p. 255.
6. NLA, MS6388, Series 9, Box 105, Folder 768. Quotes without attribution regarding the *Mayflower* voyage are from this folder.
7. This account is drawn from various sources, in particular the website http://www.gerdgruendler.de/Pamir-Untergang.html and Parrott, D.S., *Tall Ships Down*, pp. 33–53.
8. From personal diary of events on *Passat*, November 1957. Private communication, Captain Lothar Friis, September 2007.
9. *The Independent*, 22 June 2007, http://news.independent.co.uk/europe/article2692490.ece. This report has been misunderstood: the 'badly leaking deck' was the roof of the deckhouse, not the main cargo deck, and portholes could not have admitted enough water to make a difference even if they had been left open, which would be unlikely in a storm. Private communication, Captain Lothar Friis, September 2007.
10. Villiers believed that his father's widowed mother had remarried and given birth to John Villiers Farrow, who was thus Leon's step-brother. However, recent genealogical research has revealed that there is no family connection at all. Private communication, Elizabeth Sullivan, August 2008.
11. Villiers did not mention Betty again, so nothing more is known about her life.
12. NLA, MS6388, Series 4, Box 89, Folder 672.
13. NLA, MS6388, Series 10, Box 109.
14. NLA, MS6388, Series 10, Box 108, Folder 784.
15. NLA, MS6388, Series 10, Box 108, Folder 784.

CHAPTER 14: RETURN TO CAPE HORN
1. *National Geographic*, September 1963, Vol. 124, pp. 309–45.
2. Diary 106, NLA, MS6388, Series 4, Box 84.
3. Diary 106, NLA, MS6388, Series 4, Box 84
4. Diary 115, NLA, MS6388, Series 4, Box 84.
5. A second *Endeavour* replica originated with the 1988 Australian Bicentennial. It was built in Australia, with plans from the National Maritime Museum partly based on the 1960s project, and launched in 1993. She sailed to Britain, America and Europe (via Cape Horn), and back to

Sydney over eleven years, and is run by the Australian National Maritime Museum. A brigantine called *Young Endeavour* was a 1988 gift from the British government and is now a Royal Australian Navy sail-training vessel for young people.

6. Diary 123, NLA, MS6388, Series 4, Box 84.
7. Diary 127, NLA, MS6388, Series 4, Box 85.
8. *Nonsuch* was later shipped to Canada, spent several years sailing there, and is now the star attraction at a museum in Winnipeg.
9. Greenhill, B., and Giffard, A., *Women Under Sail*, David & Charles (1970).
10. Diary 141, NLA, MS6388, Series 4, Box 85.

CHAPTER 15: VOYAGE INTO THE UNKNOWN

1. Diary 144, NLA, MS6388, Series 4, Box 86.
2. Diary 148, NLA, MS6388, Series 4, Box 86.
3. NLA, MS6388, Series 1, Box 17, Folder 158 and Box 44, Folders 381–3.
4. Private communication, Peter Villiers, July 2007.
5. Diary 148, NLA, MS6388, Series 4, Box 86.
6. Diary 152, NLA, MS6388, Series 4, Box 86.
7. In which ship and aircraft losses in the Caribbean were attributed to supernatural causes. Charles Berlitz, *The Bermuda Triangle*, Doubleday (1974).
8. Diary 160, NLA, MS6388, Series 4, Box 87.
9. NLA, MS6388, Series 1, Box 55, Folder 483, and Box 63.
10. NLA, MS6388, Series 1, Box 32, Folder 279, and Box 62.
11. NLA, MS6388, Series 1, Box 62, Folder 551.
12. NLA, Manuscripts Section, Acquisitions, Alan Villiers, 203/22/00013-01.
13. NLA, MS6388, Series 1, Box 63.
14. Private communication, Peter Villiers, July 2007.
15. Private communication, Kathy Chetwynd, September 2007.
16. NLA, Manuscripts Section, Acquisitions, Alan Villiers, 203/22/00013-02.
17. Greenhill, B., and Hackman, J., *The Grain Races*, Conway Maritime Press (1986), p. 123.
18. Facey, W., Al-Hijji, Y., and Pundyk, G., *Sons of Sindbad: The Photographs*, p. 29.
19. 'Trucks' are mast-tops. 20 February 1936, diary of the *Joseph Conrad* voyage, NLA, MS6388, Series 8, Box 98, Item 2.

BIBLIOGRAPHY

Allen, Oliver. *The Windjammers*. Amsterdam: Time-Life Books Inc, 1978.

Baker, Christine. '"Tar" and "Oakum". A Sea Maid's Romance'. *The Marine Magazine*. August 1936: 39–42.

Bellamit, Philippe. Memorial Pamir. http://pamir.chez-alice.fr/ Indexm.htm#English (accessed 2005–2007).

Bourne, Pamela. *Out of the World*. Suffolk: Richard Clay and Sons, 1935.

Brock Davis, Annette. *My Year Before the Mast*. Toronto: Hownslow Press, 1999.

Bruzelius, Lars. Maritime History Virtual Archives. http://www.bruzelius.info/Nautica/Ships/Ships.html (accessed 2005–2007).

Bull, Peter. *To Sea in a Sieve*. London: Peter Davies, 1956.

Carter, Robert. *Windjammers: The Final Story*. Dural: Rosenberg Publishing, 2004.

Chapman, Sally Putnam. *Whistled Like a Bird*. New York: Warner Books, 1997.

Charlton, Warwick. *The Voyage of Mayflower II*. London: Cassell & Company Ltd, 1957.

Colton, Tim. WWII Construction Records Landing Craft, Infantry (Large). http://www.coltoncompany.com/shipbldg/ussbldrs/wwii/boatbuilders/lan dingcraft/lcil.htm (accessed 2006–2007) [alternate URL: http://www.shipbuildinghistory.com].

Conley, George. 'In the Tracks of Tradition'. *The Yachting World*. 13, 20 and 27 December 1935, 3 January 1936.

Downe, Phyllis. *Wind on the Heath*. Melbourne: Georgian House, 1946.

Egerton, F.C.C. *African Majesty*. New York: Charles Scribner's Sons, 1939.

Egerton, F.C.C. *Salazar: Rebuilder of Portugal*. London: Hodder & Stoughton, 1943.

Eriksson, Pamela. *The Duchess*. London: Secker & Warburg, 1958.

Fergusson, Bernard. *The Watery Maze: the Story of Combined Operations*. London: Collins, 1961.

Ford, Corey. *Salt Water Taffy*. New York: G.P. Putnam's Sons, 1929.

Ghys, Roger. and Neil Cormack. 'An Investigation into the Loss of the Steel Bark Admiral Karpfanger ex L'Avenir.' *Marine Technology*, Vol. 41, No. 4 (2004): 141–60.

Greenhill, Basil. 'The Alan Villiers Collection'. London: National Maritime Museum, 1998.

Greenhill, Basil, and Ann Giffard. *Women Under Sail*. Newton Abbot: David & Charles, 1972.

Greenhill, Basil, and John Hackman. *Herzogin Cecilie*. London: Conway Maritime Press, 1991.

Greenhill, Basil, and John Hackman. *The Grain Races*. London: Conway
Maritime Press, 1986.

Gründler, Gerhard. 2007. Warum ging die Pamir unter?
http://www.gerdgruendler.de/Pamir-Untergang.html (accessed 2007).

Harland, John. *Seamanship in the Age of Sail*. London: Conway Maritime Press,
1984.

Hartford, Huntingdon. 'Gone Without the Wind.' *Esquire*. October 1938: 69.

H.M. Stationery Office. 1919. *British Merchant Ships Lost at Sea Due to Enemy
Action, 1914–1918*. http://www.naval-history.net/
WW1LossesaContents.htm (accessed 2005–2007).

Hurst, Alex. *The Medley of Mast and Sail: A Camera Record 2*. Brighton: Teredo
Books, 1981.

Jacobsen, Betty. *A Girl Before the Mast*. New York: Charles Scribner's Sons,
1934.

Kahre, Georg. *The Last Tall Ships*. London: Conway Maritime Press, 1978.

Karlsson, Elis. *Mother Sea*. London: Oxford University Press, 1964.

Kemp, Peter. *The Oxford Companion to Ships and the Sea*. Oxford: Oxford
University Press, 1988.

Kendall, Nancy. 2004. Wind-some words: http://www.christianscience
monitor.org 2004/0506/p18s03-hfgn.html (accessed 2005).

Kerr, Garry. *The Tasmanian Trading Ketch: An Illustrated Oral History*. Portland
Victoria: Main'sle Books, 1987.

Kolbicz, Rainer. 2007. War diary of U-140; U-boat activity in World War Two.
http://www.uboot.net (accessed 2006).

Ladd, J.D. *Assault From the Sea 1939–45: the Craft, the Landings, the Men*.
Newton Abbot: David & Charles, 1976.

Lance, Kate. *Redbill: From Pearls to Peace*. Fremantle: Fremantle Arts Centre
Press, 2004.

Lovell, M.S. *The Sound of Wings*. London: Arrow Books Ltd, 1989.

Lowell, Joan. *Child of the Deep*. London: William Heinemann Ltd, 1929.

Middendorf, F.L. *The Masting and Rigging of Ships*, 1903. Translated by Mori
Flapan. http://home.iprimus.com.au/mflapan/MiddendorfWebpage1.htm
(accessed 2005).

Newby, Eric. *The Last Grain Race*. London: Secker & Warburg, 1958.

Padfield, Peter. *The Sea Is a Magic Carpet*. London: Peter Davies, 1959.

Pannes, Hilgard. *Diaries, 1935–1936*. MS 8304. Manuscripts Collection.
National Library of Australia.

Parrott, Daniel. *Tall Ships Down*. New York: McGraw-Hill, 2003.

Paterson, Tony. 2007. German ship which sank killing 80 was 'rust bucket'.
http://news.independent.co.uk/europe/article2692490.ece (accessed 2007).

Prager, Hans Georg. *F. Laeisz*. Herford: Koehlers Verlagsgesellschaft mbH,
1979.

Priolo, Gary P. 2005. Landing Craft Infantry (LCI): http://www.navsource.org/archives/10/15/15idx.htm (accessed 2007).

Putnam, George Palmer. *Wide Margins: a Publisher's Autobiography*. New York: Harcourt, Brace and Company, 1942.

Salter, Harold. *Bass Strait Ketches*. Hobart: St David's Park Publishing, 1991.

Scott, Peter. *The Battle of the Narrow Seas: a History of the Light Coastal Forces in the Channel and North Sea, 1939–1945*. London: Country Life Ltd, 1945.

Stark, William. *The Last Time Around Cape Horn: The Historic 1949 Voyage of the Windjammer Pamir*. New York: Carroll & Graf Publishers, 2003.

Underhill, Harold. *Deep-Water Sail*. Glasgow: Brown, Son & Ferguson, 1952.

US Navy. *Allied Landing Craft of World War Two*. London: Arms and Armour Press, 1985.

Villiers, Alan. *Papers of Alan Villiers (1903–1982)*. MS 6388. Manuscripts Collection, National Library of Australia.

Villiers, Daphne. *Diary*. D1993-134 Box 5. Maritime Museum of Tasmania.

Villiers, Peter. *Joseph Conrad Master Mariner*. Rendlesham: Seafarer Books, 2006.

BOOKS BY ALAN VILLIERS
IN CHRONOLOGICAL ORDER

To the Frozen South. Hobart: Davies Bros, 1924.

Whaling in the Frozen South. London: Hurst & Blackett, 1925. Indianapolis: Bobbs-Merrill, 1925.

The Wind Ship. London: Hurst & Blackett, 1928. [Fiction]

Falmouth for Orders. London: Geoffrey Bles, 1928. New York: Henry Holt, 1929.

By Way of Cape Horn. London: Geoffrey Bles, 1930. New York: Henry Holt, 1930.

Vanished Fleets. London: Geoffrey Bles, 1931. New York: Henry Holt, 1931.

Sea-Dogs of Today. New York: Henry Holt, 1931. London: George G. Harrap, 1932.

The Sea in Ships. London: Routledge & Sons, 1932. New York: W. Morrow, 1932.

Voyage of the 'Parma'. London: Geoffrey Bles, 1933; *Grain Race*. New York: Charles Scribner's Sons, 1933.

Last of the Wind Ships. New York: W. Morrow, 1934. London: Routledge & Sons, 1934.

Whalers of the Midnight Sun. New York: Charles Scribner's Sons, 1934. London: Geoffrey Bles, 1934. [Children's fiction]

Convict Ships and Sailors. London: Philip Allan & Co., 1936. [*Vanished Fleets* reprinted]

Cruise of the Conrad. London: Hodder & Stoughton, 1937. New York: Charles Scribner's Sons, 1937.

Stormalong. New York: Charles Scribner's Sons, 1937. London: Routledge & Sons, 1938. [For children]

The Making of a Sailor. New York: W. Morrow, 1938. London: Routledge & Sons, 1938.

Joey Goes to Sea. New York: Charles Scribner's Sons, 1939. [Children's fiction]

Sons of Sinbad. New York: Charles Scribner's Sons, 1940; *Sons of Sindbad*. London: Hodder & Stoughton, 1940.

The Set of the Sails. New York: Charles Scribner's Sons 1949. London: Hodder & Stoughton, 1949.

The Coral Sea. New York: McGraw-Hill, 1949. London: Museum Press, 1950.

The Quest of the Schooner 'Argus'. London: Hodder & Stoughton, 1951. New York: Charles Scribner's Sons, 1951.

The Indian Ocean. London: Museum Press, 1952; *Monsoon Seas*. New York: McGraw-Hill, 1952.

The Cutty Sark: Last of a Glorious Era. London: Hodder & Stoughton, 1953.

The Way of a Ship. New York: Charles Scribner's Sons, 1953. London: Hodder & Stoughton, 1953.

Pilot Pete. New York: Charles Scribner's Sons, 1953. London: Museum Press, 1953. [Children's fiction]

And Not to Yield. New York: Charles Scribner's Sons, 1953. London: Hodder & Stoughton, 1953. [Children's fiction]

Sailing Eagle. New York: Charles Scribner's Sons, 1955.

Pioneers of the Seven Seas. London: Routledge & Kegan Paul, 1956.

Posted Missing. New York: Charles Scribner's Sons, 1956. London: Hodder & Stoughton, 1956.

The Western Ocean. London: Museum Press, 1957; *Wild Ocean*. New York: McGraw-Hill, 1957.

'The Navigators' and the Merchant Navy. Glasgow: Brown, Son & Ferguson, 1957.

Give Me a Ship to Sail. New York: Charles Scribner's Sons, 1958. London: Hodder & Stoughton, 1958.

The Story of Louis de Rochemont's 'Windjammer'. New York: Random House, 1958.

The New 'Mayflower'. New York: Charles Scribner's Sons, 1958. Leicester: Brockhampton Press, 1959. [For children]

A Seaman's Collection of Great Sea Stories. New York: Dell, 1959.

Of Ships and Men, a Personal Anthology. London: Newnes, 1962. New York: Arco Publishing, 1965.

Men, Ships, and the Sea. Washington: National Geographic Society, 1962.

Oceans of the World. London: Museum Press, 1963; *The Ocean*. New York: Dutton, 1963.

The Battle of Trafalgar: Lord Nelson Sweeps the Sea. New York: Macmillan, 1965. [For children]

Captain Cook: the Seaman's Seaman. London: Hodder & Stoughton, 1967; *Captain James Cook*. New York: Charles Scribner's Sons, 1967.

With Basil Greenhill. *Nonsuch: Hudson's Bay Company Ship Replica*. London: Alabaster Passmore & Sons, 1969.

The Deep Sea Fishermen. London: Hodder & Stoughton, 1970.

The War with Cape Horn. London: Hodder & Stoughton, 1971. New York: Charles Scribner's Sons, 1971.

My Favourite Sea Stories. Guildford: Lutterworth Press, 1972.

With Henri Picard. *The Bounty Ships of France*. London: Patrick Stephens, 1972. New York: Charles Scribner's Sons, 1972.

Voyaging with the Wind. London: H.M. Stationery Office, 1975.

The Last of the Wind Ships. London: The Harvill Press, 2000.

Sons of Sindbad: The Photographs. London: National Maritime Museum, 2006.

ARTICLES BY ALAN VILLIERS

FOR THE *NATIONAL GEOGRAPHIC* MAGAZINE IN CHRONOLOGICAL ORDER

'Rounding the Horn in a Windjammer.' Vol. 59 (1931): 191–224.

'The Cape Horn Grain Ship Race.' Vol. 63 (1933): 1–39.

'Where the Sailing Ship Survives.' Vol. 67 (1935): 101–28.

'North About.' Vol. 71 (1937): 220–50.

'Last of the Cape Horners.' Vol. 93 (1948): 701–10.

'Sailing with Sindbad's Sons.' Vol. 94 (1948): 675–688.

'I Sailed with Portugal's Captains Courageous.' Vol. 101 (1952): 565–96.

'Golden Beaches of Portugal.' Vol. 106 (1954): 673–96.

'Under Canvas in the Atomic Age.' Vol. 108 (1955): 49–84.

'By Full-Rigged Ship to Denmark's Fairyland.' Vol. 108 (1955): 809–28.

'We're Coming Over on the Mayflower.' Vol. 111 (1957): 708–28.

'The Marvelous Maldive Islands.' Vol. 111 (1957): 829–50.

'How We Sailed the New "Mayflower" to America.' Vol. 112 (1957): 627–72.

'Prince Henry, the Explorer Who Stayed Home.' Vol. 118 (1960): 616–57.

'Scotland from Her Lovely Lochs and Seas.' Vol. 119 (1961): 492–541.

'Cowes to Cornwall: Sailor's Log of a Channel Cruise.' Vol. 120 (1961): 149–201.

'Aboard the N.S. Savannah: World's First Nuclear Merchantman.' Vol. 122 (1962): 280–98.

'Ships Through the Ages: A Saga of the Sea.' Vol. 123 (1963): 494–544.

'Channel Cruise to Glorious Devon.' Vol. 124 (1963): 208–59.

'Australia: The Settled East, the Barrier Reef, the Center.' Vol. 124 (1963): 309–45.

'Australia: The West and the South.' Vol. 124 (1963): 346–87.

'Fabled Mount of St Michael.' Vol. 125 (1964): 880–98.

'Wales, Land of Bards.' Vol. 127 (1965): 727–69.

'"The Alice": In Australia's Wonderland.' Vol. 129 (1966): 230–58.

'England's Scillies, the Flowering Isles.' Vol. 132 (1967): 126–45.

'The Netherlands: Nation at War With the Sea.' Vol. 133 (1968): 530–71.

'The Age of Sail Lives on at Mystic.' Vol. 134 (1968): 220–39.

'In the Wake of Darwin's "Beagle".' Vol. 136 (1969): 449–99.

'Captain Cook: The Man Who Mapped The Pacific.' Vol. 140 (1971): 297–349.

'Queen Elizabeth's Favourite Sea Dog: Sir Francis Drake.' Vol. 147 (1975): 216–153.

'Magellan: A Voyage into the Unknown.' Vol. 149 (1976): 720–53.

PHOTO CREDITS

1. Leon Villiers. Courtesy Elizabeth Sullivan.
2. Annie Villiers. Courtesy Elizabeth Sullivan.
3. Villiers children. Courtesy Elizabeth Sullivan.
4. Alan Villiers aged 16. Box 131, MS 6388, by permission of the National Library of Australia.
5. Painting of *Rothesay Bay*. 178823, John Oxley Library, State Library of Queensland.
6. Photo of *Rothesay Bay*. 178828, John Oxley Library, State Library of Queensland.
7. *Lawhill*. 133060, John Oxley Library, State Library of Queensland.
8. Villiers aged twenty-two. Jack Cato, H98.150/62, La Trobe Picture Collection, State Library of Victoria.
9. Daphne Harris. Provided by Garry Kerr.
10. Jeanne Day cleaning a lamp. A. Villiers, N61777, National Maritime Museum.
11. Port watch *Herzogin Cecilie*. N61160, National Maritime Museum.
12. *Herzogin Cecilie* officers. A. Villiers, N61137, National Maritime Museum.
13. Alan Villiers at the wheel. P49854, National Maritime Museum.
14. Programme cover for *Windjammer*. Courtesy Elizabeth Sullivan.
15. Ronald Walker. A. Villiers, N61227, National Maritime Museum.
16. *Grace Harwar*'s deck. A. Villiers, N61308, National Maritime Museum.
17. *Parma* in 1932. A. Villiers, N61359, National Maritime Museum.
18. Daphne Villiers on *Parma*. A. Villiers, N61685, National Maritime Museum.
19. Captain Ruben de Cloux. A. Villiers, N61623, National Maritime Museum.
20. Publicity shot. Box 131, MS 6388, by permission of the National Library of Australia.
21. With Betty Jacobsen, late 1932. Box 131, MS 6388, by permission of the National Library of Australia.
22. Betty Jacobsen and Hilgard Pannes. A. Villiers, N61730, National Maritime Museum.
23. The western harbour at Mariehamn. A. Villiers, N61793, National Maritime Museum.
24. *Joseph Conrad*. Box 131, MS 6388, by permission of the National Library of Australia.
25. Christine Baker. 87-9-361, Christine Baker Torgersen Collection, Mystic Seaport.
26. Villiers and boys. 87-10-2, Christine Baker Torgersen Collection, Mystic Seaport.
27. Elsie and Christine. 87-9-99, Christine Baker Torgersen Collection, Mystic Seaport.
28. *Joseph Conrad* on rocks. H.C. Pedersen, Box 131, MS 6388, by permission of the National Library of Australia.

29. *Joseph Conrad*'s dramatic figurehead. A. Villiers, P47635, National Maritime Museum.
30. Alan Villiers, 1936. Box 131, MS 6388, by permission of the National Library of Australia.
31. Crew aloft. Box 131, MS 6388, by permission of the National Library of Australia.
32. Pamela and Sven Eriksson. Courtesy Ålands Sjöfartsmuseum.
33. *Herzogin Cecilie* on rocks. 131768, John Oxley Library, State Library of Queensland.
34. Fritz Egerton. Folder 572, Box 65, MS 6388, by permission of the National Library of Australia.
35. *L'Avenir*. From the Melbourne Maritime Museum collection.
36. *Olivebank*. From the Melbourne Maritime Museum collection.
37. *Bayan*. A. Villiers, PM5251-35, National Maritime Museum.
38. The bench on *Bayan*. A. Villiers, PM5094-28, National Maritime Museum.
39. Villiers with Arab friends. N83232, National Maritime Museum.
40. Nancie and Alan, 1940. Courtesy Nancie Villiers.
41. Last moments of *Penang*, 1940. Herman Piening.
42. Alan Villiers, mid 1940s. Courtesy Nancie Villiers.
43. Examples of LCI(L)s. Anonymous, from http://www.navsource.org, courtesy Capt. Gordon G. Armstrong RCN Ret.
44. An Atlantic convoy. Image 520948, US National Archives and Records Administration.
45. View from an LCI(L). Gilbert Alexander Milne, Canada Dept. of National Defence, Library and Archives Canada, PA-137014.
46. Infantry landing on D-Day. Gilbert Alexander Milne, Canada Dept. of National Defence, Library and Archives Canada, PA-137013.
47. Villiers with crew in 1945. Courtesy Elizabeth Sullivan.
48. Nancie in 1948. Folder 564, Box 64, MS6388, by permission of the National Library of Australia.
49. Alan in the early 1950s. Box 131, MS 6388, by permission of the National Library of Australia.
50. Portugese schooners. Folder 134, Box 15, MS 6388, by permission of the National Library of Australia.
51. Villiers at the BBC. Folder 36, Box 4, MS 6388, by permission of the National Library of Australia.
52. *Mayflower II*. From the Melbourne Maritime Museum collection.
53. Alan and Nancie Villiers. Box 131, MS 6388, by permission of the National Library of Australia.
54. *Pamir*. From the Melbourne Maritime Museum collection.
55. *Passat*. From the Melbourne Maritime Museum collection.
56. *Marcel B Surdo*. Courtesy Adrian Small. Folder 130, Box 14, MS 6388, by permission of the National Library of Australia.
57. *Angiolina H*. Courtesy Adrian Small. Folder 130, Box 14, MS6388, by

permission of the National Library of Australia.

58. Alan Villiers in costume c. 1961. National Archives of Australia: SP1011/1, 4536.
59. Captain Robert Miethe, 1975. Folder 280, Box 32, MS 6388, by permission of the National Library of Australia.
60. *Polly Woodside* in Melbourne, 1989. Courtesy Lindsay Rex.
61. Four-masted *Pommern*. Courtesy Kate Lance.
62. Alan at Lucerne Road, 1970s. Courtesy Nancie Villiers.
63. Barque *James Craig*. Courtesy Lindsay Rex.

INDEX